The Words and Music of Prince

Recent Titles in
The Praeger Singer-Songwriter Collection

The Sound of Stevie Wonder: His Words and Music
James E. Perone

The Words and Music of Frank Zappa
Kelly F. Lowe

The Words and Music of Carole King
James E. Perone

The Words and Music of Bruce Springsteen
Rob Kirkpatrick

The Words and Music of Bob Marley
David Moskowitz

The Words and Music of John Lennon
Ben Urish and Ken Bielen

The Words and Music of David Bowie
James E. Perone

The Words and Music of Paul Simon
James Bennighof

THE PRAEGER SINGER-SONGWRITER COLLECTION

The Words and Music of Prince

James E. Perone

PRAEGER

Westport, Connecticut
London

Library of Congress Cataloging-in-Publication Data

Perone, James E.
  The words and music of Prince / James E. Perone.
       p. cm.—(The Praeger singer-songwriter collection, ISSN 1553–3484)
  Includes bibliographical references (p.), discography (p.), and index.
  ISBN-13: 978–0–275–99474–7 (alk. paper)
  1. Prince—Criticism and interpretation. I. Title.
ML420.P974P47 2008
781.66092—dc22   2008000540

British Library Cataloguing in Publication Data is available.

Library of Congress Catalog Card Number: 2008000540
ISBN: 978–0–275–99474–7
ISSN: 1553–3484

First published in 2008

Praeger Publishers, 88 Post Road West, Westport, CT 06881
An imprint of Greenwood Publishing Group, Inc.
www.praeger.com

Printed in the United States of America

The paper used in this book complies with the
Permanent Paper Standard issued by the National
Information Standards Organization (Z39.48–1984).

10 9 8 7 6 5 4 3 2 1

Contents

Series Foreword *by James E. Perone*   vii

Acknowledgments   ix

Introduction   xi

1. Becoming a Star   1

    The Young Virtuoso   1

    For You   2

    Prince   5

    Dirty Mind   9

    Controversy   13

2. Mixing Rock and Funk with the Revolution   17

    1999   17

    Purple Rain   24

    Around the World in a Day   29

3. Film Scores and Contractual Problems   37

    Parade (Music from the Motion Picture *Under the Cherry Moon*)   37

    Sign o' the Times   41

    The Black Album   49

    Lovesexy   51

Batman	55
Graffiti Bridge	57
4. The New Power Generation and a Name Change	**63**
Diamonds and Pearls	63
☥ ("The Love Symbol Album")	69
Come	78
The Gold Experience	82
Chaos and Disorder	91
5. The Approach of 1999	**97**
Emancipation	97
Crystal Ball	112
New Power Soul	123
The Vault: Old Friends 4 Sale	127
Rave Un2 the Joy Fantastic	131
6. The New Millennium	**139**
The Rainbow Children	140
N.E.W.S.	142
Musicology	147
3121	151
Planet Earth	155
Conclusions: The Importance of Being Prince	161
Selected Discography	167
Notes	173
Annotated Bibliography	177
Index	191

Series Foreword

Although the term, *Singer-Songwriters,* might most frequently be associated with a cadre of musicians of the early 1970s such as Paul Simon, James Taylor, Carly Simon, Joni Mitchell, Cat Stevens, and Carole King, the Praeger Singer-Songwriter Collection defines singer-songwriters more broadly, both in terms of style and in terms of time period. The series includes volumes on musicians who have been active from approximately the 1960s through the present. Musicians who write and record in folk, rock, soul, hip-hop, country, and various hybrids of these styles will be represented. Therefore, some of the early 1970s introspective singer-songwriters named above will be included, but not exclusively.

What do the individuals included in this series have in common? Some have never collaborated as writers. But, while some have done so, all have written and recorded commercially successful and/or historically important music *and* lyrics at some point in their careers.

The authors who contribute to the series also exhibit diversity. Some are scholars who are trained primarily as musicians, while others have such areas of specialization as American studies, history, sociology, popular culture studies, literature, and rhetoric. The authors share a high level of scholarship, accessibility in their writing, and a true insight into the work of the artists they study. The authors are also focused on the output of their subjects and how it relates to their subject's biography and the society around them; however, biography in and of itself is not a major focus of the books in this series.

Given the diversity of the musicians who are the subject of books in this series, and given the diversity of viewpoint of the authors, volumes in the series will differ from book to book. All, however, will be organized chronologically around the compositions and recorded performances of their subjects. All of the books in the series should also serve as listeners' guides to the music of their subjects, making them companions to the artists' recorded output.

James E. Perone
Series Editor

Acknowledgments

This book could not have been written without the valuable assistance of a number of people. I wish first to thank Karen Perone for offering moral and technical support throughout this and all of my book projects for Greenwood Press and Praeger Publishers, and for offering much-needed input at every stage of every project. Thank you, also for being about the most perceptive listener I have ever encountered: I never noticed the strange surface resemblance (the extensive use of repeated notes) between "Purple Rain" and "Cheese and Onions" from that famous 1978 Beatles send-up *The Rutles* until you mentioned it! Oh, and I promise that now that this project is done, you won't have to listen to me sing the refrain of "Sexy M.F." around the house anymore. . . .

Over the course of writing several books, I have found the entire staff of the Greenwood Publishing Group to be most helpful and cooperative. I wish to extend special thanks to Editor Daniel Harmon for his assistance in putting this book together and for his continuing support in the development of the Praeger Singer-Songwriter Collection, and to all the copy and production editors for helping me in the fine-tuning of this book. I also wish to thank Eric Levy and Rob Kirkpatrick for their assistance in getting the Praeger Singer-Songwriter Collection off the ground over the course of several years, way back at the dawn of the twenty-first century.

I also wish to send a special shout of thanks out to Ron Mandelbaum and the entire staff of Photofest for the photographs of Prince that appear in the photo essay in this book.

Mount Union College's Music Librarian, Suzanne Moushey, also deserves a special note of thanks for helping me negotiate my way through various indices and databases as I built a bibliography. She also lent a hand on some uniform title issues. Thanks, Suzy! I also wish to thank another Mount Union College colleague, Dr. William Cunion, who shared his passion for the music of Prince with me. Bill and I engaged in a number of informal conversations about Prince's intriguing, yet challenging, music over the course of a busy academic semester. I think that mutually we opened each other's ears up to things that might have remained hidden had we not talked. Thanks, Bill!

I especially wish to thank my friend and colleague, the late Dr. Kelly Fisher Lowe, for encouraging me to go as far beneath the surface as possible in looking for the real meaning of Prince's songs. As two of our friends and colleagues slaved over a practice putting green at Carolina National Golf Club in March 2007, Kelly and I stood off to the side and discussed symbolism in Prince's lyrics. Yes, I agree, Kelly, "Little Red Corvette" isn't *just* about a car! But, can't it be, at least in part, about the car? Come on, please? Despite Kelly's untimely passing in June 2007, I will continue to feel the impact of his friendship and his brilliant, take-no-prisoners style of rhetorical analysis for years to come. Godspeed, Kelly.

I also wish to thank Gary Rutkowski and the other members of the 1986 incarnation of Buffalo, New York's Maelström Percussion Ensemble for inviting me to perform as a guest clarinetist with the group for a series of concerts that year. It was on a run-out gig to Oneonta, New York, that I first encountered the fanaticism of early Prince devotees.

And, finally, a special word of thanks to Mary Cotofan for her work in helping me in the editorial stages of several Praeger Publishers projects I have undertaken. Mary and her copy editors do yeoman work with all the technical details that I manage to have left unaddressed at the manuscript stage.

Despite my own best efforts and the assistance of those named above there are bound to be errors in this book: they are solely my responsibility.

Introduction

On January 28, 1986, I was in Oneonta, New York, along with members of the Maelström Percussion Ensemble and several members of the S.U.N.Y. at Buffalo dance team—we were scheduled for an evening performance at one of the colleges in town. On the way back from a morning rehearsal, I somehow ended up in a conversation with one of the dancers about Prince. At the time my familiarity with Prince's work consisted approximately of the singles "1999" and "Purple Rain," and the album *Around the World in a Day*. As our group walked back to our lodging, the young woman with whom I was talking informed me in no uncertain terms that the psychedelic music of *Around the World in a Day* was a fluke and that if I wanted to understand the real Prince, I needed to learn his music before he became a pop hit–making sensation. I was struck by the intensity of her response to and connection with this musician with whom I had only the most superficial knowledge. As our group arrived back at our lodging, the conversation was interrupted abruptly when we saw our hosts seated at the television set, which was playing over and over again scenes of the explosion of the space shuttle *Challenger*. The explosion of the *Challenger*, the evening performance, and going out for a beer after the concert with my Maelström buddies all combined to bring my education about Prince to an end on that January 1986 day; however, I have always remembered the intensity of one young woman's response to Prince. Rarely have I witnessed such fanaticism about a pop musician. Yes, Prince started out as an underground, word-of-mouth phenomenon in the 1970s and became a cultural icon in the 1980s. Eventually, he became better known for his battles with a record company and his ensuing name change in the 1990s. Ultimately, this served to make Prince the butt of way too many jokes by comedians, professional and amateur. Regretfully, all of this took attention away from his music. Prince is perhaps the most prolific songwriter of his generation, and his work as a singer-songwriter deserves much more attention than his choice of moniker.

PRINCE AS A MUSICIAN AND CULTURAL ICON

Born June 7, 1958, in Minneapolis, Minnesota, as Prince Rogers Nelson, Prince emerged in the late 1970s with two albums, *For You* and *Prince*. These albums only hinted at the huge commercial and artistic impact Prince would have, as well as the controversies he would create both through his lyrics and through his unusual combinations of diverse musical styles. With the early 1980s albums *Dirty Mind, 1999,* and *Purple Rain,* Prince became a major force in American pop music. His combination of rock and funk on these albums and over the course of the next several years was unique. Prince then moved increasingly into film soundtracks with *Parade, Batman,* and *Graffiti Bridge.* The 1990s found Prince forming a new group, the New Power Generation, moving back in the direction of the R&B with which he had begun his career, and eventually adopting an unpronounceable symbol as his moniker. By the end of the millennium, Prince was again exploring an eclectic collection of musical styles and enjoying a resurgence of interest in his well-known song "1999." Never one to shy away from controversy, Prince became a Jehovah's Witness at the start of the twenty-first century and recorded *The Rainbow Children,* an album inspired by his new faith. Prince has also explored instrumental music—especially on his 2003 album *N.E.W.S.*—and he continues to write and record up to the present.

Prince has established himself as one of the most important singer-songwriters of the past 30 years; however, he also has been one of the busiest songwriters of the period, with a portfolio of what some estimate is more than one thousand compositions. Prince himself has recorded only a relatively small percentage of these for commercial release. Other songs have never made it past the demo stage; however, Prince has enjoyed a prolific behind-the-scenes career as a writer, session musician, and producer for other performers. Perhaps the best-known song Prince contributed to his contemporaries is the *Billboard* Pop No. 2 hit "Manic Monday," recorded in 1986 by the Bangles. Prince has also written for and/or recorded with Miles Davis, Kate Bush, Madonna, Chaka Khan, Sheena Easton, Cyndi Lauper, Carmen Electra, Chuck D., Sheryl Crow, and Maceo Parker.

In addition to the official recognition Prince received in the form of Grammy awards in 1984 (the single "I Feel for You" for Best R&B Song; the album *Purple Rain* for Best Instrumental Composition Written Specially for a Motion Picture or for Television; and the album *Purple Rain* for Best Rock

Performance by a Duo or Group with Vocal) and 1986 (the single "Kiss" for Best R&B Performance by a Duo or Group with Vocal), Prince has been a favorite of music critics. *All Music Guide*'s Stephen Thomas Erlewine, for example, characterizes Prince as "one of the most singular talents of the rock & roll era, capable of seamlessly tying together pop, funk, folk, and rock."[1] Writing in *Baker's Biographical Dictionary of Musicians,* Brock Helander characterizes Prince as, "along with Michael Jackson and Madonna . . . one of the most popular solo artists to emerge in the 1980s." Although Helander also characterizes Prince as "erratic and self-indulgent," he also acknowledges that Prince produced some of the most influential and best-selling albums of the 1980s.[2]

Prince's career certainly has not been without controversy. A fair number of his compositions have been marked by sexually explicit lyrics. It was in part in reaction to finding her daughter listening to the Prince song "Darling Nikki" that Tipper Gore founded the Parents Music Resource Center in an effort to combat sexually explicit, drug-related, and violent lyrics in popular music.[3] Prince's ability to appeal both to rock fans and to R&B fans has also created controversy: like Jimi Hendrix in the 1960s, Prince has been accused of at times ignoring black audiences in an effort to appeal to whites. An artist who has been intensely focused on artistic control of his product, Prince took the unusual step in the early 1990s of changing his name to an unpronounceable symbol as a protest against what he felt was the enslavement of "Prince" by Warner Bros. Records.

Prince was elected to the Rock and Roll Hall of Fame in 2004, and in 2006 was named the Sexiest Vegetarian Alive by the People for the Ethical Treatment of Animals (PETA). He remains active as a songwriter, multi-instrumentalist, singer, arranger, and producer. Prince's latest album, *Planet Earth,* was released in summer 2007.

THE SCOPE AND ORGANIZATION OF THIS BOOK

The focus of this volume is on the music, lyrics, and recordings of Prince; therefore, the book is arranged chronologically and has biographical information woven into the discussion of Prince's songs and recordings. I have also included a concluding chapter devoted to an assessment of Prince's work, as well as commentary on other artists' recordings of Prince's compositions.

With few exceptions, Prince has written or co-written all the material he has recorded throughout his 30-year career. A truly prolific writer and recording artist, Prince has a portfolio, according to some estimates, of more than one thousand songs. It would, therefore, be impossible to analyze all of his works thoroughly in an 80–90,000-word book. My focus in this book will be on the Prince compositions and recordings that have enjoyed official, commercial release. I will not deal with demos or bootleg recordings.

   This book's Bibliography includes many sources for further information on
Prince's life and work. Since the focus of this volume is on Prince's work as a
recording artist, I generally have not included references to concert reviews,
with a few notable exceptions. I have included annotations for most, but not
all, of the bibliographical citations.

   Note that in the Selected Discography I have included information pertaining to the principal medium for each album release (33–1/3 rpm vinyl
record and/or compact disc). Some of Prince's albums were also issued in
various tape media. I have not included information pertaining to these tape
releases because of the fact that tape was not the primary medium through
which the music was sold by Prince's record companies, and because of
the unfortunate fact that cassettes of the 1970s and 1980s are not likely to
have survived into the twenty-first century to the extent that vinyl and CDs
have. Because of what might be called the more transitory nature of singles
(they are very difficult to find in their original format in the digital age), I
have not included them in the discography.

   I have included an index of names, places, and song titles. Song titles include
those written and recorded by Prince, as well as songs by others that I discuss
in relationship to Prince's compositions and recordings. It should be noted
that I have included only the most extensive and most important discussions of
Prince's work in the various subheadings of his entry in the index.

1

Becoming a Star

THE YOUNG VIRTUOSO

Born in Minneapolis, Minnesota, on June 7, 1958, Prince Rogers Nelson entered a world filled with music. Prince's father, John L. Nelson, performed in the Prince Rogers Trio, and it was after this group that Prince was named. According to liner notes for the compact disc reissue of his second album, "at age seven, Prince first began picking out melodies to popular songs on the family piano."[1] Although John Nelson and Prince's mother, Mattie Shaw (who just so happened to be the vocalist with the Prince Rogers Trio), eventually divorced, Prince maintained ties with his father, who bought him his first guitar.

As early as junior high school, Prince was involved in the music business, playing in a number of bands. Prince's performance was not limited to the guitar; he also became a skilled piano and synthesizer player. In these prefame bands Prince also exhibited talent as an arranger, reportedly dictating the musical arrangements to other band members. A recording by one of these bands, 94 East, surfaced in the mid-1980s, by which time Prince had already become a star. Various minor labels have released the material under various names, including the British label Dressed to Kill, which issued it as *94 East,* by The Artist Formerly Known as Prince (METRO305, 1999).

The Dressed to Kill package begins with "One Man Jam," a pleasant disco instrumental. The piece is not Prince's most inspired writing—it is too repetitious to be included in a list of his best work—but it does highlight his virtuosic keyboard playing. "Dance to the Music of the World" closely resembles Prince's upbeat funk compositions and arrangements on *For You* and *Prince.*

Like the first piece on the album, however, it is an instrumental,[2] and is more reflective of the prevailing disco style of the day than the vast majority of Prince's so-called official solo work. The moderately paced "Games" is more interesting, largely because of the layered licks in the bass, guitars, and keyboards that gradually build up and eventually support a tenor saxophone solo. The next two tracks, "If You Feel Like Dancin'" and "If You See Me" continue the light funk/disco feel of the album's first two pieces. "Better Than You Think" is a not particularly interesting Quiet Storm (melodically soulful mood music, originally named after a Smoky Robinson song) ballad, except for the brief, inspired guitar solo. All in all, the album includes hints of Prince's later genius, particularly as an instrumentalist and arranger, but for the most part it consists of instrumentals that could really benefit from some other context (e.g., background music for a film, dance instrumentals, the addition of lyrics and a vocal melody) in order to work completely effectively.

By 1976, the still-teenaged Prince was working with producer Chris Moon on a solo demo record. Here, Prince was freed from the constraints of working with a band. Because of his instrumental and vocal skills, as well as skills in using the technology of the day, Prince could perform all the vocal and instrumental tracks. The finished demo record brought Prince to the attention of several record companies. He signed with Warner Bros., which took him into the studio to record an album.

FOR YOU

Recorded before Prince turned 20 years old, *For You* was released in 1978 as Warner Bros. 3150. Significantly, Prince wrote the music for all nine tracks on the album. He wrote all the lyrics for eight of the songs, and collaborated on the lyrics with Chris Moon on the other song. Prince arranged all of the vocal and instrumental tracks, played all the instruments, and sang all the vocal lines. He even designed the album's cover. While the ability to write, arrange, and perform all the vocal and instrumental parts on an album is rare enough, it is worth considering the company into which this debut effort placed the young artist from Minneapolis. Perhaps the most notable artists to completely control all aspects of a full album include Paul McCartney, Stevie Wonder, John Fogerty, and (but only on a purely synthesizer-based project) Frank Zappa. Of these four well-known musicians, only Stevie Wonder was Prince's age when first starting to fully write, produce, and perform an album's worth of material. The major difference? By the time Stevie Wonder was fully controlling his product in the late 1960s and early 1970s, he had already been a fixture in the pop music world for years, having emerged originally as a child star; *For You* was Prince's debut.

The album begins with "For You," an essentially wordless vocalise for the multitracked, *a cappella,* falsetto voice of Prince. Although the composition is barely more than a minute in length, it exhibits elements of just about every male vocal harmony style from barbershop, to gospel quartet, to doo-wop, to the *Pet Sounds* and *Smile* music of Brian Wilson, to the intricate vocal harmony of Queen's "Bohemian Rhapsody." The piece shows off the timbre (tone color) of Prince's voice and hints at the depth of his musical background; however, it is so short that the material is not as fully developed as it could be. On a micro level, the song "For You" suffers from the same problem as does the entire album of the same name: it finds Prince spread rather thin stylistically. This causes Prince's debut to show a wide range of influences, to show off Prince's considerable instrumental and vocal talents, but not to define him as a distinctive, focused, and innovative artist. Ultimately, Prince would use his eclecticism to his advantage—what appears to be a lack of focus on his debut would later be seen as incredible stylistic range on his famous albums of the 1980s.

The album's second track, "In Love," might be considered a fairly conventional upbeat R&B love song were it not for some sexual innuendos that are a tad more explicit than what the popish musical style would suggest. This is not to suggest that the only way or the best way to set graphic lyrics is to so-called graphic-sounding music. In fact, Prince himself has been quite successful at setting lyrics to music that seems to be strangely (and quite deliberately) at odds with the meaning of the text. In the best of these settings, the sense of irony that the disconnection creates becomes an important feature of the song. In the case of "In Love," it instead tends to come off as just a tad naughty. Musically, the piece is tuneful, danceable, but not a piece that digs its way into the listener's memory the way that Prince's pieces would start to do in a couple of years. The arrangement and performance also suffers somewhat from sounding too synthesizer-oriented, too canned, as it were.

Prince and Chris Moon's collaboration "Soft and Wet" moves away from the more pop-oriented R&B style of "In Love" toward funk. The slightly harder-core sexual innuendo, heavier beat, and more spontaneous sound of the arrangement and performance call to mind the popular late 1970s and early 1980s R&B funk of Rick James, an artist who emerged around the same time as Prince, but who was a decade older. Prince builds the instrumental accompaniment around a figure that uses the approximate rhythm of the phras*e soft and wet*. This gives the entire piece a feeling of rhythmic cohesion. This snappy hook is also infinitely more memorable than the broader and less-focused strokes of "In Love."

Unlike "In Love," which was sung totally in falsetto, "Soft and Wet" includes a little of Prince's lower range. This adds just a touch of machismo attitude that serves to reinforce the blatantly sexual nature of his character's interest in the woman whom he addresses. And, Moon and Prince's lyrics are plenty graphic. For example, the song begins with Prince stating that he has "a sugarcane" he can't wait to "lose in" the woman to whom he sings. Some of his references are just vague enough that it is not clear whether it is her mouth or her pubic region that is "soft and wet"; however, the sexual nature of his references is never in doubt. Although Prince's most famous—or, infamous—odes to various forms of sex (including "Darling Nikki," "Head," and "Do Me, Baby") were several years away, "Soft and Wet" shows that he was willing even at the earliest stages of his career to push the limits. Interestingly, though, because Prince sings so much of "Soft and Wet" and all of "In Love" in falsetto, there is a sense of disarming vulnerability that pervades the songs. This, in effect, sugarcoats the blatant eroticism and raw sexuality of the lyrics.

At approximately 2 ¼ minutes, "Crazy You" is the second-shortest track on *For You*. The synthesized chirping birds, gentle conga drums, slow tempo, and gentle falsetto singing of a surprisingly innocent set of love lyrics make this a popish R&B ballad. The touch of jazz influence in the guitar voicings and Prince's vocal style on the track almost suggest a musical meeting of George Benson and Marvin Gaye. It is about the sharpest contrast imaginable with the blatancy of "Soft and Wet"; however, it is erotic in its own bedroom ballad way.

Prince turns up the tempo and suggests 1970s disco in "Just As Long As We're Together." Although the lyrics and music are pleasant, they don't stick with the listener any more than any other pleasant disco song of the era. In fact, the offbeat high-hat cymbal and the bass line mark the song and arrangement as a remnant of the mid-1970s heyday of disco. The real highlight here is Prince's performance on multitracked voice, keyboards, guitars, and drums. He proves himself to be already, at the age of 20, a formidable one-man band. Even so, ultimately, "Just As Long As We're Together" turns out to be a groove piece that is just a little too long, too closely tied to a period style, and not quite distinctive enough to rank with Prince's best compositions and arrangements.

"Baby," a slow ballad, concerns a couple at a critical juncture in their relationship. The unspoken (at least until the last 10 seconds of the song) implication is that Prince's partner, to whom he sings, has just found out that she is pregnant by Prince's character. He tells her that he will abide by her decision whether they should continue to live together or "get married right away." Prince sings in a gentle falsetto, which conveys a sense of innocence and vulnerability. It is a tender approach to a complicated subject. Musically, the piece is pleasant, textbook R&B ballad material.

"My Love Is Forever" is, lyrically speaking, a more conventional, upbeat love song. And, again, while the music and lyrics might not be nearly as distinctive as Prince's work even just a few years in the future, the song exhibits a thorough understanding and mastery of contemporary popular R&B style. The song provides the first hints of Prince's virtuosity as a lead guitarist.

"So Blue," with its distinctive synthesizer and acoustic guitar textures, presents yet another side of Prince's musical personality. The chord changes and chord voicings in both the acoustic and electric guitar parts show the influence of jazz and pop standards on Prince. Prince sings with a jazz phrasing, extemporizing on the melodic material with a maturity that seems advanced for his age. Although the synthesized trombone sound seems like a dated electronic tone color today in the twenty-first century, "So Blue" as a whole holds up well because of Prince's engaging use of an incredibly wide falsetto vocal range.

Prince turns up the funk level on the album's final track, "I'm Yours." Prince's considerable talents as an arranger, producer, and lead guitarist really carry the song. The lyrics, which find Prince's character submitting to the desires of his partner for *his* first sexual encounter, play a decidedly secondary role. "I'm Yours" is really a guitar song. And, it shows Prince's mastery of rock (as opposed to purely R&B) guitar.

As a professional recording debut for a young singer/multi-instrumentalist/ songwriter, *For You* exhibits Prince's talents as a singer and instrumentalist who has a thorough understanding of contemporary R&B and (to a lesser extent) rock styles. Prince's compositions edge into some new ground with regard to explicitness of sexual material; however, rather than seeming to be on the cutting edge, they seem to be workable, solid examples of late 1970s R&B. Hints of the brilliance of Prince's work of the 1980s can be heard, but only hints.

PRINCE

Prince continues the pattern of *For You:* Prince, the young virtuoso demonstrating a command of contemporary pop music styles as a songwriter, singer, and multi-instrumentalist. On this 1979 album, however, Prince significantly expands his repertoire as a writer, arranger, and performer. He incorporates heavy metal, funk, Quiet Storm R&B, disco, pop, and (as unlikely as it may sound) elements of Charlie Daniels Band–style Southern rock. The melodic, rhythmic, and harmonic hooks of the songs are stronger, and significantly more memorable. As an instrumentalist, Prince shows off his drum and guitar playing to a far greater extent than on his debut. His arrangements incorporate a wider range of tone colors, although not always entirely convincingly. Although *Prince* did not establish the young Mr. Nelson as a superstar, the album provides significantly stronger evidence of his extraordinary talent than his debut.

The album kicks with "I Wanna Be Your Lover," a song labeled "excellent lite funk" by critic Stephen Thomas Erlewine.[3] With the song's tunefulness, Prince's vulnerable-sounding falsetto singing, and the love theme of the lyrics, this track takes the basic framework of Smoky Robinson's up-tempo songs of the 1960s and updates them with late 1970s instrumentation and accompaniment rhythms. There is, however, a huge catch. After the first verse, in which Prince places himself in opposition to the other men who vie for the attention of the woman he addresses—they have money, he does not, and so on—he sings in the chorus that he wants to be "the only one that makes [her] come running." Then, at the end of the chorus he repeats the sentiments, but with the altered wording, "I wanna be the only one you come for." The listener can hear this as a simple rephrasing of the first statement; however, given the explicit sexual sentiments expressed by Prince literally throughout his entire career, it is easy to understand this line to mean that he wants to be the only one who brings this woman to an orgasm. Sexual double entrendre of this level was never heard in the work of Smoky Robinson. Sexual double meaning or not, "I Wanna Be Your Lover" is stronger than any track on Prince's debut album, although the long fadeout tends to dissipate some of the energy of the song.

The album's second track, "Why You Wanna Treat Me So Bad?" stands as one of the best early examples of Prince's integration of disparate pop musical styles. The double lead guitar lines suggest the Southern rock of groups such as the Charlie Daniels Band and Lynyrd Skynyrd; Prince's vocal phrasing and the double-time rhythms of the vocal line come straight out of R&B; there is even a hint in the guitar and piano figure heard at the end of several phrases of the pop-rock of the late-1960s/early-1970s band Badfinger's "Day after Day." All of these stylistic hints are fully integrated to the extent that "Why You Wanna Treat Me So Bad?" truly becomes a genre buster: it refuses to fall into a pigeonhole.

The music, instrumental arrangement, and instrumental performance are really the highlights of the song. Prince's major-key melody weaves its way down from the dominant (fifth scale-step) to tonic (first scale-step) in the chorus providing an easy-to-remember popish hook for the song's title line. He harmonizes this hook in the double lead guitar line that pervades the piece. Every detail of the arrangement is worked out for maximum affect and appeal, right down to the powerful downward glissandi in the keyboards. The slightly distorted guitar solo Prince plays at the end of the song sounds thoroughly his own, but it is possible to pick up the repeated figures of Southern rock, the wide vibrato and tremolos of Jimi Hendrix and early 1970s hard rock and heavy metal guitarists. The single release of "Why You Wanna Treat Me So Bad?" reached No. 13 on *Billboard*'s Black Singles charts—successful, but not nearly as successful as "I Wanna Be Your Lover," which hit No. 1 on the Black Singles chart and No. 11 on the pop charts.

Prince is an album that seems to be mostly about Prince writing and performing genre pieces. "Sexy Dancer" clearly falls into that category. The *ostinato,* pretty-much-one-chord rhythm guitar figure that runs throughout the entire piece screams "James Brown" to any listener familiar with Brown's groove-based songs of the mid- to late 1960s and early 1970s. There are hints of Sly Stone's brand of funk from the same time period. Prince's lyrics say little aside from identifying the object of his attention as a "sexy dancer," whose body he "want[s]." The lyrics, however, are not really what the piece is about; it is about the rhythmic groove. One of the perhaps unexpected highlights of the piece is Prince's piano solo, which makes reference to the swing-era Glenn Miller hit "In the Mood." Whether the listener gets the so-called joke ("in the mood"—wanting the dancer's body) clearly depends on the listener's ability to recognize the source of the musical quote. It probably can strike the astute listener, though, either as a sly, clever, wink-wink-nudge-nudge in-joke, or as a too-obvious groaner. In my ears, it wears less well with repeated hearings; it is both clever and funny the first time, though. The solo itself exhibits such technical command and rhythmic precision that it suggests sequencing, as opposed to a live improvisation.

The next two tracks, "When We're Dancing Close and Slow" and "With You," are straightforward ballads. Since several of the up-tempo pieces on *Prince* are so distinctive—particularly "I Wanna Be Your Lover," "Why You Wanna Treat Me So Bad," "Bambi," and "I Feel for You"—the two ballads tend to come off as pleasant-enough album tracks, but not as highlights of the album. They just do not possess the kind of recognizable musical and lyrical hooks that would make them stand out.

The next track, "Bambi," exhibits Prince's command of the hard rock/heavy metal genre better than any of his other early songs. The electric guitar tone color and some of the melodic figurations—most notably the wide trills—suggest Led Zeppelin's Jimmy Page and other British metal bands of the early 1970s, such as Black Sabbath. The lead guitar hook, with its short, easy-to-remember tune, also recalls some of Jimi Hendrix's more memorable guitar riff–based compositions, such as "Fire." The virtuosity of the solo and Prince's use of a sustained tone also suggest the influence of Carlos Santana. Musically, however, the piece so fully integrates these various influences from the late 1960s and early 1970s that it never sounds derivative of any one particular guitar god of the previous generation. It is, however, a genre piece. One of the more interesting structural features is the close motivic resemblance between the vocal refrain in the chorus and the lead guitar answer. A lesser writer might have answered the vocal line with an exact instrumental repetition. In Prince's hands, the answer is varied just enough that it takes on its own identity, while being closely related to the vocal line that precedes it.

The lyrics of this heavy metal song of love and physical desire find Prince's character telling young Bambi that she will never fully understand love and life until she's had a lover who is a real man (presumably, like Prince's character). The lyrics here do not break new ground; however, the lyrics in and of themselves are not what the piece is about. As Prince would do increasingly in the early 1980s, he creates the whole *gestalt* of the piece more through the arrangement and overall feel than through motives, melody, harmony, rhythm, or lyrics.

It should be noted that Prince's work is not alone in contemporary music in the importance of arrangement and feel in delivering the ultimate meaning of the piece to the listener. As rock composer, lyricist, guitarist, and singer Frank Zappa notes:

On a record, the overall timbre of the piece (determined by equalization of individual parts and their proportions in the mix) tells you, in a subtle way, *WHAT* the song is about. The orchestration provides *important informa- tion* about what the composition *IS* and, in some instances, assumes a greater importance than *the composition itself*.[4]

Prince's next song, "Still Waiting," presents a complete sonic contrast. This song has an easygoing, moderate-tempo, lightly gospel-influenced feel. Prince's lyrics present him as a man who hears his friends telling him about how wonderful finding love has been in their lives. Prince's character, how- ever, is "still waiting for [his] love to come around." The lyrical style, with its complete focus on the emotional—as opposed to physical—side of love is at odds with just about everything on Prince's first several albums. In addition, most of Prince's lyrics, whether of love or lust, clearly define the object of his desire. Here, in contrast, his character has not met his future lover, nor does he objectify her in any concrete way. And, the musical style, which suggests more than anything else Crystal Gayle's 1977 country and pop hit "Don't It Make My Brown Eyes Blue," is also well outside the bulk of Prince's best-known work. All of this, along with the fact that Prince sings all the lead and backing vocal lines high in his falsetto range, adds up to sug- gest that this may have been a song that was meant to be shopped around, perhaps for recording by a female artist.

There certainly is nothing wrong with that. In fact, "Still Waiting" shows command of this pop ballad genre. There are elements that go well beyond a mere exercise in the (for want of a better term) "Don't It Make My Brown Eyes Blue" genre. For example, Prince uses a repeating, largely diatonic (only the pitches of a single major scale) chord progression throughout the vast majority of the song; however, in a couple of places—which will be noticeable even to the musical novice—he moves to harmonies that are outside the immediate key. These secondary-dominant-function harmonies snap the complacent listener back to attention, thereby reminding him or her of the urgency of the plight of Prince's character. In the chorus section, Prince uses harmony, melodic motion, and a consistency of lyrical phrase structure to build up the expectation that the chorus will end at a particular point. He then turns to chromatic chords (harmonies outside the key area) that allow him to extend the ending of the chorus. This allows him musi- cally to portray the idea of "still waiting."

One of the more popular bands of the late 1960s and early 1970s, Sly and the Family Stone combined elements of funk and rock. The group included black and white, male and female musicians, and it appealed both to tradition- ally pop and R&B audiences, so it managed to break stereotypes both musi- cally and demographically. Sly Stone's best-remembered songs—"Everyday People," for example—featured simple, easy-to-sing and easy-to-remember melodies. Prince's "I Feel for You" calls to mind the work of Sly Stone and his band on a couple of levels. The song has an easily singable, hook-laden melody in both verse and chorus, and it features Prince singing in his natural range as well as in falsetto, which suggests a mixed-gender ensemble. Although Prince's recording of "I Feel for You" is not his best-known work on this particular album, Chaka Khan, Kylie Minogue, and other pop singers later recorded cover versions of the song. Khan's recording of the song was such a success in 1984 that she won a Grammy Award for Best R&B Vocal Performance, Female, and Prince won the Grammy for Best Rhythm and Blues Song for "I Feel for You."

Prince concludes with the song "It's Gonna Be Lonely," a Quiet Storm R&B ballad. Here, Prince uses his falsetto to portray a vulnerable character that is trying to recover from a failed relationship. It is a pleasant album track; however, it is not nearly as distinctive as Prince's great, later ballads would be. "It's Gonna Be Lonely" includes too many lead vocal and instrumental accompaniment references to earlier songs to succeed fully. In particular, there are brief figures that suggest the 1973 Spinners hit "Could It Be I'm Falling in Love" and the 1966 Smoky Robinson and the Miracles hit "I Second That Emotion."

Prince's second album made considerably more of a commercial impact than did his debut, largely on the strength of "I Wanna Be Your Lover" and "Why You Wanna Treat Me So Bad?" It found him exploring several disparate styles of the 1970s, including various subgenres of R&B, Southern rock, pop, and heavy metal. However, he also made this unusual combination of styles sound more personal and more natural than on his debut. Still, though, in hindsight, *Prince* suggests the work of a highly talented singer-songwriter-multi-instrumentalist who was just one small step away from putting together a completely personal package in a thoroughly convincing way so as to firmly etch himself into mass public consciousness.

DIRTY MIND

Dirty Mind found Prince returning to the more explicit sexual references of *For You,* his debut album. As he had done on both *For You* and *Prince,* he continued to defy musical categorization. Here, he includes funk, pop, new wave rock, and references to early rock and roll in his mix of styles. On the 1980 album *Dirty Mind,* however, the material overall is more memorable, and more sexually explicit. In short, Prince takes more musical and lyrical chances, and in doing so, he takes a positive step toward establishing himself as an unique artist of major importance. In fact, *All Music Guide*'s Stephen Thomas Erlewine calls the album a "full-blown masterpiece."[5]

The title track, "Dirty Mind," finds Prince telling a young woman that whenever he is around her, he gets "a dirty mind," and is consumed by his desire to "lay [her] down." It is raw; it is clear; it is explicit. Prince dispenses with the niceties of the courting ritual and any pretense of emotional attachment. His use of the word *love* is entirely within the context of raw sex, and then entirely for his own physical pleasure. At the same time as Prince dispenses with customary metaphors for sex, or even with sly double entendres, his music is just as groundbreaking. This is an upbeat funk track, somewhat airier and lighter in sound than much of the other sexually oriented funk music that was around at the time, principally because of Prince's falsetto singing and emphasis on mid-range and higher-pitched accompaniment. Prince's setting of short declamatory statements in what are close to speech rhythms is echoed in Rick James's 1981 hit "Super Freak." Where Prince's music in "Dirty Mind" really breaks free of the constraints of textbook funk style, though, is in his use of a chromatically rising melodic line between scale-steps five and eight at the ends of some of the sections. This rising line is accompanied by a chromatic chord progression that breaks free of the traditional tonal system. The harmonic progression is goal-directed toward the tonic chord; however, the traditional fourth- and fifth-related root movement of much pop and classical movement is absent. It is thoroughly modern sounding, yet also thoroughly accessible. Incidentally, the same rising chromatic line and accompanying harmony would be heard in the late 1990s at the end of the theme music in numerous television infomercials produced by infomercial guru Kevin Trudeau's organization.

Prince turns from funk to the then-current new wave style for "When You Were Mine." The twangy electric guitar and Farfisa organ texture, as well as the drum part—with its Ringo Starr–ish snare drum on beat two, the "and" of two, and on beat four—all practically scream "new wave" to the listener. The new wave's embrace of the sound of prepsychedelic 1960s music (1964 and 1965, in particular) is also confirmed by the simple melodicism of the tune, as well as the song's simple harmony. In contrast to most of the new wave material of the day, "When You Were Mine" is fairly sexually graphic. The woman who Prince's character now loves more than he did when she was his used to cheat on him in his bed and then "didn't have the decency to change the sheets." The song is the kind of backhanded declaration of love that one might expect to hear from, say, an Elvis Costello; however, it does take a step toward the explicit beyond what Costello was writing at the time.

The largely synthesizer-based "Do It All Night" finds Prince stepping back somewhat from the explicitly sexual references. It's clear enough just what he wants to "do" all night; however, the title line itself is about as graphic as this song gets. It is a melodically interesting, upbeat soul song, reminiscent somewhat of the popular blue-eyed soul of Daryl Hall and John Oates.

"Gotta Broken Heart Again" finds Prince playing the role of a jilted lover, who has a "broken heart again." It is a thoroughly commercially viable, radio-friendly (that is, tuneful and lyrically innocuous) shuffle-rhythm

R&B song. The song is brief, weighing in at less than 2 ½ minutes, but it demonstrates—perhaps even better than the songs of *For You* and *Prince*—Prince's command of contemporary commercial styles. Because the song is so focused on Prince's lead vocal, it is easy to overlook his brief electric guitar solo. Serious students of Prince, however, will want to pay attention to this solo, since it demonstrates a side of Prince's playing not often heard: a blues-based (as opposed to soul or rock) tone and articulation.

The album's next song, "Uptown," is considerably more substantial. Here, Prince portrays an urban character that catches the eye of a beautiful woman. Once the two begin a conversation and he starts throwing pickup lines, she asks, "Are you gay?" Prince's character is momentarily taken aback, but then returns the same question to her. The passive/aggressive encounter Prince describes points out some of the game playing of dating and courtship, especially as two attractive individuals initially feel each other out to see just what lies beyond surface appearances. Despite the game playing, and Prince's feeling that the woman is mixed up and too focused on conforming to society's norms (unlike Prince's character, who is secure in his counterculture lifestyle), the two ultimately hook up for a sexual encounter later that day. Prince's conclusion is that the Truth (with a capital "T") of going uptown is being free.

All of the intricacies of the story and implications of "Uptown" are wrapped in catchy music that suggests an integration of R&B and new wave. In a way, it suggests some of the work of the early 1980s of the band Talking Heads in this respect. Prince uses conventional harmonies, and his melody is built from short, simple phrases. The song is catchy, with a singable chorus hook and a straightforward dance beat. It illustrates Prince's command of the contemporary dance idiom of the day.

"Head" finds Prince turning up the level of explicit eroticism a couple of notches. In this song, Prince portrays a young man who meets up with a virgin, who is dressed in her wedding dress on her way to the wedding ceremony. She gives Prince's character oral sex in the back of the limousine; however, he ejaculates on the wedding dress. Yes, it is graphic, and definitely deserves an R rating; however, the story probably represents a dark male fantasy to which at least a few of Prince's listeners could relate. Songs such as "Head" are all about exploring repressed sexual fantasy. Writers have done this sort of thing for years; however, pop songwriters prior to Prince's time generally shied away from such graphic sexual material. Prince's exploration of the male psyche does not pass judgment on such fantasies; it simply acknowledges that, whether or not polite society wishes to admit it, it is part of reality.

It is far too easy to focus on the lyrical content of "Head" and ignore Prince's work as an instrumentalist, arranger, bandleader, and producer. Dr. Fink's keyboard work on the track is impeccable, and the production is exceptionally clean and clear. Lisa Coleman's deliberately understated vocal work on the song suggests that her character wishes to control, but cannot control, her dark desire to bring oral gratification to Prince's character on her wedding day. The effect is that of a fully formed composition, from lyrics, melody, and chords, to arrangement, performance, and recording production. As one example of the fully formed nature of the piece, I would cite the close motivic ties between the keyboard hook and the vocal melody, both of which emphasize the minor third scale-step and the lowered seventh scale converging on the tonic (first) scale-step.

Exceptionally brief at 1 minute, 31 seconds, "Sister" is still one of the most provocative songs on *Dirty Mind*. To fast-paced new wave rock music (with a touch of neo-rockabilly), Prince sets a story about incest. The premise is that his 16-year-old character first had sex with his sister, who at the time was "thirty-two, lovely, and [pause] loose." While neither the story nor the music is as fully developed as it might be, this paean to incest breaks at least a couple of pop song taboos. First of all, Prince's character is underage (16) when a woman twice his age seduces him. And, of course, secondly, she just happens to be his sister. The song makes a direct segue into "Partyup."

"Partyup" combines the urge to party ("got to partyup") with antiwar sentiment ("fightin' war is such a fuckin' bore"). As an antiwar statement, it comes off as pretty shallow. The obvious question that arises is, if you are so against the draft (which Prince mentions, but which was not in place at the time) and "the war," why not do something about it, instead of dropping out and partying? Prince would take a similar juxtaposition (partying vs. dealing with the end of the world) in "1999." In "1999," Prince's intent would be much clearer than it is in "Partyup." Perhaps he is not being shallow here; perhaps he is pointing out the apathy he sees around him. The fact is that the lyrics and the overall feel of the song are so unclear that it is difficult to tell.

In light of Prince's eventually infamy as one of the principal artists who motivated Tipper Gore and other members of the Washington, D.C., elite to establish the Parents Music Resource Center, it is easy to focus too much on the so-called dirty part of *Dirty Mind*. Certainly, part of the importance of the album was in the way in which it opened up formerly taboo pop song subjects at the start of the 1980s. Other subsequent artists would pick up on this in their work increasingly throughout the decade. The thing that makes *Dirty Mind* stand out among the sexually explicit albums of the past nearly three decades, however, is the music. In particular, Prince sets the explicit texts—and all of his texts on *Dirty Mind*—to music that is tuneful and thoroughly commercial sounding. Prince's production is crisp and clear, making it radio-friendly, even if the lyrics are not. The musical component of *Dirty Mind* is perhaps more interesting to the listener, though, than the explicit sexual references, or even the commerciality with which Prince coats those references. If one completely disregards the lyrics, the songs showcase Prince's command of new wave, soul, R&B, and hybrid mixes of styles. His singing and playing is more confident and wide-ranging than on his first two albums, too.

CONTROVERSY

Prince has been the most prolific singer-songwriter of his generation, so it should not be a surprise that his fourth album, *Controversy*, appeared in 1981, hot on the heels of *Dirty Mind*. *Controversy* found Prince once again writing, producing, and performing almost every vocal and instrumental part; however, as had been the case with *Dirty Mind*, there are important contributions from collaborators. On *Controversy*, keyboardist/vocalist Lisa Coleman, drummer Bobby Z., and keyboardist Dr. Fink (Matthew Fink) contribute to varying degrees on all of the tracks. It goes a long way toward defining Prince's soon-to-be band, the Revolution. The album also plays an important role in defining Prince as a lyricist. *Dirty Mind* was so ground-breaking in its exploration of sexual taboo that it could have defined Prince as a narrow, single-subject songwriter—much like some of the 1950s so-called blue comedians were usually defined solely as dirty comics, despite their ability to present convincingly a variety of types of material. *Controversy* finds Prince exploring a richer variety of subjects. He had already established himself as a composer, singer, and multi-instrumentalist who defied genre categories; *Controversy* helped him to establish himself as a multidimensional lyricist. On the musical level, the album has created some, well, controversy. While some view it as a rehash of *Dirty Mind*, others—including myself—consider it to be more of an extension and refinement of *Dirty Mind*. Prince writes in the same sort of unique combination of funk, new wave, R&B, and rock that marked *Dirty Mind;* however, the styles are more fully integrated, and the pieces are more consistently fully developed.

The title track, "Controversy," leads off the album. The song finds Prince exploring a theme that he has continued to explore throughout his career: his desire that the things that keep people apart, such as religion, race, and sexual orientation (to name a few), would vanish. He suggests that the listener live in the here and now; life is a party and while we are here on earth, we should enjoy the experience and allow others to do the same. "Controversy" explores the theme more thoroughly and in a more metaphorically elegant way than any of the songs on Prince's first three albums. To the extent that "1999," the title track for the album that would follow *Controversy*, would represent something of an apex in Prince's exploration of the theme, then "Controversy" represents an important step in the development of the theme. In addition, Prince mentions that he does not understand people's fascination with the sordid details of others' personal lives. Although it would be several years before George Harrison would refer to gossip metaphorically as "the Devil's radio" in a particularly memorable way on his 1987 song "Devil's

Radio" (*Cloud Nine*, 1987), Prince's "Controversy" points out the danger of gossip and fascination with others' personal lives nearly as effectively—but in different terms.

Musically, "Controversy" is a 7 ¼-minute funk workout. The rhythm guitar style is clearly descended from James Brown. The melody, which is made up of short, narrow-range, easy-to-remember motives sung in octaves, suggests the writing and arranging approach of Sly Stone. Speaking of Stone, the lyrical theme is a direct lineage from Sly and the Family Stone's "Everyday People." Despite these obvious ties, the piece is thoroughly contemporary sounding—easily right at home in the dance club idiom of the early 1980s. In fact, David Bowie's 1983 hit "Let's Dance," with co-production from disco star Nile Rodgers of Chic, is not all that far removed stylistically from this 1981 Prince song. The recording includes some hard rock–style lead guitar figures from Prince, something that steps beyond the usual stylistic constraints of the era. It is because of this kind of integration of styles on the songs of *Controversy* that I hear this album as much more than the musical rehash of *Dirty Mind* that some listeners hear.

There is one other aspect of "Controversy" I would like to discuss. In approximately the last 1 minute and 45 seconds of the song, Prince presents a brief repeated spoken refrain that breaks into a canon (or round). At first glance, Prince's sentiments might seem a little too obvious and sexually oriented ("I wish we all were nude") to be given serious consideration. However, there is some intangible quality about the rap—perhaps it is just the fact that Prince treats it in a strict canon—that suggests something beyond the obvious might be contained therein. It seems not to be too much of a stretch to hear the phrase about being nude to refer to Prince's desire to see the external trappings of life stripped away, so that each person can relate to every other person without reference to any of the things that pull people apart. In other words, Prince seems to be saying—to quote a 1972 John Lennon and Yoko Ono song—"We're All Water," basically the theme of Sly Stone's "Everyday People."

On the surface, the sentiments of "Sexuality" are much more to the point and less metaphorical. Here, Prince says in not so many words that all he ever needs is sexuality. Throughout the song, however, he expounds upon several issues (the intoxication provided by television and the way in which so many people seem to "experience" life as though they are tourists—observing, but not truly participating). As the song progresses, it becomes increasingly clear that "Sexuality" is much more than a song about sexuality; it is really about the importance of living life in the here and now and interacting with people, rather than simply watching a second- or third-hand simulation of life. That Prince develops his theme on several fronts and that he does so using music that effectively bridges the gap between new wave rock and R&B show the progress that he had made as an innovative and accomplished songwriter from the time of his first two albums, just a couple of years before.

"Do Me, Baby" is less successful. This Quiet Storm–ish R&B ballad finds Prince replacing the sexual metaphors of traditional R&B ballads with fairly explicit references to playing "with my love," which in context sounds an awful lot like a reference to his penis, and "doing" him. Near the end of the song, Prince tells his lover that he wants to continue making love to her until "the war is over." In the context of the early 1980s, this is a problem: America was not in the midst of a long, protracted war at the time. This fact weakens the song, making it seem like a period piece from another time. The problem is, had it been from an earlier time (such as the Vietnam era), the lyrics would have been too out of place stylistically.

The album's next track, "Private Joy," is an up-tempo dance track that mixes R&B and new wave rock styles. This tale, in which Prince tells his "little orgasmatron" that she is the only one who will "play with [his] toy," is a more effective song of graphic eroticism than "Do Me, Baby." Largely, this is a result of the tempo of the piece: frankly, it is in more of a sex tempo than a sweet-talking tempo. Prince makes the sexual references completely disarming, however, by means of the simple, sing-along, Sly Stone–ish melody. Prince's electric guitar solo near the end of the track breaks down into some distortion and feedback that provides a segue into "Ronnie, Talk to Russia."

Prince's previous album, *Dirty Mind,* contained one very brief, fast-paced (almost Ramones tempo) rock song: "Sister." "Ronnie, Talk to Russia" plays the same role on *Controversy.* Here, Prince turns to retro-style rock as he addresses U.S. President Ronald Reagan. He urges the president to "talk to Russia" in an effort to disarm tensions between the world's two principal nuclear powers. The sentiments were certainly topical, particularly in the context of Reagan's infamous (what he thought was) off-microphone comment, "Let the bombing begin." The song suffers somewhat, though, from the recorded gunfire that is heard at the end of the short piece—the gunfire effect is just too derivative of Vietnam-era songs such as the Fugs' "Kill for Peace" and the early studio version of Country Joe and the Fish's "I-Feel-Like-I'm-Fixin'-to-Die Rag." Besides, were the United States and the Soviet Union of the early 1980s actually to get into war, it would not be small arms fire that would have provided the soundtrack. Curiously, that is just what Prince's lyrics say. Why, then, effectively downplay the message with the sound of small arms fire?

Prince returns to the theme of sex in "Let's Work." Here, though, sex ("let's work") is considerably more metaphorical. It is straight-ahead funk, and, while not the most memorable Prince song, works effectively as a dance track. The next piece, "Annie Christian" is more substantial lyrically. In this composition—which can't really be labeled a song, since it is completely spoken with instrumental accompaniment—Prince creates his own version of the New York City performance art sound, the scene parodied to great effect in the 1982 cult film *Liquid Sky.* Accompanied by a drum machine and a repeated, simple chord progression, Prince recites his narrative about

Annie Christian, a character that represents Evil. Annie is responsible for racial discrimination (killing black children), the murder of John Lennon, the attempted murder of Ronald Reagan, and other atrocities. She cares only for power and the material things in life.

The piece's chorus is especially interesting for one reference that Prince makes. He states that until Annie Christian is "crucified," he will live his life "in taxicabs." This image is especially rich. On one hand, the image of Prince's character being forced to live his life in taxis can be understood to mean that he, a black man, will only be able to earn a living through jobs such as driving a cab: not exactly a white-collar occupation. The image can also be understood as a statement of Prince's character's economic plight: as long as Annie Christian practices her racial discrimination, Prince will not be able to afford his own vehicle; he will have to pay for taxicabs for his longer-range intra-urban travels. Prince would resurrect the Annie Christian image several years in the future in the song "Sign o' the Times."

Prince concludes *Controversy* with his ode to manual sexual stimulation, "Jack U Off." Basically, Prince describes a series of private (in the back of a parked car) and public (in the back row of a movie theater, or in a crowded restaurant) situations in which he might be able to manually stimulate (jack off, in the vernacular) his female lover. This song features a snappy neo-rockabilly style. It is a solid musical effort from the standpoint of Prince's writing and performance; however, the song is easy to interpret as mere sexual titillation—a song lacking a whole lot of substance. It may fit the theme of "controversy" that is at the heart of the album, but it does not add significantly to the Prince canon.

Controversy showed Prince's continuing development as a composer, arranger, and performer. As a lyricist, he tackled some sensitive issues on the album, but at times turned to mere titillation. The album capped off the first phase of Prince's career. He had grabbed the attention of a sizable public, but had not quite entered into the realm of the pop culture icon—that step was quickly to come.

Mixing Rock and Funk with the Revolution

Prince's early singles and albums had earned him a fairly sizable fan base; however, they had not resulted in widespread fame throughout the whole of U.S. popular culture. The next phase of his career found Prince continuing to mix R&B and rock in unique ways; however, it also found him turning increasingly to rock, and especially, psychedelia. In doing so, Prince's white audience expanded as his black audience diminished somewhat. As a lyricist, Prince became more subtle and metaphorical in this period. Although he continued to expand his range as a writer, arranger, singer, and instrumentalist, he also developed a fairly democratic band for a period. And, perhaps most notably, he at last achieved the status of pop culture icon.

1999

Prince had enjoyed some commercial and critical success before the 1983 release of the album *1999*. The album and the singles it spawned ("1999," "Delirious," and "Little Red Corvette"), however, placed Prince in an entirely different league. Although neither the album nor any of the singles actually hit No. 1 on *Billboard*'s pop or R&B charts, the album made it to the Top 10 on both the pop and R&B charts, and the three singles made it into the Top 20 of *Billboard*'s Black Singles and Pop Singles. More significantly than sales, however, the songs, especially "1999" and "Little Red Corvette," defined the year 1983: both found their way onto several lists of the most significant songs of the 1980s.[1] Moreover, *1999* was Prince's masterpiece of production and instrumental work up to that point in his career—it is a guitar- and synthesizer-driven album, with Prince himself playing nearly every instrument.

That by itself is nothing new: he had been the sole or primary songwriter, producer, arranger, singer, and instrumentalist on all of his previous efforts. Here, for the first time, the songs sound entirely organic. For one thing, Prince eschewed his previous wild stylistic swings for a more unified funk approach. The lyrics, too, reach a higher level than on any of Prince's previous albums: there is a more cohesive view of the universe that is presented, and some truly interesting religious and philosophical subtext to the songs.

The album kicks off with the voice of God (presumably) telling the audience not to worry because he "won't hurt you," he only wants the hearer to "have some fun." This otherworldly introduction begins the song "1999." Unfortunately, in retrospect, the electronic processing of Prince's voice in assuming the persona of God does not wear well. Like some of the synthesizer work on various recordings of the 1970s and early 1980s, the processed voice of the "1999" introduction just seems kind of cheesy in light of subsequent technological achievements in sound synthesis and sound manipulation. Be that as it may, it does not significantly detract from what is one of the masterpieces of late twentieth-century pop music. The status of "1999" as a classic is a result of three main features: (1) the music and arrangement; (2) the totality of the world and personal philosophical view that the lyrics present; and (3) Prince's sense of timing in writing, recording, and releasing the song.

The melody of the verses and the chorus of "1999" suggest a higher level of sophistication than in Prince's earlier work. The verse consists of four phrases, each sung with a distinctive timbre (tone color) and range, as if to suggest Sly and the Family Stone–style shared lead vocals (in the manner of "Everyday People"). The first phrase begins on the fourth scale-step, descends to the first scale-step, and then moves up to conclude on the third scale-step. The second phrase emphasizes the second scale-step at its conclusion. The third and fourth phrases emphasize scale-step three. Prince's avoidance of scale-step one at the end of all four phrases gives the verse an unresolved quality. A melodic move to tonic (scale-step one) only comes at the end of the chorus. In this respect, the chorus makes (musical) sense of the verses, just as the lyrics of the chorus make sense of the details of Prince's dream, which he describes in the verses.

The other structural feature of "1999" that stands out is the sense of ongoing variation that Prince provides, especially as the coda section repeats over and over. He makes subtle changes to the instrumental accompaniment, and adds a spoken question ("Mommy, why does everybody have a bomb?") to the texture. So, even as the song seems to establish a groove that repeats over and over, the listener actually receives new musical and lyrical information throughout the extensive coda section.

In some of his earlier recordings and album cover art Prince had alluded to some of his philosophical and religious beliefs; "1999" the song and *1999* the album find him focusing in on presenting his view of the universe to an extent not found in any of his earlier work. The song "1999" begins with Prince describing a dream in which the sky was clothed in purple on Judgment Day. The imagery provided by the color purple is interesting. For one thing, purple traditionally has been associated with royalty. In mainline Christianity, however, purple is also commonly associated with the season of Lent, a time of preparation for the crucifixion and resurrection. Both of these images of the color purple fit in with Prince's image of purple as the color of the end of the world: it is a time of the arrival of the Kingdom of God, and it is a time when humans will experience the afterlife *en masse*. In fact, Prince alludes to his belief in God and in the afterlife not only in "1999" but in lyrics from later songs on the album. The other—and what some people might consider conflicting—message of "1999" is that one's purpose on earth is to "party" and generally enjoy oneself. Prince expresses a view that runs completely counter to mortification of the flesh as a means of doing God's will. Prince's religious philosophy is that God put people on earth to have a good time, to enjoy themselves. The unspoken message of "1999" is that redemption from sin and eternal life will come solely through one's beliefs and the grace of God.

The other lyrical feature of "1999" that stands out, especially in the post–September 11, 2001, world, is the spoken question, "Mommy, why does everybody have a bomb?," which occurs near the end of the song. Prince seems to have changed his assessment of exactly what would be most likely to happen at the end of the world. On the album *Controversy*, he expressed fear that a nuclear holocaust between the United States and the Soviet Union would signal Judgment Day. Here, however, he seems to suggest that the wholesale slaughter of humanity will take place at the hands of a whole lot of people wielding smaller bombs—an image that seems especially eerie in light of the rise of international terrorism, with its reliance on suicide bombs and car bombs.

Another part of the genius of "1999" is the song's timing. Prince is to be given credit for effectively merging the spirit of the time, the musical style of the time, and the coming of the millennium in such a way as to create a song that resonated in 1983 and in 1999 just as strongly. The year 1983 was crucial at least in part to the success of "1999" because of its proximity to 1984, the temporal setting of George Orwell's famous novel *1984*. Around the United States people pondered just how close the country and the world was to the Orwellian concept of "1984," and Prince's dream of the apocalypse fits right in with that "1984" theme. That the song was written and released during the Reagan administration was also significant. For one thing, there had been an earlier attempt to assassinate the president, which left Americans somewhat nervous about the state of the nation and the world—if a would-be assassin can get that close to the heavily guarded President of the United States, how can anyone be safe? It was also significant that the song appeared during the Reagan administration because some liberals feared that a conservative leader such as Reagan would be more inclined to start World War III than a more moderate or a left-wing leader.

The song "1999" had a resurgence of popularity at the end of the millennium. The party theme, the unease at the possible religious implications of the end of the millennium, struck a chord with audiences as the year 2000 approached. In the years between the release of the song and the year 1999 there had been a number of devastating and well-publicized terror attacks with bombs (the 1985 bombing of Air India Flight 182, the December 1988 bombing of Pan Am Flight 103, the February 1993 bombing of the World Trade Center, the March 1993 bombings in Mumbai, India, the April 1995 Oklahoma City bombing, the 1996 Centennial Olympic Park bombing, and the 1998 bombings of U.S. embassies in Kenya and Tanzania) that seemed to confirm Prince's suspicions. The thing that really sealed the continuing popularity of "1999," however, was its easy-to-remember melodic hooks, and its minimalistic rhythmic groove. It is a dance piece that, because the recording is not overproduced like some 1980s material, sounds musically vital into the twenty-first century.

It would also be appropriate to mention Prince's composition "Manic Monday" at this point.[2] This song, which was a huge commercial success for the Bangles (*Billboard* Pop No. 2) in 1986, is clearly derived from "1999." In fact, from a long-range structural standpoint and from a small-scale motivic standpoint, the verses of the two songs are very similar. In "Manic Monday," however, Prince bases the four phrases of the verse on exactly the same melodic motion. The song therefore lacks some of the melodic richness of "1999." The relative simplicity of the verses and the chorus (which is also based on, but more simple than, the chorus melody of "1999"), however, is offset by a middle-eight section that includes more elaborate melodic and harmonic melody. The presence of a heard-one-time middle-eight section reflects back to British Invasion (1964–1965) pop-rock songs. In fact, the melodic simplicity of the rest of "Manic Monday" can give the listener the sense that Prince was taking material from "1999" and deconstructing it— taking out the funk rhythms, the funk shared lead vocals, and building the fragments back up into a fully realized mid-1960s pop-rock song. It should be noted, however, that the sung and spoken lyrics of the middle-eight snap the listener into the realization that this is no remnant from 1964; the purely physical sexual desire that is expressed when the singer's lover tells her in his "bedroom voice," "come on honey, let's go make some noise," is more pointed than what would usually be heard in 1964 Top 40 pop, especially in a song sung by a woman, given the more narrowly defined gender roles of the first half of the 1960s. It should also be noted that one of the more obvious differences between "Manic Monday" and "1999" is the clarity of production and the immediacy of the instruments on the Bangles' hit: the Prince recording of "1999" loses some potential potency because of its somewhat amorphous synthesizers.

The second track on *1999*, "Little Red Corvette," is one of Prince's best uses of metaphor. This moderate-tempo R&B and pop hit actually finds Prince using a psychedelic mix of metaphors to describe his reaction to a casual sexual encounter with a woman who was more willing than his character to take sexual chances. All of this is bathed in synthesizer-based pop music.

In "Little Red Corvette," Prince uses two primary images: (1) the little red Chevrolet Corvette of the song's title, and (2) horses, to create a delightfully rich mix of metaphors. The woman with whom Prince's character enjoys a casual sexual encounter without the protection of condoms seems at the same time to drive a little red Corvette and to be the personification of the sports car. At the start of the song, Prince refers to the woman parking sideways, which suggests that she drives the little sports car; however, later in the song, he uses the image of the Corvette to suggest that it is a metaphor for the so-called fast woman. Similarly, Prince uses the images of horses in a deliberately confusing way. First, he equates horses with Trojans, the brand of condoms. Later, however, he intimates that the woman agrees to unprotected sex, which he connects to the image of the woman's horses running free. The horses, then, in a curiously mixed metaphor, refer to the vehicle by which the couple's casual sex could have been protected from pregnancy and sexually transmitted diseases, *and* to the wild sexual abandon of Prince's partner. The most interesting thing about Prince's use of mixed (or even contradictory) metaphors is that the listener knows exactly what is going on. Prince knows that his audience can experience lyrics on more than one level and he takes advantage of that sophistication in his lyrical references.

Musically, "Little Red Corvette" is distinguished by Prince's use of heavy contrast between the *parlando* (nearly speech rhythm style), low-register singing in the verses—in which he describes the sexual encounter of the couple—and expressive, more melodic, higher-register singing in the chorus—in which he tells the little red Corvette that "she" moves way too fast. Ultimately, what Prince has created, then, is a complex web of metaphors and feelings: he knows that what he is doing is not right and that it in fact is dangerous, but he willingly engages in a casual, unsafe sexual encounter.

The next track, "Delirious," is a catchy dance song, which primarily is distinguished by a theremin-like synthesizer lick that 1980s-izes what sounds like a 1950s rock and roll song in a variant of blues form. It is another of Prince's sex-focused songs, with a number of quickly stated, fairly graphic references to just what kinds of activities with his lover makes him "delirious." It reprises the metaphor of an automobile for a woman that marked "Little Red Corvette." The album's next track, "Let's Pretend We're Married," is another of Prince's sex-focused songs. This one, however, is more interesting musically. The groove is stronger and Prince provides interesting variations in the instrumentation as the song progresses. Prince's lyrics find him playing the role of the recently jilted lover who is content to find the quick rebound.

He tells a new woman that he meets, "Let's pretend we're married, and go all night," and later, "come on baby, let's ball." Nearly seven minutes into the song he changes his tack and becomes pointedly graphic, telling the object of his desire that he wants to "fuck the taste right out of [her] mouth." As the song reaches its conclusion, he reaffirms the religious/philosophical beliefs he first espoused at the opening of the album in the song "1999." He changes from a singing to a speaking voice, as if he is now addressing the audience and not the woman he had been addressing earlier. He says that he loves only God, that he believes in the afterlife, that he will reach that afterlife, but while he is here on earth, he will have fun "every motherfuckin' night." On a less graphic note, once again, he subtly references popular music of an earlier era. He invites the multivoiced chorus to join him in the song's refrain with the line, "all the hippies sing together," a reference to the counterculture lifestyle of the late 1960s. This direct lyrical reference to the lifestyle of the psychedelic 1960s directly anticipates the entire *gestalt* of Prince's 1985 album, the psychedelic *Around the World in a Day.*

The album's next track, "D.M.S.R.," is nearly eight minutes of potent James Brown–ish/Rick James–ish funky dance music. The title refers to "Dance, Music, Sex, Romance," Prince's formula for enjoying life on earth. Like the dance-oriented music of the period by Rick James, it is not as timeless as earlier funk by James Brown, mostly because the reliance on synthesizers make it sound too much like a 1980s period piece. The next song, "Automatic," weighs in at an even heftier nearly 10 minutes. It is another groove piece. This time, Prince addresses a woman who seems something of (to use the vernacular) a cock tease. Her attractiveness makes Prince's sexual desire "automatic." By the end of the piece, the sounds of lovemaking make it clear that Prince's partner was only a temporary tease. It is not as memorable as most of the songs on *1999.*

Prince moves into the realm of techno music for "Something in the Water (Does Not Compute)." Prince provides lyrics that establish that his character encounters rejection from every woman with whom he has been involved. The piece confirms that Prince is at his best when he uses melodic and harmonic hooks to establish a musical groove. This piece is not particularly memorable musically or lyrically.

The next song, "Free," is a slow-paced ballad in which Prince praises freedom. He questions whether we realize the importance of freedom, and if "we will fight for the right to be free." The vocals by Prince and his backup singers are emotional, passionate even; however, the synthesizer-based instrumental arranger is sonically weak. This renders the entire song less effective than it could have been, had the arrangement been different.

To say that many of Prince's compositions are based on sexual fantasy would be an understatement. The song "Lady Cab Driver" finds Prince exploring the darker side of male sexual fantasy. On the surface, his character literally takes a ride with an attractive female cab driver. As the ride proceeds and he asks the cab driver to keep driving him, it becomes deliberately unclear whether he is asking for a ride or for sex. In fact, eventually the ride turns into a sexual encounter. As Prince's character begins the sex act, he delivers an angry-voiced rap in which he dedicates each thrust to a different image, including discrimination, egoists, Disneyland tourists. The song approaches aural rape—it is clear that Prince's character has crossed the line between sex as lovemaking and sex as violent expression of inner rage. Prince's juxtaposition of the angry rap with the breathy, singsong vocal melodic material supported by horn-like synthesizer lines is truly striking, and it makes the angry, violent side of sex stand out in especially sharp relief. What is perhaps most disturbing about the song is the quickness of the move from physical attraction to rape: it is immediate and without cause. Prince does not condone sexual violence in the composition. What he does is to shock the listener; he raises the issue and the uncomfortably close ties between love and hate.

According to *All Music Guide*'s music critic Stephen Thomas Erlewine, "All the Critics Love U in New York" is "a vicious attack on hipsters."[3] Prince's lyrics really can be understood on a richer level than that. Prince actually takes on artists who use hipness in order to appeal to critics, naïve artists who believe that if they can make it in the big city, their artistic worth is somehow confirmed, as well as (to a lesser extent) the critics themselves. The unspoken statement that Prince makes in the song is that the external validation of seeing one's name mentioned favorably in a review is of greater importance than pleasing the audience. The fine line between making one's art with personal integrity, pleasing critics just for the sake of this external validation, and pleasing a commercial audience is complex. Prince's song exposes some of the dangers of leaning too heavily in the direction of the critics. By doing so, he also exposes the tremendous power that critics can exert over the arts. Ultimately, Prince seems to conclude that the truest form of musical art comes from the exploration of the real human experience, which, for him, is sexuality.

"All the Critics Love U in New York" is about much more than the lyrics. Although Prince speaks/raps the verses, which mention some of the excesses of the New York arts scene, he includes a memorable melodic hook in the chorus. His singing is accompanied by interesting tone colors in the synthesizer. Prince provides some great lead electric guitar licks, which come out of an intriguing combination of heavy metal, acid rock, and the avant-garde playing of figures such as Robert Fripp. The combination of rap, rock guitar, a tuneful chorus, crystal clear and powerful record production, and lyrics that raise a wealth of issues about the meaning and purpose of art and arts criticism makes "All the Critics Love U in New York" one of Prince's strongest tracks up to that point in his career.

The album ends with "International Lover," an R&B ballad that is essentially one 6 ½-minute pickup line. Prince's emphasis on falsetto singing and his single-minded focus on picking up the object of his affection for a flight on "the seduction 747" suggest his work on his earlier albums. His use of sexual metaphor is stronger than on the rather more pointedly explicit songs of *For You, Prince,* and *Dirty Mind;* however, it is clear that his interest in the young woman he addresses is almost exclusively physical in nature. The music is pleasant, but not as memorable as Prince's best work.

The album *1999* was an important step in Prince's musical development. Although it does not show off his command of as many disparate styles as his earlier albums, there is still plenty of stylistic richness. It is Prince's lyrics, complete with increased use of metaphor and religious imagery—not to mention a variety of subjects that go beyond sex—that really make the album stand out. Songs such as "Little Red Corvette," "Delirious," and "1999" were high charting pop and R&B hits. Although not as well known, "All the Critics Love U in New York" also shows Prince's growth as a social observer. *1999* was the product of a true star; with Prince's next project, he would become a true pop culture icon.

PURPLE RAIN

In one of the most memorable scenes from a 1980s pop music–related film, a crowd of diverse young people in a Minneapolis nightclub slowly begins to sway and wave their hands over their heads as they become immersed in a new song "The Kid" debuts. This mysterious character, "The Kid," had seen his family disintegrate, his standing in the musical hierarchy of local big-name bands recently diminish, his new girlfriend and potential bandmate break ranks to form another act (and become involved with The Kid's archrival). And, to top it all off, The Kid was on the verge of losing his long-standing gig and seeing his band disintegrate. The song that showed the nightclub owner, his just-about-ready-to-split bandmates, and the masses that previously had begun to shift loyalties that he was indeed *the* star of the local scene was "Purple Rain." This concert scene was the grand finale of Prince's film *Purple Rain.* Prince and the Revolution had the No. 1 film, pop single, and album in the same week. This put the group in the most exclusive of clubs: only Elvis Presley and the Beatles had a simultaneous No. 1 album, film, and single. But, *Purple Rain,* the album, is about much more than commercial/popular success. The songs, written by Prince alone or in collaboration with the Revolution, aim at a wider audience than any previous Prince material, and succeed across the board. Two of the songs, "Purple Rain" and "When Doves Cry," have become true classics of late twentieth-century popular music, and as such were included in various millennial lists of the most significant music of the entire rock era. The production, apparently influenced by the Revolution, is more powerful and punchier than that on earlier Prince solo albums.

The album's opener, "Let's Go Crazy," begins with a slow synthesized organ chorale, which supports Prince's spoken introduction. Prince portrays a preacher in his monologue. He confirms the afterlife and the bliss that it will provide. He concludes, however, by observing that in this earthly life, "you're on your own." The song itself is an upbeat party song, featuring a stylistic blend of new wave rock and R&B in the mold of early 1980s material by the J. Geils Band ("Freeze Frame" and "Centerfold" are the closest stylistic precedents). Like the songs of the 1981 J. Geils Band album *Freeze Frame,* the melody is built in short, easy-to-remember phrases. Perhaps the most notable feature of the melody is the syncopated descending figure that accompanies the words, "take us down." While this represents just a touch of musical text painting, it is not the last example on the album. The song's melody is supported by a powerful instrumental accompaniment on a minimal, *ostinato*-like chord oscillation. Prince adds strong rocking lead guitar, especially notable for a Jimi Hendrix–like cadenza at the conclusion of the song.

Since "Let's Go Crazy" is credited to Prince and the Revolution it is difficult to ascertain exactly who came up with what. However, the lyrical style represents a shift from the bulk of Prince's earlier material. It takes on a much more impressionistic air than is customary for Prince. Images of the grim coming "to take us down" in his "de-elevator" and purple bananas provide rich imagery in the verses and the chorus. The chorus, with its implied message to "hang tough" against the lure of drugs, but to enjoy the fun we can have with the friends we have in this life by punching "a higher floor" on the elevator of life, confirms the message of the preacher in the introduction: "Get through this thing called life," but keep in mind that "He's coming," so the even greater glory of the afterlife will be upon us soon. It is a 1980s blend of the Old Testament *Song of Solomon* with Christian imagery in which the pursuit of physical pleasure—through the enjoyment of the natural highs (such as sex)—is viewed as God's gift to humankind. It is a mix of the kind of religious philosophy Prince expressed on *1999* and the kind of psychedelic impressionism that he and the Revolution would explore even more thoroughly on their next album, *Around the World in a Day.*

"Take Me with U," a duet with Apollonia Kotero, serves a clear function in the film, in which it confirms the love part of what becomes a love-hate relationship between Apollonia and Prince's character: The Kid. This is certainly not among Prince's most famous songs, and it is not among the best-known songs on *Purple Rain.* That is because of the strength of songs such as "Purple Rain," "Let's Go Crazy," and "When Doves Cry," and not because of any weakness in "Take Me with U." The song is, in many respects, one of the most effective pure love songs Prince has ever written and recorded. It is catchy, like the best pop music. One of the best hooks in the song comes as a result of the metrical placement of the title line. The line is presented with each word directly on each of the four beats of the *penultimate* measure of the musical phrase. Since the line ends the chorus, its placement captures the listener's attention. The "missing" bar of singing stands out sharply. It also helps that the child-like tune to which the line is set (it moves from scale-step three, up to scale-step five, down to scale-step seven, and up a half-step to the tonic, scale-step one) is so simple. This makes it easy to remember, easy to sing along with, and its child-like quality suggests the innocence of the love between Apollonia and The Kid in the film.

Purple Rain includes three songs composed, performed, and produced by Prince, without the collaboration of the Revolution. The first of these, "The Beautiful Ones," is a Quiet Storm ballad in which Prince plays the classic role of a man whose lover has to choose between him and another man. For a Prince song, the lyrics are uncompromisingly romantic—as opposed to physical—and it is supported by a beautiful melody and full-sounding synthesizer arrangement and production. As Prince sings, "Is it him or me?" in a vulnerable falsetto, he is entirely believable. Although it may be something of a stereotype, this kind of falsetto singing fits a song in which the hero is in danger of losing his lover better than in a song praising the purely physical side of sex, something Prince had done with mixed results on his early albums.

"Computer Blue" combines elements of R&B and heavy metal rock. Prince addresses a woman, "Computer Blue," that he believes needs to "learn love and lust." One of the notable features of the song is the synthesizer figure that tops each line of the chorus. This chromatic figure bears some resemblance to a figure in Jonathan Richman's song "Pablo Piccaso."[4] It is just otherworldly enough to suggest the unfeeling, computer-like nature of the woman Prince addresses. The real highlight of the song, however, is Prince's technically brilliant and musically powerful electric guitar playing. The recording's production, by Prince and the Revolution, gives Prince's guitar solos and the entire sonic landscape a greater feeling of depth than anything on Prince's earlier solo albums.

The next track on *Purple Rain*, "Darling Nikki," gained notoriety through its association with the movement to adorn recordings that included explicit references to sex, violence, or drug use with parental warning labels. It was after finding her young daughter listening to "Darling Nikki," a song in which Prince refers to Nikki's "bumping and grinding" and masturbation, that Tipper Gore, working with other members of the Washington, D.C., political elite, founded the Parents Music Resource Center to combat references to sex, violence, and drugs in popular song lyrics.

"Darling Nikki" is a powerful, rhythmically heavy, slow, bluesy, rock piece. Prince's melody for the verses has a singsong quality. He presents this in a sly voice that suggests that the child-like innocence of the melody is meant to be ironic. The harder rock-oriented chorus, in which Prince describes Nikki's highly erotic grind, features more powerful vocals and distorted hard rock lead guitar. Nikki is a "super freak," in the sense of the Rick James song of the same title, and she can be understood in this way through Prince's musical setting. Prince abruptly switches gears for the final 45 seconds of the song. Here, he turns to a combination of a gospel-esque vocal chorale and Laurie

Anderson–influenced minimalism. This comes as a shock after the hard-rock setting of Prince's tale of Nikki's sexual escapades. This music finds Prince turning from a focus on Nikki to a lyrical focus on the even greater fulfillment that will come in the "Purple Rain," the afterlife. From a purely musical standpoint, the minimalistic coda to "Darling Nikki" anticipates a bit of the style of the next track, "When Doves Cry."

Prince has enjoyed a number of strong commercial hits on the pop and R&B charts over the course of his career. His most successful single to date, however, is "When Doves Cry." The single was No. 1 on the *Billboard* R&B charts for eight weeks, and it held the No. 1 position on the pop charts for five weeks. "When Doves Cry" found its way into several surveys of the most important songs of the rock era.[5] The song represents Prince's coming of age as a songwriter. The music, however, is not entirely without precedent: there is a melodic resemblance in the verses to the chorus of the 1966 Supremes hit "You Keep Me Hangin' On," and Prince's use of synthesized classically inspired synthesizer lines clearly has precedence in some of Stevie Wonder's mid-1970s work (including "Village Ghetto Land"). The *ostinato* chord oscillation and Prince's incorporation of sustained synthesizer chords suggest just a touch of the hip New York loft minimalism of the early 1980s work of Laurie Anderson. The song, however, mostly achieves the status of timeless pop/R&B classic by virtue of its lyrics and the intersection of its music and lyrics.

Prince's lyrics find him addressing his lover about their passionate, albeit turbulent, relationship. The down sides of the relationship are entirely the fault of Prince's character. In the film, in fact, the lyrics about being "just like my father" take on a deeper meaning. In the story's context, the lyrics clearly refer to the scene in which, in a fit of passionate anger, The Kid strikes Apollonia. At that moment, he realizes that he in essence has become his physically abusive father. The song accompanies Prince's lonely motorcycle ride that follows the episode of violence. Even outside the context of the film, the images of Prince's character caught in a fight between taking on the behavior of his dysfunctional parents and doing what he knows to be the right thing are poignant. And, the image of the sorrow he feels about his actions and the breakup of his own turbulent relationship being just like "what it sounds like when doves cry" remains one of his strongest lyrical metaphors.

The simple nature of the musical setting allows the lyrics to stand out. While there is nothing entirely innovative about the style, the melody, or the harmony, there is one aspect of Prince's arrangement that is likely to capture the attention of the listener: not what is there, but what is absent. This is one of the very few pop songs of the entire rock era that has no bass line—Prince includes no bass guitar and no bass line in the keyboards. This suggests the influence of classical music, which tends to emphasize the mid-range and higher-range instrumental sounds more than musical styles such as rock and R&B.

Although Prince and the Revolution's "I Would Die 4 U" might not be part of the standard canon of contemporary Christian music, it is one of the purest religious songs from this part of Prince's career. In the film *Purple Rain*, the live performance tends to allow the song to take on a double meaning: Prince's character can be understood at once as a personification of the Messiah, and as a man who tells the love of his life that he would give the ultimate sacrifice (his life) for her. In the context of the album, however, the song's religious meaning is stronger. The combination of Christian imagery in the lyrics and disco-influenced dance music supports the overall religious philosophy Prince espoused on the songs "1999" and "Let's Go Crazy": the Messiah will appear at the end of the world, and take believers with him, but God's purpose for us on earth is to enjoy ourselves.

The album's next track, "Baby, I'm a Star," fits well into the context of the film. To the extent that the listener considers *Purple Rain*, the album, as a standalone artistic statement, however, the song contributes little. That being said, it is interesting that the song makes a direct segue from "I Would Die 4 U." The combination lends some support to the understanding of "I Would Die 4 U" as a song in which Prince represents a human being who thinks of himself as his lover's Messiah. The juxtaposition seems mostly intended to raise the issue; in any case, it is not resolved.

Throughout the rock era there have been a number of especially notable mammoth slow-tempo anthem-like hits, perhaps most notably the Beatles' "Hey Jude," Foreigner's "I Want to Know What Love Is," and Prince's "Purple Rain." While not the biggest hit single on the album—"When Doves Cry" unquestionably holds that title—it is perhaps the most memorable song on the album. Certainly, it plays a most prominent role in the film. It is this song—the music of which is composed by The Kid's bandmates Wendy and Lisa[6]—to which The Kid finally acquiesces to add lyrics and perform at what would be his band's make-or-break performance. The lyrics, which express Prince's regrets at hurting his former friend/lover, fit easily into the context of the film: they are both an apology to Apollonia for striking her in a fit of anger, as well as an apology to Wendy and Lisa for ignoring their attempts to contribute songs to the band's repertoire for so long. The image of "purple rain" was introduced earlier on the album. It seems to signify the appearance of God at the end of the world. As The Kid apologizes to Apollonia and/or the members of his band, he gives perhaps the ultimate expression of devotion, that he only wanted to see them "standing in the purple rain," in other words, making it safely into heaven.

Musically, "Purple Rain" is a mixture of the familiar and the unexpected. The chord progression of the verses and the oft-repeated chorus include the most basic of harmonies, triads (three-note chords) built on the first, fourth, fifth, and sixth notes of the major scale. This collection of harmonies would fit entirely into pop and gospel music of the 1950s. Given the style of the setting, however, the harmony seems more timeless than retro. Likewise, the melody is generally fairly stepwise and simple. The setting on the recording finds the band breaking into gospel-style harmony on the choruses, which in part lends the song its anthem feel. Adding to this is the ultralong coda section: a repeat, over and over, of the chorus's chord progression with ever-changing instrumental lines.

Just as "Take Me with U" had featured a feeling of unusual melodic phrase structure, "Purple Rain" does the same. The end of each verse includes what sounds like an extra measure of music. Since the overall melodic shape and the harmonic material is so typical of simple pop music, this phrase extension instantly stands out. It sets up a focus on the start of the chorus that cannot help but draw even the most casual listener in.

Although it is tempting to focus on trying to find the influence of Jimi Hendrix on Prince's compositions, singing, and guitar playing in his hard rock songs, I believe that "Purple Rain" is one of the best examples of the influence of Hendrix in the entire Prince repertoire. Slower-tempo Hendrix recordings such as "Little Wing" and even "Hey Joe" (the latter of which Hendrix recorded but did not write) include double-time, *parlando*-style phrases in the verses—something that Prince adopts in "Purple Rain." The phrase "but you can't seem 2 make up your mind" has a rhythm and a pitch fall-off on the word *mind* that sound just like Hendrix. Even Prince's use of the entire range of the electric guitar, including some tasty low-register lines, suggests the influence of songs such as "Little Wing." Jimi Hendrix is not the only late 1960s, early 1970s guitar god whose influence can be felt in "Purple Rain." The more highly technical high-register figures bear the stamp of Carlos Santana. Prince assimilates these influences and creates a solo lead guitar style that sounds entirely personal. The feeling of his guitar work is that it is an instrumental representation of the passion felt in the words of his apology.

The album *Purple Rain* has become a pop culture classic. The fuller arrangements, wider range of subject matter, melodic pop hooks, Prince effectively portraying a wider range of emotions, and the strong instrumental work from the entire band represent a step above Prince's best previous work. Add to that the impact of the film, and *Purple Rain* remains a defining work for Prince.

AROUND THE WORLD IN A DAY

In the wake of the megahit *Purple Rain,* Prince and the Revolution turned back the clock to the second half of the 1960s for the psychedelic *Around the World in a Day.* The album took Prince's fans by surprise; the structure, lyrics, arrangements, and style of the songs bore little resemblance to any of Prince's pre–*Purple Rain* solo work. Critics, too, did not take to the album. On the positive side, *Around the World in a Day* found Prince expanding on his philosophy of life, and it showed that he and the Revolution could branch out into a 1960s-rock style and jazz more fully than before. It is easy for music critics and fans of Prince's funk work to denigrate the album; it was, after all, very different in all respects from Prince's previous work, and it was terribly out of step with any of the prevailing pop styles of the mid-1980s. I suspect, though, that if one takes one's expectations of what a Prince album is supposed to sound like out of the mix and experiences *Around the World in a Day* as a revisitation of the peace, love, and understanding philosophy and musical styles of the 1960s, it succeeds to a greater extent than conventional wisdom would suggest.

The album begins with the title track, "Around the World in a Day," a song written by Prince, David Coleman, and Prince's father, John L. Nelson. The lyrics find Prince describing a wonder journey "around the world in a day" that will take place if the listener only consents to open her or his heart and mind. It is a call to openness and the good feelings it can bring. It can also be taken to mean that the album will represent a journey of sorts through different emotional states. The lyrics speak to the universality of the journey by contrasting the "purple" nature of the trip with the "red, white, and blue." Previously, in songs on both *1999* and *Purple Rain,* Prince equated purple with the reign of God on earth. By saying that this journey will take the passenger from the "red, white, and blue" to the "purple," Prince, Coleman, and Nelson suggest a spiritual basis (without political boundaries) to the album. This theme of spirituality may not fully permeate *Around the World in a Day* in a classic concept-album form; however, a mix of religious imagery comes through in most of the songs. What is clear is that this journey through emotional states, faith, love, and lust is meant to be universal and experienced on multiple levels: everything that follows on the album can be found anywhere one travels around the world, or in one's own neighborhood.

The song "Around the World in a Day" includes a few musical signifiers that emerge as ties between the songs of the album. The song includes plenty of references to world music, including chord organ, sometimes heard in Indian music, and oud, finger cymbals and goblet drum from the Middle East. The finger cymbals, in particular, play a prominent structural role on the album: they are heard on several of the album's early tracks, thereby linking the songs. The later songs on the album contain other song-to-song instrumental ties.

Melodically, "Around the World in a Day" sets the stage for the most successful songs of the album. The melody of the verses winds its way from the major third scale-step up to the lowered seventh scale-step. This lowered seventh step plays an important role in suggesting the Middle Eastern nature of the song: some of the commonly used modes (scales) of the Middle East and of India include this note in what otherwise sounds like the context of the European major scale. These modes of the Middle East and Indian subcontinent resemble the Mixolydian mode,[7] but sometimes do not include all seven different notes of the Mixolydian mode. They also include or imply certain specific melodic patterns, a trait not found today in the European modes. The other important feature of the lowered seventh scale-step is that the song's writers set it up as an upper melodic boundary. The most memorable songs on this album feature a clear, oft-repeated upper melodic boundary note. In fact, other especially popular and memorable Prince melodies find him firmly establishing an upper melodic pitch through repetition: "1999" and its closely related cousin "Manic Monday" emphasize scale-step four, for example.

In later years, Prince would also turn to the Mixolydian mode from time to time. Generally, his use of this scale is associated with spirituality or universal brotherhood/sisterhood. In the case of "Around the World in a Day," he addresses both themes. Incidentally, the use of the Mixolydian mode, with its distinctive combination of major third scale degree and minor (or lowered) seventh scale degree, in popular Western music did not begin with the 1966–1967 psychedelic era's fascination with the music of India; there are earlier examples. I would cite as an example the 1961 rock instrumental "Jack the Ripper" by guitarist Link Wray. This piece makes extensive use of the lowered seventh scale-step in what is otherwise clearly a major key context. However, Wray's focus—and title—is on aggressive, edgy beat music, about as far away as possible from the peace-love-and-understanding aesthetics of the psychedelic era. I raise the example of the Link Wray composition to illustrate that there need not be anything inherently spiritual with the Mixolydian mode or with harmonies derived from it. So, for Prince to associate the scale with spirituality and universal agape-type love is a conscious decision and ties pieces such as "Around the World in a Day" with the 1966–1967 associations of the scale with Hindustani music and philosophy.

The 1960s saw a connection between urban parks and the hippie movement: San Francisco's Golden Gate Park, in particular, is indelibly etched into the story of the year 1967's so-called Summer of Love. Prince and the Revolution's "Paisley Park" is a metaphorical "place" of peace, love, and understanding. As the song's lyrics state, "Paisley Park is in your heart." The lyrics contain a reference to the "profound inner peace" that can be found in this park, and the suggestion that "there are many rooms in Paisley Park." Both of these references use language that is just spiritual and religious enough in nature that the religiously attuned listener can hear the song as a call to live the peace that is preached by the major world religions. In the case of this song, the world of peace is not the afterlife—a subject of more than a few Prince compositions—it seems more to be a heaven on earth. Although this philosophy might seem to be more in line with Buddhism than with what one commonly finds in Prince's work, it can be understood within the Christian tradition: give one's cares and problems over to God, and one will find peace. It should be noted that one of the characters is invited to the park to overcome his sorrow at being homeless because of his poverty. This subfocus on the urban poor is echoed in the song "America," four tracks later on *Around the World in a Day.*

"Paisley Park" suggests the psychedelic music of the 1960s, right from the deliberate addition of distortion to the opening chord. The instrumentation, too, which includes what sounds to be a mellotron, also comes right out of the late 1960s. This keyboard instrument goes just slightly out of phase with the prevailing background rhythm, another characteristic of psychedelic music. The melody of "Paisley Park" features an easy-to-remember hook, as well as the clear definition of a central upper-limit pitch—in this case, scale-step five. The melodic writing is also interesting because of the clear motivic ties between the verses and the chorus. The chorus takes one phrase of the verse melody and develops it. This gives the entire piece a feeling of unity that supports the idea of the universal nature of achieving a better state of being through faith. The song is tied together with the album's opener by means of the finger cymbals. In addition, the violin *obbligato* that enters late in the song anticipates the fuller use of orchestral string instruments on some of the album's later songs, thereby providing an instrumental link that overlaps with the use of the finger cymbals, but continues longer.

The song "Condition of the Heart" is performed in its entirety by Prince. It begins with impressionistic piano and synthesizer figures. Curiously, the first improvised-sounding melody that Prince plays on the synthesizer begins with a reference (whether intentional or accidental) to the opening bassoon solo in Igor Stravinsky's *Le Sacre du printemps* (which also begins with a downward arpeggiation of a major-seventh chord). Interestingly, the Stravinsky ballet score concerns ancient Russian pagan rituals, including the sacrifice of a virgin in order to please the gods so that the land will yield abundantly. Ironically, Prince's lyrics, once they appear, concern the extent to which men sacrifice themselves to love, an emotion that, according to the lyrics, invariably leads to a terrible "condition of the heart." The ambient wash of sound that precedes the text suggests some of Stevie Wonder's 1979 incidental music for *Journey for the Secret Life of Plants.* Approximately two minutes into the composition, Prince transitions into a sad ballad style. It is curious that in this song, which contains no other discernable references to 1960s psychedelia or world music, Prince includes more finger cymbals. While this instrumental touch makes sense on songs such as "Around the World in a Day," "Paisley Park," and "Tamborine," it seems illogical here. Because the instruments do not fit as naturally here, the orchestration tends to come off as an attempt to force a concept-album–like feel to a collection that includes some songs that are thematically linked through their lyrics and some songs that seem more standalone.

The next song, "Raspberry Beret," concerns a young woman who dresses in a funky manner (her beret is "the kind you find in a secondhand store"), enjoys wearing skimpy clothing, and instantly commands the attention of Prince's character. She ends up taking a ride with him on his motorcycle, and the two make love. Although Prince includes a few sexual innuendos—enhanced by the sly-sounding speaking voice he adopts on several lines—this is a song of sexual metaphor. As such, it is very different from the explicit songs of *For You, Prince,* and *Dirty Mind.* This, along with the catchy, popish music, makes "Raspberry Beret" instantly radio-friendly. One of the more unusual and more effective attributes of the song is the way in which Prince moves between singing and speaking in the verses. This, combined with his use of soft rhymes (as opposed to exact, hard rhymes), gives his story of meeting and taking up with the girl who wears the raspberry beret an authentic-sounding conversational tone. Orchestrationally, the song is linked to the previous three songs through the finger cymbals, and is linked to "Paisley Park" and "Pop Life" through its inclusion of a violin section.

The song, "Tamborine," on which Prince performs all the vocals and plays all the instruments, is notable for Prince's use of the percussion instrument of the song's title (*tambourine* is the more common spelling) as a metaphor for both female and male sex organs. It is not particularly subtle; however, the lyrics are not the highlight of the song. It is primarily a vehicle for Prince the performer: he covers an incredible pitch range in the multitracked vocal lines, and his drum set performance is inventive. In fact, the inventiveness of the drum track stands out starkly, mostly because it is so much more human sounding than the rock steady, but mechanical-sounding drum machine tracks on songs such as "Paisley Park."

Overt political and social commentary emerges in the song "America." Here, Prince paints a picture of the poor and oppressed in contemporary U.S. society, some of whom—as they lost the American dream of economic prosperity—also lost whatever love for and allegiance to America they once possessed. The lyrics make it clear that the biggest threat to the United States lies within: the only way that all Americans can come together to protect the country from foreign enemies is to ensure equality for all citizens. The lyrics also project a Cold War–era disdain for Soviet-style communism, acknowledging that the freedom and hope that American democracy promises is far superior. The song includes lyrical and rhythmic hints of the well-known patriotic hymn "America, the Beautiful."

"Pop Life" is a moderate-tempo funk piece in which Prince and the Revolution (with drummer Sheila E.) describe some of the harsh realities and minor disappointments of life and suggest that people find an alternative to drugs and violence as ways of dealing with them. They extol the virtues of staying in school and getting a natural high from pop music. It does, however, take some time for the meaning of "pop life" as a natural high to come through—it is not until the final 30 seconds of the 3-minute, 43-second song, in which audience sounds from a live rock concert take over the texture, that the "pop life" is completely understood as pop music. The song includes the orchestral strings (violins, violas, cellos, and double basses), as arranged by the Revolution's Lisa Coleman and Wendy Melvoin. This provides an orchestrational link with

"Paisley Park" and "Raspberry Beret." Musically, "Pop Life" is notable for its monothematic melody: the verses and the chorus consist of the same music. In the context of the entire album, this comes across as the logical extension of the structure of "Paisley Park" and "Raspberry Beret," the two songs that feature the clearest melodic links between verse and chorus. It is significant that the three songs ("Paisley Park," "Raspberry Beret," and "Pop Life") are linked by means of their verse-chorus relationships, use of the orchestral strings, and by something of a common theme. All three songs deal with escaping from major and/or minor problems of life and suggest a "natural high" as a solution: in "Paisley Park" the natural high comes through faith ("say you believe"); in "Raspberry Beret" it comes through a love/sexual relationship; and in "Pop Life" salvation comes through music. This song, however, tends to come across as lightweight. The singsong monothematic melody tends to reduce all of the disappointments that are described to the level of trivialities. This is especially noticeable in the context of the album—"The Ladder," which follows "Pop Life," is considerably stronger musically—which can present the listener with an interesting subtext: pop music and the fan's perception of the glamour of the pop life may offer some relief from the drudgery of day-to-day existence, but it is not a relief Prince and the Revolution would have the listener value on the level of faith in God.

"The Ladder," a gospel-style piece, reinforces the idea that throughout history, people of diverse cultures and places have been looking for "the ladder" that leads to redemption and eternal life. It is very much a genre piece, in that it includes numerous melodic, harmonic, and structural signifiers that come right out of the black gospel music style. As a standalone work, it does not seem to be distinctive enough to become a standard. However, "The Ladder" continues the emphasis on spirituality and the striving for redemption that marks earlier songs on *Around the World in a Day,* notably "Paisley Park" and (in contrasting metaphorical terms) "Pop Life." The piece takes on added meaning when paired with the album's final track, "Temptation," because the two songs share a thematic link: the classic human dialectic of good versus evil, faith versus temptation. Whereas in "The Ladder" Prince sings about the desire to find heaven (by climbing the metaphorical ladder), in "Temptation" he sings of "animal lust." Ultimately, though, his character resolves the inner conflict by concluding that, "love is more important than sex." Musically, the two pieces emphasize the dialectic, too: "The Ladder" practically screams "gospel music" at the listener, while the up-tempo funk of "Temptation" strongly suggests the pleasures of the flesh. As mentioned throughout the discussion of *Around the World in a Day,* one of the organizing factors that plays a structural role is the use of instrumental links between songs (e.g., finger cymbals and orchestral strings). Both "The Ladder" and "Temptation" feature *obbligato* saxophone solos from Eddie M., which emphasizes to the listener that they are meant to go together—as if the themes of the songs' lyrics did not make that clear.

Around the World in a Day is an album that is too easy for critics and fans of Prince's more funk-oriented work to dismiss: it seems to be aimed at a fundamentally different audience base than Prince's earlier work, because it finds Prince incorporating styles drawn from 1967-era psychedelic music (not the most fashionable style for the mid-1980s pop culture aesthetic); it includes a mix a spiritual and religious imagery that draws from disparate world religions; and so on. The album contains so many clever musical and thematic ties and oppositions that seems difficult to imagine that they all happened by accident. Prince and the Revolution should receive credit for trying to develop musical and lyrical themes throughout *Around the World in a Day*, even if the touches of psychedelic rock that mark the first half of the album are not exactly the listener's cup of tea. The rhetorical styles are fairly wide-ranging—not on the level of *Purple Rain*—but more varied and more subtle than the material on Prince's first couple of solo albums: sometimes the lyrics are clear, sometimes hazy, and sometimes somewhere in the middle. A song such as "Raspberry Beret" shows that Prince can include sexual innu-endo (something for which he had always been known), but now in a muted, more radio-friendly form—in fact, more than just about any other Prince song, with the possible exception of "Manic Monday," it shows his total command of conventional pop songwriting. It may not be his most substan-tial song, but it is one that is almost impossible to get out of one's head. The world music touches of "Around the World in a Day" might not fit into the conventional stereotype of what people think Prince's music is supposed to sound like, but they work within the context of the song and the album.

Film Scores and Contractual Problems

More than perhaps any other famous musician of his generation, Prince has been a prolific songwriter and recording artist. Not only does he write a lot of songs, but they (especially his funk/groove compositions and his anthem-like ballads) easily can be five, six, seven, eight minutes (or more) in length. The combination of the two—lots of songs and long songs—can create a marketing problem, especially when the norm for many artists might be one album per year. The second half of the 1980s and the start of the 1990s saw Prince expanding his work on motion picture soundtracks and increasingly running into conflicts with Warner Brothers Records over his desire to release the huge catalog of recordings he was amassing. This period also found him disbanding the Revolution and resuming to record as a solo artist: a solo artist, however, still known as Prince.

PARADE (MUSIC FROM THE MOTION PICTURE UNDER THE CHERRY MOON)

Given the success of *Purple Rain,* perhaps it was only natural that Prince would soon star in another film. *Under the Cherry Moon* found him portraying a suave ladies man, Christopher Tracy[1], who plays the piano on the French Riviera and seduces wealthy European women. Absent the semi-autobiographical appeal of *Purple Rain,* this film was far less commercially and critically successful. The soundtrack album itself (which I will henceforth label simply *Parade*) exhibits some ties to Prince and the Revolution's previous album, *Around the World in a Day;* however, Prince and his collaborators rely less heavily on pseudo-1960s psychedelic techniques and include more funk. However, there is plenty of musical experimentation, which includes both an extremely economical, minimalistic approach to funk, and references to New Age–style ambient music. The album is not as strong as *Purple Rain,* but it appealed to fans and critics more than *Around the World in a Day,* and it received far more favorable critical commentary than the film from which the material is drawn.

The album kicks off with "Christopher Tracy's Parade," a collaboration of Prince and his father, John L. Nelson. The song sets the stage for the film's storyline by extolling the virtues of Christopher Tracy's piano playing and his "parade," presumably a parade of beautiful rich women. The Nelsons, father and son, include simple, popish melodic material in the verses. Clare Fisher's orchestration and the Revolution's instrumental contributions create a swirl of sounds that suggests grandiosity at times, as well as deliberate confusion. The arrangement clearly follows in the tradition of George Martin's arrangements of the Beatles' psychedelic era; the song "Magical Mystery Tour" immediately comes to mind. Structurally, the song breaks out of the stereotypical 1980s pop song mold: it does not include a chorus, *per se;* instead, the verses are separated by a longish instrumental interlude. The song's structure and its brevity—"Christopher Tracy's Parade" is slightly less than 2 ¼ minutes long—suggest that the piece was designed entirely with the purposes of the film in mind. Outside of the soundtrack context, particularly given Prince's normal tendencies to fully develop his material and often to include fairly lengthy "groove" sections, it seems underdeveloped.

"Christopher Tracy's Parade" clocked in at less than 2 ¼ minutes, and the album's second track, "New Position," barely tops 2 ¼ minutes. "New Position" is a funky song of seduction with a decidedly minimalistic approach to the funk style. Prince evokes the feel of James Brown's great funk performances of the late 1960s and 1970s with his exclamations of a guttural "huh." The combination of the male and female voices of the Revolution also suggests a nod in the direction of Sly and the Family Stone. Instrumentally, however, the piece represents funk stripped to its bare essentials—it is a uniquely "Prince" approach to the genre. The inclusion of a single-note steel drum lick links the piece to "Christopher Tracy's Parade," which also included steel drums. As was the case with "Christopher Tracy's Parade," the brevity of "New Position" may have fit Prince and the Revolution's needs for the film *Under the Cherry Moon,* but as a standalone funk number, the song is way too short. Part of the attraction of this genre is the extended groove; the groove of "New Position" just gets established when the song abruptly slows down and makes a direct segue into "I Wonder U."

The song "I Wonder U" finds Prince and the Revolution exploring the psychedelic style of *Around the World in a Day;* however, it is a very brief mood-setting piece. As is the case sometimes with incidental music, absent the context of the film, it does not function particularly effectively as a standalone composition. The next track, "Under the Cherry Moon," however, is more substantial. This slow, jazz-influenced torch song, co-written by Prince and his father, John L. Nelson, places Prince in the company of other 1980s musicians, such as Elvis Costello and Sinéad O'Connor, both of whom wrote and/or recorded songs in the torch ballad tradition. O'Connor, in fact, recorded Prince's composition "Nothing Compares 2 U," another song that falls into the torch song category—a recording that *Rolling Stone* critics included in their millennial lists of the most significant singles of the rock era.[2] "Under the Cherry Moon" is not as significant as "Nothing Compares 2 U." Melodically, however, the song is quite memorable. Prince bases the verses principally on a melodic motive in the key of E minor that is bounded on the bottom by E and on the top by B, thereby emphasizes the tonic (E minor) triad (E, G, B). The verses conclude, however, with a phrase that starts with a four-note chromatically descending figure from the flatted-seventh scale-step (D). The chromatic figure (D, D-flat, C, B), is followed by another step-wise descending figure that leads the end of the verse to the unexpected resolution on D major. The tonal ambiguity, the move from minor to major, the balance of winding melodic figures with completely descending melodic figures all combine to place emphasis on the conflicted nature of Prince's character. He is willing to die of a broken heart, yet he yearns for salvation from this plight in the form of a woman.

"Girls & Boys" is the one *Parade* track that contains the most obvious 1960s cues that were found fairly abundantly on *Around the World in a Day*. The simple, monothematic singsong melody and the vocal arrangement suggest the work of Sly and the Family Stone. The spare, repetitious figures also suggest early 1980s new wave rock. It might not be Prince's most sophisticated composition melodically, harmonically, lyrically, and structurally, but it is instantly infectious and betrays Prince's unique ability to create material that is slyly sexual, yet thoroughly commercially appealing. It is one of the rare tracks on *Parade* in which Prince and the Revolution and the guest musicians have the chance to completely establish a rhythmic groove and work in some interesting textural variations. Chief among these textural variations is the introduction of a curiously dissonant synthesizer countermelody near the end of the song. The dissonance of this instrumental figure captures the bittersweet nature of the relationship between the two characters Prince describes: the man is deeply in love with the woman who is "promised 2 another man." The rest of the musical setting suggests optimism, both in the past and present state of the couple's affair. The dissonant synthesizer countermelody suggests that the harsh reality of the situation (that the relationship very well may have to end soon) snaps back into the immediate consciousness of the male character.

The song "Life Can Be So Nice" features a wide mix of psychedelic imagery to describe the wonderment of love. Included among these are such phrases as "no one plays the clarinet the way u play my heart" and "kisses never lie when delivered with milk from your lips." The groove-oriented music includes an *ostinato* synthesizer figure that has the same unifying effect of the synthesizer *ostinato* in the Human League's song "Fascination."

"Venus De Milo" is a mood piece that finds Prince venturing into the world of light, New Age–style ambient pop jazz. The composition is just less than 2 minutes long, so it is not as fully developed as it might otherwise be (e.g., if Prince and the Revolution had recorded an entire nonsoundtrack album of such material); however, it suggests a convincing understanding of the relaxed, ambient nature of the so-called smooth jazz genre. As it stands, "Venus De Milo" is a trifle of soundtrack incidental music.

"Mountains" is a Bee Gees–ish four-to-the-bar disco song in the "love will conquer all" mold, most distinguishable because of the metrical truncation of the verse as it moves into the chorus. It is the kind of rhythmic stumble that plays games with disco dancers—the genre was notable for squarely symmetrical phrase structure back in the 1970s—perhaps best-known through Blondie's "Heart of Glass" and that song's occasional measures of five beats. The song "Do U Lie?" is a tidbit of vaudeville-flavored silliness that falls roughly in the same realm as Brian Wilson's *Smile* track "Vegetables" and the Holy Modal Rounders' "If You Want to Be a Bird" (easily the strangest-sounding song on the 1969 *Easy Rider* soundtrack).

"Kiss" revisits the emphasis on falsetto singing that Prince used on his first two solo albums. In fact, the main attributes that set "Kiss" apart from Prince's early work are (1) his lyrical focus on kissing, as opposed to the more graphic forms of sexual interaction he explored almost exclusively early in his career, and (2) stronger melodic and arrangement hooks than on most of his early compositions. "Kiss" has been a song loved by fans and critics alike: the single release was a No. 1 pop and R&B hit and it won a Grammy for Best R&B Performance by a Duo or Group with Vocal. The falsetto singing—which, incidentally, is much more effective than the Prince-does-"Stayin' Alive"-falsetto of "Mountains"—the relative innocence of Prince's expression of attraction, and the catchy melodic phrases connect the song to the 1960s work of Smoky Robinson; however, Prince sings with more rhythmic funkiness than Robinson and includes almost stereotypical, James Brown–derived seventh and raised-ninth chords. These disparate influences, however, somehow sound entirely original, in part because of the 1980s sparseness of the arrangement.

"Anotherloverholenyohead"[3] finds Prince's character reacting to the breakup of a relationship: "U need another lover like u need a hole in yo head." He, as the character Christopher Tracy, touts his sexual prowess in an effort to convince the woman he addresses that he, Tracy, is all that she needs to "do the duty in [her] bed." This message is set to moderately uptempo funk that finds Prince breaking with standard R&B—and with standard Prince—structure. First of all, each phrase of the melody of the verses features a step-wise ascending figure. While this is not necessarily anything new in pop music, it is unusual for Prince, a composer who seems to favor arch-shaped phrases (a melodic rise and consequent fall), or descending melodic figures. The rising melody in "Anotherloverholenyohead" suggests the urgency Christopher Tracy feels at his predicament. More interesting, however, is the fact that these ascending melodic phrases are each three measures in length, something most unusual in twentieth-century pop music. In fact, deviation from two-, four-, and eight-measure phrase structure is so unusual that examples tend to stand out in sharp relief to other songs of their era: the three-measure instrumental introduction and the deliberate metrical stumble of the verses of the Beatles' "All You Need Is Love," and the seven-measure phrases of the verses of the same group's hit "Yesterday," for example. Prince and the Revolution's phrase structure in this song snaps the listener's ears to attention. It also works with the rising melodic phrases to suggest the urgency of the character's appeal to his love—he is in such a rush to make his appeal that he defies and truncates conventional R&B phrase structure. Aside from the unusual phrase structure, the song is notable for Prince's vocal phrasing, which sounds strangely reminiscent of some of Stevie Wonder's low-range singing, particularly in his work of the mid-1970s through the 1980s.

The story of Christopher Tracy, lecherous cabaret pianist, ends with "Sometimes It Snows in April," a gentle ballad of mourning. It is an interesting song from the structural standpoint. The verses, in which Prince sings of some of the specifics of his friendship with Tracy, are marked by a conventional rhyme scheme: ababcdcd, which is supported by a meandering, almost through-composed sounding melodic line. The melody makes it sound as if Prince's character is improvising, pouring his heart out spontaneously. Of course, the studied rhyme scheme runs counter to this feeling of spontaneity, but this is a pop song. Interestingly, though, the chorus finds Prince almost studiously avoiding a conventional rhyme scheme; here, he turns metaphorical, comparing the loss of Christopher Tracy to an unexpected snow in April, a snow that prevents lovers from walking in the springtime rain.

Parade showed that Prince could use his well-known eclecticism to create music that would support a wide range of emotions and situations in the context of a film. Unfortunately, the film *Under the Cherry Moon* was neither a critical nor a huge commercial success. The soundtrack album itself is probably best remembered for the superb song "Kiss," although "Girls & Boys" and "Under the Cherry Moon" are also notable tracks.

SIGN O' THE TIMES

The 1987 album *Sign o' the Times* represented the start of a problematic period for Prince: Prince reached a new high level of creative output that at times put him at odds with Warner Bros. Records. *Sign o' the Times* is a double compact disc collection, and it was to be quickly followed by another 1987 album, the so-called *Black Album*. The amount of material Prince was writing and recording broke every rule in the recording industry about the amount of time that needed to elapse between releases in order for albums to be commercially successful. Prince wanted his material released as it was produced, and his record company wanted to maintain the space that was the corporate paradigm of the time. It is important to note that *Sign o' the Times* and the albums that followed it in quick succession were not written, recorded, and produced by Prince so quickly because they were in any way thrown together. Some of the material, recording, and production—on *Sign o' the Times,* especially—was state of the art: Prince managed to be both the most prolific artist of the era and a perfectionist at the same time. *Sign o' the Times* has been compared to some of the other famous, mammoth, multidisc packages of the late 1960s and early 1970s. In particular, critics noted its structural resemblance to the Beatles' 1968 double album *The Beatles* (commonly known as the White Album) and the Rolling Stones' 1972 double album *Exile on Main Street.* Like those earlier collections by the Beatles and the Rolling Stones, *Sign o' the Times* includes songs that cross numerous stylistic boundaries and that deal with a wide array of lyrical subjects. *The Beatles, Exile on Main Street,* and *Sign o' the Times* all present the listener with so much material and such diversity of styles that the totality is challenging to take in. Despite this, *Sign o' the Times* is one of Prince's greatest achievements.

The album begins with the title track. Here, the musical emphasis is on a melodic descent from the flat seventh scale-step. A long step-wise melodic descent was nothing new: the famous Christmas hymn "Joy to the World," with music attributed to the Baroque-era composer George Frederic Handel, begins with a step-wise descent through an octave. Other composers have made noteworthy use of the flatted seventh step and/or the flatted seventh of the dominant-seventh chord: Hank Williams's 1947 song "Move It on Over" features a melodic arpeggiation up to the flatted seventh step, a melodic figure that was copied almost verbatim for the 1954 song "Rock around the Clock." Leonard Bernstein's song "Somewhere," from *West Side Story,* opens with a leap of the interval of a minor seventh. The old Chuck Berry hit, "Reelin' and Rockin'," begins with a melodic figure that moves step-wise up to, and then back down from, the flatted seventh scale-step. In more recent times, Badfinger's 1971–1972 hit "Day after Day" moves dramatically up to the flatted seventh and then settles back down in the opening of the verses. And, Elvis Costello's 1979 song "Green Shirt" opens with a similarly dramatic leap up the interval of a minor seventh. The Costello song then features a step-wise descent. What really marks "Sign o' the Times" is the amount of almost insistent emphasis Prince places on the flatted seventh step. All the other songs mentioned above eventually move off in other directions: "Sign o' the Times" reemphasizes the note again and again. This constant fall from what would ordinarily be considered an unstable, slightly dissonant scale-step gives it rare emphasis as the principal melodic tone of the piece. Prince's arrangement is not quite as minimalistic as the drum and bass (DnB) style that would become fashionable in the 1990s, but it is quite sparse. This allows the subtle details of Prince's bluesy electric guitar solos to stand out in sharp relief to the rest of the texture. It also allows the message of the lyrics to emerge easily.

Prince addresses a number of social issues in "Sign o' the Times," some that clearly define the song as a product of the 1980s, and some that are more universal. At the time of the song, the disease AIDS had been recognized for only approximately a half-decade. The song begins with Prince's description of a "skinny man" who dies of a "big disease with a little name." He does not identify AIDS by name, but his description leaves no doubt what the cause of death of the young man (and his girlfriend, who shared his needle) was. There is even an easy-to-miss subtext to Prince's lyrics. Back in 1987, AIDS was still thought of as largely, if not exclusively, a disease of homosexual men among a fair number of Americans. Prince, by means of choice of characters, tells the listener (in not so many words) that AIDS is a danger to heterosexuals (the skinny man's *girlfriend* dies of the disease, too).

Prince also takes on gang violence in "Sign o' the Times," as well as the proliferation of guns among youth, the *Challenger* disaster, terrorist attacks on airliners, weather disasters, inner city poverty, crack cocaine, illegal drug usage in general, the international arms race, the human tendency to inflict and risk death, and so on. He contrasts this gloomy scenario with a reference at the end of the song to the stereotypical American dream of getting married, having a baby, and living in a house with a white picket fence (actually, he does not mention the house with the picket fence). Prince's singing style in the verses is deliberately offhanded—almost conversational—which gives the listener the impression that he plays the role of the dispassionate social observer. One of the structural "kickers" of the song, though, is that Prince uses the last line of each verse to deliver a sort of punch line. Perhaps the best example of this is the verse about his cousin's drug abuse.

The song is powerful, and is considerably more effective than Prince's earlier stabs at social commentary, principally because of the musical setting and arrangement and Prince's performance. The overall effect is stark, thought-provoking, and somewhat eerie, especially in light of the events of the two decades that have passed between this recording and today.

The next song, "Play in the Sunshine," finds Prince combining elements of J. Geils Band–style party rock and Stray Cats–style neo-rockabilly. The lyrics speak of having fun; however, without the aid of alcohol and drugs. Prince also warns against the sins of envy and the collection of wealth for wealth's sake metaphorically by stating that, "the color green will make your best friends leave you." Prince's conception of partying and fun revolve around dancing, enjoying music and love. Musically, the piece is a combination of the conventional and the experimental. The harmonic progression and melody are standard rock-and-roll fare. The arrangement and production, however, make use of speaker-to-speaker panning, Prince's hard rock/heavy metal guitar solo, sparse sections with stop-time drumming, and the sound of the marimba. The near-sonic overload of the arrangement in the middle of the song suggests the extent to which Prince wants the listener to believe that consciousness expansion and a so-called high can be achieved strictly through nonchemical means. It is very easy, however, to miss the antidrug, antienvy, and anticonsumerism message of the song, as the lyrics tend to be overshadowed by psychedelic dance music setting. Fortunately, *Sign o' the Times* includes a lengthy booklet with all the lyrics printed.

Over the years, Prince has been taken to task for his perceived inability to sound thoroughly convincing in the hip-hop genre. Especially, he has been on the receiving end of derisive comments about his attempts to incorporate rap into his music. The third track on *Sign o' the Times,* "Housequake," can be read in two ways: (1) a serious attempt by Prince to create a dance track in the prevailing club style of the late 1980s, or (2) as a parody of the style. To the extent that the listener reads it as the former, it reinforces every negative stereotype about Prince's place in the dance genre. As a parody of house party music, however, it is successful—maybe not quite brilliant, but successful. Prince includes just about every kind of stereotypical dance music phrase in the lyrics one can imagine, from "rock this mother," to "in this funky town," to "U put your foot down on the 2," to references to rock-steady music, "let's jam y'all," and "the baddest groove." There are enough off-the-wall references in some of the rhyming couplets, such as "green eggs and ham" (rhyming with "jam") and "the saxophone is the fault" (rhyming with "check it out") to let the listener know that this is not a piece to be taken seriously.

On the other hand, "The Ballad of Dorothy Parker" is a song that is meant to be taken seriously. Here, Prince describes his rather fetish-like sexual encounter with a waitress named Dorothy Parker. Dorothy's character mentions that Joni Mitchell's "Help Me" is her favorite song. Prince quotes a melodic phrase from the 1974 Mitchell song, but more interestingly, he sets his entire song to the kind of light, jazz-influenced music that marked the work of artists such as Mitchell and Carole King (on her 1972 *Rhymes and Reasons* album) in the first half of the 1970s.

Given Prince's reputation for fixating on sex in his lyrics, the listener might assume that the song "It" is about, well, "it." That assumption is absolutely correct. Prince's lyrics are not particularly substantial, consisting mostly of phrases such, "gonna do IT all night long," "I wanna do IT every day," and "feels so good, IT must be a crime." The funky music, too, establishes a heavy rhythmic groove (balanced with a lighter, high-pitched synthesizer overlay), but avoids the subtleties of Prince's more interesting songs. Simply put, this is visceral music, and as such, it suggests an absolute emphasis on physical pleasure for its own sake. This is at odds with the ultimate conclusion of the *Around the World in a Day* track "Temptation," in which Prince states that, "love is more important than sex." This apparent conflict, however, has been at the core of Prince's treatment of love and sex throughout his career. He has explored every extreme of love and sex, their differences, and their interrelationship. To the extent that he is inconsistent, Prince reflects the very real human confusion of the intersections of love and sex, emotional desire and physical desire.

"Starfish and Coffee" is a very different kind of song. Here, Prince's character describes a girl he knew in school: Cynthia Rose. She is a girl with an open and active imagination (she says that she starts everyday with a breakfast consisting of "starfish and coffee"), and a simple innocence (she enjoys drawing smiley faces on the wall) that contrasts sharply with the attitudes of her classmates. Prince's music is simple, with few chords and a narrow-range, child-like melody. The musical simplicity complements the way in which the lyrics portray the character. While Cynthia Rose perhaps is not as vivid a character as the subject of "Raspberry Beret," her personality, and the ways in which it makes her stand out from the other students at school, is clear.

"Slow Love" is a moderately slow 12/8-meter ballad in which Prince tells his lover that tonight is a night for "making slow love." It is unabashedly romantic, and is most notable for the jazzy saxophone and trumpet arrangement. It is not a piece without its peculiarities: in particular, the clang of the finger cymbal at one point in the song reminds the listener of Prince and the Revolution's use of that particular percussion instrument to link the first several songs of *Around the World in a Day*. The next track, the funky "Hot Thing," calls to mind the work of Rick James. The lyrics are not substantial: they mostly find Prince telling the "Hot Thing" of the song's title how she turns him on. Musically, it breaks out of the straight 1980s funk mold by means of some interesting vocal harmony by Prince—in open fifths and octaves—that provides yet another suggestion that Prince was not yet ready completely to leave behind the pyschedelia of *Around the World in a Day*.

Disc 1 of *Sign o' the Times* concludes with "Forever in My Life," a song in which Prince tell his lover that he is finally ready to settle down and make a commitment to one woman. Since the lyrics are filled with clichés, the most interesting features are in the performance and arrangement. With its steady, repeated eighth-note bass part and Prince's soulful vocals, "Forever in My Life" is an amalgamation of Police-like new wave (the repeated bass notes of "Every Breath You Take") and R&B.

Disc 2 of the two-disc set begins with "U Got the Look," a rare Prince song that falls pretty much into twelve-bar blues form. Actually, Prince takes a somewhat minimalistic approach to the form, by simplifying the conventional twelve-bar blues chord progression in the last of the three phrases.[4] It is certainly not the most profound song Prince ever wrote: it finds him simply telling a young woman that he finds her sexually desirable because (to paraphrase) she has the look. Sheena Easton provides backing vocals. Obviously, she is a flashier singer than either Lisa or Wendy of the Revolution, and certainly part of the appeal of the song is her vocal counterpoint to Prince. The sentiments expressed by the two singers ("Your body's jammin' / let's get to rammin'") seem on the surface to be quite simple. On the most surface level, the song speaks of visual appeal leading to sexual attraction and physical desire. As one goes a little deeper into deconstructing the lyrics, however, it becomes clear that this attraction, and indeed the "pretty" qualities of Easton's character, are not quite as "natural" as they might seem. Prince sings that it looks as though the woman "took an hour just to make up [her] face." Therefore, this is a painted on—artificial—beauty, despite Prince's description of it as "natural." So, on the deeper, more hidden level, Prince tells us that his character confuses "natural beauty" and fashion; he is a product of consumerism to the core.

"U Got the Look" is an appealing song, with impressive pop hooks. It was one of the two big hit singles on *Sign o' the Times*, the title track being the other. "U Got the Look" reached No. 2 on the *Billboard* pop charts, besting the title track by one position. Despite its popish nature, however, "U Got the Look" includes a few traces of Prince's still-present neo-psychedelic inclinations, including some deliberately discordant electric guitar and synthesizer licks, and some spoken material (with electronic processing) that proclaims Prince's come-on lines as yet another episode in the "boy versus girl" game. Incidentally, it should be noted that Prince had been in part responsible for Sheena Easton's career transformation from that of a somewhat lightweight pop diva ("Morning Train") to that of sassy sex symbol when he wrote (under the pseudonym Alexander Nevermind) the song "Sugar Walls" for her in 1984.

The next track, "If I Was Your Girlfriend," reprises the basic theme of the early Prince song "I Wanna Be Your Lover," in that it finds Prince thinking across gender lines. In "I Wanna Be Your Lover" Prince's character intimated that he wanted to be everything to the woman of his desires: a lover, a mother, a sister, and so on. Here, he wishes that he could share the kinds of things with his former lover that female friends share. Prince leaves the reference vague enough that it is never clear whether he means the term to refer to lesbian lovers or to platonic girlfriends. On one hand, then, the song can be read as a desire to break down the barriers that gender and previous sexual involvement can place in a relationship. On the other hand, the song can be read as the ruminations of a man whose lover has left him for another woman, although that is probably quite a bit of an interpretational stretch. After the sound of orchestral string instruments tuning up (a reminder of the opening of the Beatles' *Sgt. Pepper's Lonely Hearts Club Band*) and a snippet of Felix Mendelssohn's "Wedding March," Prince establishes a gentle R&B feel. It is truly an intriguing song, mostly because of the ambiguity with which Prince treats the meaning of the phrase "if I was your girlfriend." It forces the listener to grapple with questions of gender roles and sexual orientation.

Prince jumps headlong into an even more controversial aspect of sexuality in "Strange Relationship." In this song Prince's character apologizes to his "lover," for using her sexually. The implication is that his continuing treatment of her revolves around sex as control, if not outright violence. Even if one gives Prince's character the greatest possible benefit of the doubt, this is certainly an unhealthy co-dependent relationship: he is a user, and she seems subconsciously to thrive on being on the receiving end of his use. The thing that really makes the song alarming is the fact that Prince sets his tale of such a clearly dysfunctional relationship to such catchy, vaguely Caribbean-sounding music. The more one delves into the possible implications of the lyrics, the more unsettling the song becomes. It is the kind of song that is much too easy to hear purely as a musical statement on first listening: the musical setting is so catchy that it dominates the message at first. The song, then, evolves with each listening, as the implications of the lyrics gradually come into greater focus.

Prince moves firmly into the new wave pop style of the 1980s for "I Could Never Take the Place of Your Man." The happy-sounding music setting is very similar to the Bangles' arrangement of Prince's composition "Manic Monday," a recording of the previous year. Interestingly, though, this song dates from the early 1980s, with the original 1982 version evolving over the years. Despite its genesis at the height of the popularity of new wave in the early 1980s and its ties to the style of "Manic Monday," structurally, "I Could Never Take the Place of Your Man" breaks out of the pop, new-wave mold at the 3:47 mark of the recording. At that point, Prince moves into a sparse, minimalistic jam, in which he suspends the song's chord progression and trades multitracked, economical, bluesy electric guitar licks with himself. Prince then counts off the lead-in into the song's brief coda section, which lasts the final 25 seconds. This coda recaps the hook-heavy instrumental introduction. In the album version of the song, the proportion of the first section to the second section is relatively close to the classical proportions of the Golden Mean, a relationship in which one section of a work of art is approximately 1.618 times as large as another section. While this numerical proportion and its importance in the arts dates back to Ancient Greece, it was especially important to artists in the European Renaissance, and to some twentieth-century composers, most notably Béla Bartók.

The lyrics of "I Could Never Take the Place of Your Man" tell the story of a woman whose lover has left her. Prince's character meets her in a bar on a Friday night. After he asks her to dance, she intimates that she is looking for someone to take the place of the man that left her, but he knows (1) that neither one of them ultimately will be satisfied with that, and (2) that he will never be able to replace her former lover in her heart. As is the case with many of his songs, "I Could Never Take the Place of Your Man" finds Prince's character in command of his sexual destiny; however, this is a rare example of Prince portraying a character who declines a sexual encounter.

It is possible, in fact to draw connections between this story and the story of Adam and Eve's fall from grace in the Old Testament Book of Genesis. Interestingly, though, while Adam yields to Eve's temptation, Prince's character in this song rejects a cheap sexual encounter because he realizes that it cannot lead to a fulfilling long-term relationship. The song reinforces the message of the *Around the World in a Day* track "Temptation" ("Love is more important than sex"). Because of the song's contrasting musical style and the way in which Prince's character contrasts from all of the other characters on *Sign o' the Times*, "I Could Never Take the Place of Your Man" places an important structural role on the album: it adds to the rich diversity of the album.

Overall, *Sign o' the Times* does not include a large amount of the spirituality of its immediate predecessors or Prince's twenty-first-century albums. This tends to make "The Cross" stand out for the listener. It is impossible to take it for granted since it contrasts so starkly with the material that surrounds it. The song is marked by Prince's simple sustained electric guitar melodic figure, which closely resembles one of the Hindustani ragas and the Western Mixolydian mode.[5] "The Cross" begins quietly, but just over 2 minutes and 30 seconds into the piece, Prince repeats the entire text, singing with more intensity over a hard rock feel in the drums and distorted rhythm guitar. The contrast between the quiet two-beat feel of the opening and the heavy, and louder, four-beat feel of the hard rock section[6] resembles what alternative and grunge bands would be doing in a couple of years. Certainly, the style was already somewhat in the air in the late 1980s, but this high level of dynamic and intensity contrast would be a regular feature of bands in the 1990s. In the last minute of the nearly 5-minute song, Prince doubles the Hindustani-influenced/Mixolydian-mode guitar figure with what sounds like a sitar, emphasizing the musical ties to the Indian subcontinent even more. The final 10 seconds of the song consist of a chorus singing the words, "the cross" in complex, barbershop-style harmony. The lyrics of the song look at "the cross" in two contrasting ways: (1) it is a metaphor for the burdens that people have to bear in life, and (2) it symbolizes the release that God provides from those same burdens in the Christian tradition.

The next song, "It's Gonna Be a Beautiful Night," is a collaborative composition of Prince, keyboardist Dr. Fink, and saxophonist Eric Leeds. The recording is an 8-minute-plus live performance by Prince and the Revolution. In fact, it is the only track on the album on which all members of the Revolution appear. The song itself is a James Brown–style funk dance jam, stylistically suggesting both some of the groove-type songs of Prince's first two albums and the dance-based work he would do on *The Black Album*.

The album concludes with "Adore," a Quiet Storm R&B love ballad. The composition and arrangement are marked by a couple of unexpected chromatic harmonic shifts and a slightly unpredictable collection of musical instrument timbres. The piece meanders melodically and moves from a predictable verse structure into a more unpredictable mid-song semipsychedelic section. It is a recording that would probably very rarely find itself on the radio or even on the stereo as "make out" music: it is just too quirky. It is best appreciated as Prince's experimentation with a specific type of genre piece. If listened to that way, it is brilliant how Prince moves out of and back into the structural confines of the genre. His use of unusual instrument textures and a horn section that seems to appear and disappear at unexpected times also plays around with the genre.

So, in two compact discs' worth of material Prince explores sex as part of love, sex for purely physical pleasure, the dangers of drug usage, various other social ills, child-like innocence, the emotional side of love, religious salvation, a vulnerable-sounding decline of sex, co-dependency, and parodies contemporary dance music. *Sign o' the Times* is a terribly eclectic mix of lyrical themes and musical styles. The material covers a fairly wide range of time, from the 1982 song "I Could Never Take the Place of Your Man," new songs, and songs that were left over from the shelved triple-disc set *Crystal Ball*. Prince ties it all together, though, through the implications of the album's title. If studied as a wide-ranging snapshot of emotions, sexual mores, social issues, and musical styles of the 1980s, it is one of the most intriguing albums of the era. It also remains one of Prince's most essential albums.

The Black Album

Called "The Legendary Black Album" for good reason, this collection originally was meant for release in late 1987. However, it fell victim to either Prince's or Warner Bros.'s axe, just like the later-rumored *Crystal Ball* album. Although some of the material soon found its way into some of the songs of the 1988 album *Lovesexy*, *The Black Album* was eventually released by Warner Bros. in limited quantities in its original intended version in 1994. Since there were several bootleg permutations of *The Black Album* that appeared starting at the time the album originally was supposed to be released in its legitimate form, hardcore Prince fans were probably already at least partially familiar with the material. Whatever motivated the original shelving of the album—rumors about this run a wide gamut, and Prince has not necessarily been entirely forthcoming about his possible reasons—it would seem unusual that an album of new material appear so quickly after *Sign o' the Times*. Prince's prolific writing and recording work was resulting in too much material in order for his release schedule to fit into the recording industry paradigm of the time. Since *The Black Album* was intended for release in November 1987, it will be dealt with here, in order to put it into the context of the chronological study of Prince's writing and recording. All in all, it is a significantly more funk-oriented and dance rhythm–oriented album than anything Prince had put together previously. Therefore, it has a more unified feel than Prince's previous albums; however, that is something of a double-edged sword: it lacks the richness of stylistic diversity of Prince's earlier albums. It represents Prince's first foray into hip-hop musical and lyrical style. There is a lyrical darkness (particularly on the song "Bob George") that is rare in the Prince canon. It is also an album that clearly finds Prince dealing with the reality that his black fan base had diminished since *Purple Rain* brought him more fully into white popular culture.

The album kicks off with "Le Grind," an upbeat funk track that uses "le grind" to represent a demonstrative dance as well as sexual intercourse. Prince's lyrical references to the funky beat of the song, the use of call and response vocal lines, as well as the balance of *ostinato* instrumental parts with ever-evolving instrumental parts, exhibit clear ties to the music of James Brown, George Clinton, and other funk pioneers. "Le Grind" is a powerful dance track—not the most lyrically interesting piece Prince has ever composed—but that's not the point of a piece such as this.

"Cindy C." is Prince's come-on to supermodel Cindy Crawford. His character hopes both to bed her and to photograph her in the nude. It is explicit, but with an infectious, infinitely danceable groove. The next track, "Dead on It" fits firmly within the hip-hop style and is most notable for Prince's rhythm and lead guitar parts and the rhythmic interplay between the various layers of instruments and vocals lines. Prince's lyrics parody rappers and the hip-hop genre, despite the fact that the music is so firmly part of the genre. It is an interesting experiment in genre writing and performance, but ultimately is not a particularly successful track. "When 2 R in Love," which critic Stephen Thomas Erlewine labels "an urban ballad as nondescript as the genre,"[7] is another piece that would make an ideal album cut for any R&B ballad singer of the era. However, as Erlewine suggests, it is easily lost in the Prince canon, since he has written and recorded so many songs that are more distinctive.

The next track, "Bob George," shares some tone color and rhythmic characteristics with "Le Grind," but it is entirely different in mood. This is a decidedly dark piece. Through electronic manipulation, Prince takes on a deep, low-pitched voice for his rap. The lyrics find him as a foul-mouthed, paranoid, and violent man who believes that his woman is cheating on him with Bob George, the song's title character. The piece is so dark, with Prince's character taking a gun to get back at those who he believes have wronged him, that it seems to be a serious-minded parody of the hardcore violence of some hip-hop songs. It is, however, not without its moments of levity. For example, Prince's badass character mentions "Prince" at one point in his rant, referring to him as "that skinny motherfucker with the high voice."

In "Superfunkycalifragisexy," Prince establishes a fast tempo funk groove that owes more than a small debt of gratitude to George Clinton and Parliament/Funkadelic. The lyrics find Prince's character picking up a woman on the dance floor and then enjoying a night of casual sex (she can't remember his name in the morning). There is not enough to the song to hold the listener's interest as well as most of the rest of the songs on *The Black Album*.

Although "Superfunkycalifragisexy" is one of the weakest songs on the album, it is followed by one of the strongest: "2 Nigs United 4 West Compton." Despite the programmatic-sounding title, this is not a song, but an instrumental piece. It is introduced by an impressionistic montage of faux party conversation. Prince takes on the character of Frankie, a musician who is asked to "serve it up." All of this, along with a statement of the title of the piece, takes approximately 38 seconds. That's when the instrumental portion of the composition begins. Prince then provides nearly 6 ½ minutes of up-tempo funk jam. There are technically impressive keyboard and bass (possibly synthesized) solos. It is perhaps the single greatest showpiece for Prince's arranging, production, and instrumental skills. Prince provides plenty of contrasting synthesized tone colors and constant rhythmic variation to make this the strongest piece on *The Black Album*. As an instrumental piece with a social/political title (West Compton is a predominantly African American town in Los Angeles County, California, perhaps most closely associated in the late 1980s with street gangs and gangsta rap) it follows in the tradition of some of the jazz compositions of John Coltrane ("Africa" and "Alabama"), Charles Mingus ("Haitian Fight Song"), Branford Marsalis ("Brother Trying to Catch a Cab [On the East Side] Blues"), and others.

The horn arrangement on the album's final track, "Rockhard in a Funky Place," exhibits the influence of bebop jazz, something that was in the air in late 1980s R&B. The jazz references, elaborate arrangements, and metaphorical and explicit lyrical references to Prince's character's erection suggest the influence of the work of Frank Zappa. It is an entertaining piece, but does not wear particularly well with repeated hearings the way that Prince's best songs do.

The name of *The Black Album* clearly is no accident: all of the songs find Prince working in the prevailing African American styles of the mid- to late 1980s. Prince's lyrics run the gamut from tender to violent. Because there is such a wide range of emotional states and several subgenres of R&B represented, it is not as cohesive as it might be. Some of the songs are either too generic sounding ("When 2 R in Love"), or too deliberately over-the-top ("Bob George") to be fully successful from the commercial standpoint. If, however, the album is understood as Prince's home studio experimentation with and unspoken commentary on prevailing black music styles of the period, it is a success. The main problem is that Prince had previously been at his best and his most commercially successful when he defied racial and genre boundaries. The irreverent *Rough Guide to Cult Pop* perhaps put it best: "When it [*The Black Album*] was finally released, those who hadn't bought the previously sought-after bootleg discovered why it wasn't issued in the first place."[8]

LOVESEXY

Prince's 1988 album *Lovesexy* is instantly recognizable for its cover, which features a photograph of the naked Prince in a send-up of a cheesecake pose.

As a somewhat gender-bending photo, it falls in line with Prince's appearances in frilly clothing and/or with his purple motorcycle on the cover of albums in the mid-1980s. There is more to *Lovesexy*, however, than the cover photo. Musically, it finds Prince eschewing the focus on R&B and hip-hop of *The Black Album* for a balance of R&B and rock music, as well some intriguing hybrid pieces. Prince also stretches himself harmonically and structurally on some of the songs—considerably more than on the more straightforward R&B music of *The Black Album*. Curiously, the album was released on compact disc as a single, 45-minute-plus track. The individual songs are not indexed on the disc, because Prince felt that the album needed to be experienced in sequence. The obvious problem for the listener is that this tactic makes it inconvenient to pick and choose individual tracks to listen to. Interestingly, *Lovesexy* provides the earliest Prince material to receive serious academic study: Stan Hawkins published an article on the song "Anna Stesia" in the journal *Popular Music*.[9]

Although Prince presents *Lovesexy* as a sequentially exact song cycle that needs to be experienced all the way through, I will treat the individual songs. The album begins with "I [Eye] No."[10] Here, Prince expresses his belief in God, heaven and hell, and that God wants people to enjoy love and sex. In Prince's worldview, there is no need for drugs. All the high that is needed comes from love, sex, and belief in the Almighty. It isn't so much that Christian spirituality can co-exist with sexual desire as that the two are intertwined—in other words, the Prince philosophy clearly is that God gave humans the gifts of emotional and physical love for a reason: that they be enjoyed. Incidentally, during his rap, a female voice addresses Prince as "Frankie," thereby reviving the persona he first took on for the song (a similar party-like track) "2 Nigs United 4 West Compton" on the temporarily shelved *Black Album*. Like "2 Nigs United 4 West Compton," this is party-like music that surrounds a serious subject. The music is bright-sounding, both in the tempo sense and in the tone-color sense: the orchestration features a catchy muted trumpet figure and the overall arrangement is less bass-focused than the arrangements on *The Black Album*. Prince balances the harmonic emphasis on a single chord in the guitars, bass, and keyboards with more adventurous chromatic harmonies in the saxophones and brasses. Melodically, the song is reminiscent of early hits of Motown artists the Jackson Five. So, Prince balances Motown-like R&B pop with jazz and funk.

"Alphabet St." continues the lyrical theme of "I [Eye] No." Prince sings about going down "2 Alphabet Street," picking up the first girl he meets and giving her a ride in the backseat of his dad's 1967 Thunderbird. As is customary in the lyrics of Prince, the ride in backseat can be taken literally or metaphorically (to represent sexual intercourse). As the song develops, it becomes clear that while he may be giving her a ride to some remote location in the literal sense, his main objective is to give her a ride in the backseat in the metaphorical sense. Once they have arrived at the location where Prince's character intends to do the deed, however, she is reluctant to have sexual intercourse, so he is willing "to go down" (have oral sex), "if that's the only way." Again, he emphasizes that with "Lovesexy" one has no need for drugs for a high. Along with his glorification of sex, Prince includes a paraphrase of Jesus of Nazareth's command to love one's enemies, thereby reinforcing the linkage between love, sex, and religion that was at the core of "I [Eye] No." Prince's use of a slight variant on the simple I-IV-V-I chord progression, a simple, narrow-range falling melodic motive, and the rhythmic figures and tone color of the prominent rhythm guitar all call to mind the kind of prefunk, presoul, uptown R&B songs that white Brill Building teams such as Goffin and King and Mann and Weil wrote for both African American and for blue-eyed soul artists of the early to mid-1960s. Only the funk-style slap bass, the explicit lyrics, and a couple of hip-hop stop-time production effects make it clear that this is not a mid-1960s popish R&B song at the beginning. As the music progresses, the instrumental accompaniment gets progressively heavier, and eventually the female rapper Cat delivers a rap, thereby bringing the song squarely into the hip-hop style. The horn section, which was not part of the arrangement at the start of the song, also gradually emerges, thereby linking the orchestration of "Alphabet St." to "I [Eye] No." It is a truly interesting musical transformation.

The next song, "Glam Slam," is a take-off on the phrase "Wham, bam, thank you, Ma'am," used to denote an anonymous, casual sexual encounter. Here, Prince's character contrasts the relationship he is in with casual sex. The relationship "transcend[s] the physical," and Prince prays that his lover "will always stay." With its vocal harmonies, use of reverberation on the vocals, synthesized string lines, and simple pop-oriented melodic hooks, the verses and chorus of the song emphasize emotional attachment—the love part of the relationship. Prince includes interlude sections that are much more disjunct melodically. In these he provides brief snippets of some of the physical/sexual pleasures his character enjoys in the relationship. The song also increasingly strays from a pop feel near the end as the synthesizer melodies move somewhat out of the prevailing key. This can leave the listener with a sense of conflict, especially in the context of the focus on the purely physical side of love found in some of the other songs and in numerous songs from throughout Prince's earlier career. As I hear this move into somewhat more experimental instrumental music as the song progresses, I sense that the physical urges Prince's character feels may cause him (and not his lover) to be the one to stray. The lyrics do not imply this; however, the music itself provides a contrasting feel that all may not be right with the relationship, despite the glorious terms with which Prince's character describes it.

In "Anna Stesia," Prince seemingly juxtaposes a desire for a girl named Anna Stesia with a desire for God. At least, that is the reading put forth by Stan Hawkins in his article "Prince: Harmonic Analysis of 'Anna Stesia,'" in the journal *Popular Music*.[11] Hawkins's analysis finds that Prince almost exclusively uses the C Aeolian mode (also known as C natural minor) in the section of the piece that ostensibly deals with carnal desire, and then uses a richer harmonic palette in the spiritual section. Certainly, Hawkins's findings about Prince's changes of melodic and harmonic material between the two sections are valid. I would propose, however, that there is another way to read the first section. To the extent that one reads the title and object of Prince's desire as a play on the word *anesthesia,* then one can read the character as a metaphor for a desire for or addiction to drugs. Perhaps this reading better explains why the two contrasting desires are set to such harmonically contrasting musical material and why the desire for God seems to end the desire for the supposed "woman" Anna Stesia. Certainly, the linkage of love, sex, and God is the main theme of *Lovesexy.* It is not, however, the only theme, since Prince also communicates a clear antidrug message as part of the spoken introduction to "I [Eye] No" ("The reason why my voice is so clear is that there's no smack in my brain") as well as in the lyrics of the album's first track.

Prince turns to clearer social commentary in the song "Dance On." In short, one-line statements and observations, he describes some of the evils he sees, including gang violence, robbery, murder, and nuclear proliferation. According to Prince, the only solution to these social problems is "a power structure that breeds production instead of jacks who vandalize." In the end, he identifies greed as the root cause of the local and global social problems. The funky musical setting includes vocal lines sung in a variety of pitch ranges, which suggests some of the songs of social commentary of Sly and the Family Stone's 1969 album *Stand!* and 1971 album *There's a Riot Goin' On.* It is not, however, as memorable or successful a song as the late 1960s work of Sly Stone.

The song "Lovesexy" is perhaps the ultimate expression of Prince's worldview, in which worship of God and sex are intricately tied together. I say this because it is one of his starkest songs in terms of contrast between the purely physical and the purely spiritual. Images of race cars burning rubber in Prince's pants and "intelligent" curves to one's "behind" seem particularly at odds with falling in love "with the heavens above"; it is just all too extreme.

"When 2 R in Love" may not have fit the hardcore funk style of *The Black Album,* but it works better in the context of *Lovesexy.* To the extent that *Lovesexy* is Prince's exploration of the many aspects of love (its spiritual side, emotional side, and physical side), and their interrelationships, the sheer romanticism of "When 2 R in Love" certainly has a place. Although the easygoing melodic hooks run closer to the more romantic 1980s ballad work of singer-songwriters such as Lionel Richie and Stevie Wonder than what one might (stereo)typically associate with Prince, it works. And, despite the fact that it fits so firmly in the middle-of-the-road love ballad genre, it clearly exhibits some traits that identify the song as a Prince composition and production. This is most apparent in the vocal arrangement, which includes background harmony writing that finds Prince referencing 1960s psychedelic music, particularly the complex 1967-era work of bands such as the Beatles.

The song "I Wish U Heaven" is one of Prince's unique combinations of new wave rock and R&B. In it, Prince suggests that the ultimate expression of love is to wish his lover "Heaven," which is understood here in the literal/religious sense. The song ties Prince's sex-love-God philosophy together pretty well from a lyrical standpoint. It succeeds better than "Lovesexy" because it does not rely on the starkest extremes of what some listeners might call sacred and profane. It is not, however, the best example of a Prince song in the area of melodic, harmonic, or arrangement hooks.

The message of the album's final song, "Positivity," is clear: one needs to keep one's focus on God in order to make it through this earthly life and to eternal life; one must not stoop to "kiss the beast" and give in to worldly temptations of greed and violence. The disconnected lyrical images and disconnected vocal lines provide the listener with overall impressions of the kinds of evils that must be resisted. In the chorus, Prince drives home the point of a positive outlook by asking the question, "Have you had your plus sign today?" Given the close visual relationship between a plus sign and the cross, it is easy to make the metaphorical connection.

An exploration of Prince's life philosophy that links God, love, and sex in unconventional ways, *Lovesexy* exhibits a range of emotions and musical styles. Some of the songs, however, suffer either because they are not particularly distinctive musically, or because they do not explain Prince's unconventional philosophy of life.

BATMAN

Prince provided songs for the soundtrack of the 1989 Hollywood blockbuster *Batman*. The movie was a huge commercial success and the synergy between Prince's songs and the original score by Danny Elfman in establishing mood throughout the film is strong. The soundtrack album is strong; however, the connections between specific characters and parts of the storyline that are included in the liner notes and in the short snippets of dialogue from the film are not particularly helpful, nor ultimately meaningful. In at least one case—"Vicki Waiting," in particular—the film version of the character Bruce Wayne seems to be strangely at odds with Prince's take on the character. Other songs, such as "Partyman," may provide a feeling of mood that surrounds a particular character—in this case, the Joker—but seem like they go on longer than they should. Other songs, such as "The Future" and "Batdance," either work very well outside the context of the film (the former), or they are brilliant musical/mood constructions that tie many aspects of the film together (the latter). The individual songs range from the funky to the sappy.

The album's first song, "The Future," comes from the viewpoint (according to Prince) of Batman. It is a song with a mix of emotions: on one hand, Batman sees the temptations and the reality of drugs and youth violence; however, on the other hand, he holds hope for the future. It would seem to be a somewhat tenuous hope. The message and the somber nature of the music (repetitive melodic motives, narrow melodic range, and careful use of musical space), despite its moderately fast tempo, matches the character of Batman as he is developed by director Tim Burton and actor Michael Keaton. Unlike the 1960s television program version of Batman, Burton's version focuses on the darkness of the character, as found in Bob Kane's original comic books.

In contrast to Batman, who seems throughout the film to be waging an internal war between good and evil, the Joker is much more of a caricature. Prince captures this in "Electric Chair" and (especially) in "Partyman." Because the two songs are so wrapped up in the character's over-the-top, flamboyant nature, they work fine as mood pieces in the context of the film, but really require the context of the film in order to be fully effective. Prince and pop chanteuse Sheena Easton collaborated on the writing and singing of "The Arms of Orion," a pop love ballad that is supposed to represent *Batman* characters Vicki Vale and Bruce Wayne. In the film, the relationship of these characters does not seem as sappy as this ballad makes it out to be.

"Trust" is one of the more curious songs in the collection in that it finds Prince interacting with the Joker. The song begins with the Joker (sung by Prince) making his bid for trust. Later, Prince tells the listener that the only entity one can truly trust is God. By commenting on the Joker (who represents the greedy, gluttonous side of human nature), Prince steps outside the traditional role of the soundtrack composer: he places himself as a character (or at least, a commentator) in the drama. This is not likely to be noticed in the film itself, but it is crystal clear in the context of the album's liner notes, in which the characters are identified. Since there is nothing in the *sung* lyrics to suggest that they come from two different characters, the Joker-Prince interplay (which is evident from the printed lyrics sheet) is confusing. The music is pleasant dance pop, but tends not to stick in the listener's mind. Similarly, "Lemon Crush," which supposedly comes from the viewpoint of Vicki Vale, does not make a particularly strong impression. It is interesting to note, however, just how much mileage Prince gets out of the oscillation between the tonic pitch and the minor third scale-degree in the verses of the song. The lyrics feature fairly obvious rhymes.

"Scandalous" is a curiosity. Prince sings this ballad, which is about being so aroused that he wants "2 skip the 4 play" and "get down here on the floor," in a high falsetto. The sentiments and the vocal characterization are totally out of character for the Tim Burton/Michael Keaton concept of Batman, from whose viewpoint the song purportedly comes.

The album's last track, "Batdance," however, is quite effective. Here, Prince weaves together various images from the film, from the album's previous songs, and personal references to his style and the name of his new band (the New Power Generation). Musically, he references some of the other songs of the album, the theme song from the 1960s television version of *Batman*, techno, hard rock, Steve Reich–style minimalism. It is much more, though, than a pastiche of these various reference points. It is a *tour de force* for Prince as a composer and studio producer. It is also a showpiece for Prince as a guitarist. "Batdance" is a 6-minute and 13-second expansion of ABA form. The first major section (A) consists of 2:42 of a hybrid of fast hard rock and hip-hop–influenced funk; the second section (B) consists of 2:14 of a slower-tempo, monothematic funk guitar riff, over which the relationship of Bruce Wayne and Vale, the Joker's abduction of Vale, and Prince's desire for Ms. Vale's body are explored through spoken snippets; there is a return to the A material for approximately the final 1:17. It is fascinating exploration of repetition and contrast. However, the piece is not as likely as some of Prince's more dramatic compositions to enjoy a long life span because it is so closely tied to the *Batman* story.

The *Batman* soundtrack showed that Prince could work successfully within the confines of a commercially based Hollywood motion picture that did not revolve around himself as an actor. "Batdance," in particular, is a well-structured and aurally fascinating piece of composition and production work. The soundtrack album seems to be one Prince work that could find its relevance wane over time, however, because it is so context-driven: someone with no exposure to the characters just would not get it.

GRAFFITI BRIDGE

When Prince first portrayed "The Kid" in his film debut *Purple Rain,* he created a sensation. The film was a commercial success, and the soundtrack album and its singles, including "Purple Rain" and "When Doves Cry," brought Prince up to the level of superstar and pop culture icon. The 1990 film *Graffiti Bridge* found Prince reprising the semiautobiographical character. Morris Day and the Time, costars of *Purple Rain,* again appeared. While *Purple Rain* revolved around the inner turmoil The Kid felt largely as a result of his dysfunctional family life, *Graffiti Bridge* revolved around The Kid's desire to express spirituality in his music, in the context of the club scene. The film was a critical and commercial disaster. Despite this, the soundtrack album contains some fine and memorable music. One more notable feature of the soundtrack is that it finds Prince breaking free of traditional pop music genre boundaries more than he had done recently, primarily because the fictional Kid's music blended so many influences—black, white, R&B, rock, jazz, pop—just like Prince had at one time routinely done.

With the spoken introduction, "Dear Dad, things didn't turn out quite like I wanted them to," the soundtrack to *Graffiti Bridge* begins. The introduction itself refers back to the personal maturity and commercial success The Kid found at the end of the film *Purple Rain.* He had come to grips with his inner demons, he had finally accepted the music of his bandmates, and in the process, had won the hearts of the patrons of the club at which he was on the verge of losing his long-time gig. It wasn't enough for The Kid, though.

The first song on the album, "Can't Stop This Feeling I Got," is an up-tempo neo-rockabilly–influenced piece. The melodic rhythmic and pitch motives bear a superficial resemblance to the music of the 1984 Kenny Loggins hit, "Footloose." "Can't Stop This Feeling I Got" is most notable for Prince's rockabilly guitar playing, and for its harmonic subtleties (especially the use of unexpected minor chords) and formal contrast (especially the brief half-time interludes).

The New Power Generation was the name of Prince's best-known fan club, and soon after the release of *Graffiti Bridge*, it would be the name of his new band. Some of the members of the new band perform on the *Graffiti Bridge* soundtrack; however, not under the group name. The song "New Power Generation," which appears twice on the album (first, as the second track and then in briefer form as the last track), provides the listener with the philosophy that, "makin' love and music's the only things worth fightin' for." The message that conflict can lead nowhere is universal enough, and the lyrics are general enough that the message does not rely on the context of the film. Musically, Prince combines a hard medium-tempo funk groove with music that is harmonically and melodically catchy, in a Stevie Wonder-esque way. The club/party atmosphere of the recording comes out of the film; however, Prince had already included faux live party sounds on several previous albums, so, again, the song's arrangement and production can be effective outside the context of the movie.

Although "New Power Generation" is on one level an invitation to the dance floor, the song's message of peace and understanding give it another level of significance. Prince distinguishes between the dance-focused music of The Kid and that associated with Morris Day and the Time in the film. For example, the songs "Shake!" (written by Prince) and "Release It" and "Love Machine" (co-written by Prince) all exist pretty much just on a visceral level. In this way, Prince helps to define the characters through his words and music.

In the brief poem of "The Question of U," Prince creates a wonderful masterpiece of double meaning in the tradition of some of George Harrison's work, in particular, Harrison's 1987 song "Fish on the Sand." Prince asks several questions about how he needs to go about answering "the question of u," while leaving the nature of just who "u" is vague. He could be addressing a person or God. Yes, he includes religious imagery that reflects back to Jesus of Nazareth's parables, but throughout the lyrics Prince remains just one little step away from making the meaning obvious. Musically, the piece is a slow, blues-influenced rock ballad, which is most notable for Prince's almost exclusive use of ascending melodic phrases. This reflects the questioning nature of the text. Prince's sustained electric guitar solo exhibits the subtle influence of Carlos Santana, both in tone color and in some of the melodic figurations.

Although Prince's arrangement on "Elephants & Flowers" practically screams "late 1980s and early 1990s" (especially the drum machine line and the lead electric guitar tone color), the aesthetics of late 1960s soul also cannot be missed. Prince paints the picture of a young man who is torn between the loveless sexuality he sees all around him and his desire for a "quiet" lover, and for a relationship with God. This dialectic is at the very heart of the story of the film *Graffiti Bridge;* however, the song's message of the conflicts between sacred and secular society is universal enough that the song can fully function outside the context of the film. While it may not be Prince's best-remembered song in terms of lyrics, melody, or structure, "Elephants & Flowers" certainly is notable for the vocal arrangement, in which the many-times-overdubbed "voices" of Prince sound like a full gospel chorus.

The next selection on the *Graffiti Bridge* soundtrack album is "Round and Round," a Prince composition that is sung by Tevin Campbell, and accompanied by the composer on backing vocals and all of the instruments. The basic gist of Prince's lyrics is that dreaming about the future and talking about the future are not going to achieve anything: one must *do,* rather than dream. To the extent that Prince can sometimes be a bit quirky in the philosophy he espouses in his lyrics (his combination of sex and religiosity, for example, would be considered highly controversial, if not blasphemous, by some), this song is surprisingly straightforward. The song "We Can Funk" finds Prince writing and performing with funk pioneer George Clinton. It is not the most memorable song with which Prince has been associated, especially considering that this was the meeting of two true giants of funk style.

Prince's solo composition and performance (he provides all instruments and voices) of "Joy in Repetition" is actually more memorable. Prince builds his paean to repetition using a very distinctive tune in the verses in which he repeats a descending step-wise minor third. Although the use of music repetition might seem a bit obvious, the descending phrase is distinctive enough that the song holds the listener's attention, while making the point that repetition can—in some circumstances—be a good thing.

While the lyrics of "Tick Tick Bang" tend toward the totally visceral—they are about the sexual excitement Prince's character feels when he is in the presence of the bombshell that turns him on—the way that the songs that the Time perform in the movie all tend to be, this song is a product entirely of Prince. What really distinguishes this song from the vehicles Prince provided for the Time in *Graffiti Bridge* is the intriguing combination of Prince's Jimi Hendrix–influenced hard rock rhythmic and lead guitar feel with his vulnerable-sounding, Smoky Robinson–influenced falsetto singing.

Although "Thieves in the Temple" might not be Prince's best-known composition, its lasting quality can be seen in the fact that it continues to appear in new arrangements into the twenty-first century. For example, while attending the 2007 annual convention of the Ohio Music Education Association, I heard a jazz ensemble consisting of educators from across the state play a new arrangement of the piece that was recently composed for high school jazz groups. It is important to note that 2007 high school students were just born at the time Prince composed and recorded "Thieves in the Temple!" In the *Graffiti Bridge* soundtrack, Prince plays all the instruments and sings all the multitracked vocal lines. Prince's lyrics concern the age-old story of betrayal by one's closest friends, the "thieves in the temple." He calls on "Love" to come quickly and protect him. On one level, "Love" represents God, although one can easily understand the song as being directed to Prince's lover. The music is mysterious, with accompaniment suggests of Asian music in the open-interval harmonization in the synthesizer figure upon which the opening phrases of the verses are built. This melodic figure itself outlines a G minor triad, the key on which the song is based; the minor tonality and the unpredictable nature of the opening rhythms add to the somewhat ominous, mysterious feeling of the song.

"The Latest Fashion," which Prince performs with the Time, is a catchy funk piece with strong melodic and accompaniment hooks, although the melodic phrases tend to be more repetitious than Prince's strongest melodies. More than anything else, the song sets up a strong rhythmic groove. The rap on the song is not particularly strong, but it anticipates the more interesting song "My Name Is Prince," which Prince and the New Power Generation would record a few years later.

Mavis Staples makes a guest appearance as the lead vocalist on "Melody Cool." The Steeles provide the gospel-influenced backing vocals and Prince plays all the (mostly synthesized) instruments. Prince's lyrics use the same kind of general metaphor of such songs as "Ebony and Ivory," in which harmony in music becomes a metaphor for harmony in life. While this might strike some listeners as trite, as might some of the instrumental licks from 1980s pop songs Prince throws in, the performance by Staples and the Steeles helps the song succeed better than it might have in the hands of performers less well versed in the gospel genre.

Graffiti Bridge is not exactly a ballad-filled album, so the song "Still Would Stand All Time" is bound to stand out. In terms of the use of tonality, it is one of Prince's more interesting songs. The melody of the verses is built almost entirely on one short, often-repeated phrase that emphasizes the tonic pitch, actually almost relentlessly. For the chorus, however, Prince moves into a new key and uses lush, jazz-inspired chromatic harmonies that tend to obscure the tonality. Prince's lyrics contrast the hope and desire for a time when humankind will experience "heaven on earth" with his belief that that reality does not have to be just a concept or a hope for some future generation, but that it could come about just as soon as people would turn to "the Light," or "Love" (read "God"). Prince's use of contrasting degrees of tonal focus in the music highlights the dialectic between idle hope and working reality he sets up in the lyrics. While the song just does not have the stamp of "classic" written on it, particularly because the verses are so repetitious and the chorus is so meandering, it works as an expression of Prince's character's view of the universe.

"Still Would Stand All Time" is not the first song, nor would it be the last song, that Prince wrote that revolves around the concept of finding heaven on earth through belief in and submission to the will of God. Although some Prince's fans were taken aback at the 1966/1967-style psychedelic touches of *Around the World in a Day,* that album's "Paisley Park" is clearly another song in which Prince states that all that is needed to find heaven on earth is to "believe." The song "Graffiti Bridge" looks more widely at the concept of heaven than either "Still Would Stand All Time" or "Paisley Park." For example, while Paisley Park is accessible through belief, and is described as a place that living human beings have found and in which they live, Prince provides images of the Graffiti Bridge for which humans strive to make it possible to understand the place as the afterlife and/or heaven on earth. Some of the images are scattered to the extent that the song loses focus. For example, a couple finding true love is one realization of Graffiti Bridge, but the listener is also told to "let democracy take u higher." Prince's use of the phrase "a future worth fighting for" in such close proximity to his praise of democracy is a bit problematic in that it could be taken to be an endorsement of warfare. The problem is that there are too many of these images for the listener to get a clear vision of Prince's Graffiti Bridge. It is an interesting song musically, particularly in Prince's use of asymmetrical phrase lengths. The melodic quote of a phrase from the famous tune Australian composer and folksong collector Percy Grainger collected and arranged, "English Country Garden" (Prince quotes the phrase "In an English country garden" in Grainger's original), is curious and somewhat confusing. It can tend to force the listener to somehow equate Graffiti Bridge with London Bridge.

While *Graffiti Bridge* (the film) was not well received, and while the soundtrack album is not as strong as the soundtrack from Prince's film *Purple Rain,* the *Graffiti Bridge* album proves—as *Batman* had done—that Prince can use his musical and lyrical eclecticism to fit the needs of films. Taken solely as a Prince album, *Graffiti Bridge* clearly is not nearly as graphic sexually as most of his work from the 1980s and 1990s, and because of the presence of the Time, Mavis Staples, and other guests, as well as because some of the songs relate so strongly to the story of the film, it does not hang together as well as Prince's best albums. Still, some of the songs, such as "Joy in Repetition," "Thieves in the Temple," and "Still Would Stand All Time" are interesting compositionally, and the songs Prince wrote for the Time work well as dance numbers.

Another important milestone of the end of this phase of Prince's career was Sinéad O'Connor's 1990 recording of Prince's "Nothing Compares 2 U." To label this song a *hit* is to understate its popularity and its importance. O'Connor's single held the No. 1 spot in the *Billboard* pop charts for four weeks and it found its way onto several end-of-the millennium lists of the most significant recordings of the rock era. For example, *Rolling Stone* magazine listed "Nothing Compares 2 U" at No. 16 in its December 2000 list of the top 100 pop songs.[12] Certainly, the emotional impact of O'Connor's performance and the hauntingly stark arrangement on the recording played roles in the tremendous popularity of the recording, as well as in the critical notice it received from publications such as *Rolling Stone*. Prince also deserves a great deal of credit as a composer. In "Nothing Compares 2 U," he created a song that fits squarely into the tradition of torch songs of the Tin Pan Alley and classic Broadway eras; however, it is a composition that also sounds thoroughly contemporary.

Both the words and the music of "Nothing Compares 2 U" deserve mention. In the lyrics, which find the singer describing all the things that she (in the case of Sinéad O'Connor—the song lyrics themselves are fairly gender-neutral) can now do since her former lover is gone, there is a wealth of insight the listener receives about the nature of the relationship through Prince's inferences. In the "seven hours and fifteen days" since he left, the singer has been out partying all night and sleeping all day; she "can eat [her] dinner in a fancy restaurant," do anything she wants, and see whomever she chooses. On one level, she is trying to kill the pain with her activities—with her indulgence. On the other hand, the inference (whether intentional or not) is that she was not able to go to fancy restaurants, she could not do what she wanted to do, and she could not necessarily see whatever friends she chose to see while she was involved in her former relationship. Without saying it in so many words, Prince infers that O'Connor's character has a new-found freedom, possibly suggesting that her former lover exercised control over her life. This adds weight to the strength of her sense of loss: she loves him this much, despite perhaps having been under his thumb.

As the singer describes her partying, and the fine restaurants, friends, and new lovers she can experience, the melodic phrases generally trend upward. In contrast, the repetitions of the line "nothing compares 2 u" include difficult-to-sing, disjunct intervals, and it trends downward at the conclusion of most of the statements. In this way, Prince highlights the emotional contrast between the state of trying to kill the pain and the overriding sense of loss the character feels. It is also notable that the melody at the end of the chorus section of the song comes within one step of the tonic pitch. The harmony cadences on the tonic chord only after the formal conclusion of the chorus proper. This suggests the sense of incompleteness the singer feels as she sings, "nothing compares 2 u." This kind of melodic text painting falls very much within the torch song ballad tradition. Still, in Sinéad O'Connor's recording, a thoroughly modern, 1990 feel comes through in the melodic rhythms and the drum track, both of which owe a debt of gratitude to the prevailing hip-hop style.

The New Power Generation and a Name Change

The next phase of Prince's career found him cementing his recording work with a new band, the New Power Generation, changing his name to an unpronounceable symbol, and eventually coming into even greater conflict with Warner Bros. Records, despite the fact that the contract he negotiated with the company gave him a seat on the Warner Bros. Board of Directors in 1992. Throughout the process of changing his name to a symbol, signing a huge multimillion dollar contract, and then claiming to be a slave to his record label, Prince was widely parodied.

DIAMONDS AND PEARLS

The 1991 album *Diamonds and Pearls* was the first album formally credited to Prince and the New Power Generation. While Prince would continue to include a few choice selections on which he was the sole instrumentalist and the sole vocalist, his next several releases showed that the New Power Generation was a force (primarily instrumentally) to be reckoned with. The jazz and R&B-based "chops" of the players complemented Prince's funk and hard rock tendencies. *Diamonds and Pearls* was generally better received than Prince's most recent previous work (*Batman* and *Graffiti Bridge*), and it found him moving significantly closer to the prevailing urban R&B style of the day. He continued to incorporate a number of experimental musical and lyrical tricks as a writer, performer, and producer throughout the album. *All Music Guide*'s Stephen Thomas Erlewine captured the essence of the overall impact of *Diamonds and Pearls* in one particular sentence from his review, in which he wrote, "Although he [Prince] still has a problem with rap—'Jughead' is simply embarrassing—he manages to skillfully reinvent himself as an urban soulman without sacrificing his musical innovation."[1]

Diamonds and Pearls kicks off with a grand song that borrows from the black gospel tradition: "Thunder." Curiously, even though the song begins the first album credited to Prince and the New Power Generation, this song finds Prince supplying all the voices and instruments. And, it is a musical *tour de force* for him. The melody is fairly simple; for the most part it turns around the pitch B, the tonic note in the song's key of B minor. There are melodic and harmonic connections to "Thieves in the Temple"; however, the two songs very much retain their individual identities, in the same way that "1999" and "Manic Monday" clearly share musical material, yet have individual "personalities." The sitar-like riff and the brass-like synthesizer lines are catchy and commercial hooks. Prince performs all of the multitracked vocals and instrumental parts flawlessly.

Like Prince's richest songs, there are several ways in which the lyrics of "Thunder" can be interpreted. He sings of finding Love, with a capital "L." However, he is somewhat open as to whether he refers to the religious ecstasy or to physical love: there are catch words that suggest both. Yes, Prince does sing about his "promise 2 see Jesus in the morning light"; however, it is unclear precisely how this promise relates to the experiences of the night before. On one hand, Prince's promise could stem from the religious enlightenment he experiences, or it could be a way to atone for the perceived misdeeds of the night before. The combination of the deep hip-hop–related drums, mystical-sounding sitar, and multitracked gospel chorus tends to favor the purely religious interpretation of the lyrics, but still allow the listener ample wiggle room. This represents a new, higher level of subtlety and sophistication for Prince as a lyricist, something that would tend to distinguish some of his work of the 1990s from his earlier, generally more cut-and-dry lyrics.

The album's second track, "Daddy Pop," takes the twin influences of James Brown (most obviously "Papa's Got a Brand New Bag" and "Sister Popcorn") and Sly Stone and updates them into a 1990s R&B context, while simultaneously maintaining the feel of a tribute to the 1960s pioneers of soul and funk. Prince makes the tribute aspect of the song obvious enough, especially through his quote of the famous brass chord that begins Brown's "Papa's Got a Brand New Bag."[2] Despite the obvious references to Brown and Stone, Prince's lyrics and (especially) Rosie Gaines's backing vocals suggest a more direct sexuality than one would typically find in the soul of the 1960s.

The ballad "Diamonds and Pearls" is notable for the metrical ambiguity that the accompaniment rhythm and overlapping phrases provide. Prince matches this with lyrical ambiguity when he asks his lover if a gift of diamonds and pearls would make the person "a happy boy or a girl." The later lyrical references to colorblindness (in the racial sense) combine with the gender ambiguity to turn the song into a universal abstraction. Prince is not singing to a particular lover: he is any man singing to any lover, male or female, black, yellow, red, brown, or white. His message, that all he really gives that is truly meaningful is his love then, is meant for any love relationship: gay, straight, monoracial, interracial, and so on. The song doesn't quite match the natural feel of the gender ambiguity on Prince's earlier song "If I Was Your Girl-friend," or the gender-neutral elegance of the songs on David Bowie's three twenty-first century albums, but it is noteworthy.

The album's next song, "Cream," sounds as though it comes right out of the Marc Bolan/T. Rex songbook: it is an obvious cousin of "Bang a Gong (Get It On)." The tempo, minimalistic instrumental setting, and melody clearly pay tribute to the 1972 glam-rock classic. The overall theme of the Bolan song, of love for a woman who is a bit on the sleazy side ("You're dirty sweet, and I love you"), is also adopted by Prince ("U're filthy cute and baby u know it"). Interestingly, while the T. Rex single only made it to No. 10 on the *Billboard* pop charts, the single release of "Cream" became Prince's last pop No. 1 to date.

Prince's exploration of the T. Rex glam classic is particularly interesting because of the extent to which the glam movement aligned with Prince's work. Although the specific lyrical themes and the musical style of art-ists such as Marc Bolan, David Bowie, and the New York Dolls only show up occasionally in Prince's songs, the overarching themes of shock and ambiguity—central to glam—are common in Prince's music. It is easy to see how Prince uses shock, especially considering his many songs with frank, sexually explicit lyrics. The ambiguity of glam, which has at its core the com-bination of what might commonly be assumed to be opposites, however, is less obvious, but just as important in Prince's work. The glam-era use of ambiguity caused by the combination of what at first glance seems to be polar opposites can be seen in "Bang a Gong (Get It On)." The girl of whom Bolan sings is "dirty sweet," in the most literal sense, a contradiction. Similarly, ambiguity and shock caused by combining polar opposites can be seen in the sexual ambiguity of performers such as Bolan, and, especially David Bowie, with Bowie's androgynous Ziggy Stardust persona. In the case of Prince, the sexual ambiguity sometimes appears, for example, in a song such as "If I Was Your Girlfriend" and "Diamonds and Pearls." There are also touches of ambiguity of traditional gender roles in Prince's use of fal-setto voice and some of his stage, film, and album cover costumes. The most important connection to the combination of apparent opposites in Prince's work, however, is his dual exploration of the graphic, purely physical sexual-ity and spirituality, and—to top it off in true glam fashion—his sometimes disconcerting combination of the two.

"Stollin'" finds Prince moving in an entire different musical and lyrical direction. Over an easygoing popish jazz background, he touts the entice-ments of escaping from the drudgery of daily life and just "stollin'." It might not be Prince's most substantial song, but it serves as an example of the influence of jazz on his work, something that the New Power Generation clearly gives him more freedom to explore than the Revolution. One of the challenges, though, that Prince presents to the listener with his stylistic range is the question of sincerity. For example, in his detailed analysis of Prince's work of the 1990s, writer Stan Hawkins suggests that Prince "is poking fun at this [the jazz] idiom"[3] in the song. I hear the song more as an exploration of a mood that is meant to contrast with the other songs of the album.

The next song, "Willing and Able," concerns the lead character's willingness to "lay his cards on the table," and let the listener know exactly how he feels. The thing is, Prince does not move to the next step and actually tell the listener what he's going to "lay on the table." Musically, it is a minimalistic combination of a slightly country-influenced boom-chuck beat and references to gospel. It conjures up images of some of Paul Simon's work of the early 1970s—sort of a combination of "Kodachrome" and "Loves Me Like a Rock." On "Willing and Able," the backing vocalists the Steeles play the same role the Dixie Hummingbirds did on Simon's "Loves Me Like a Rock": they lend the song much of its gospel credibility.

Several of the songs of *Diamonds and Pearls,* most notably "Thunder," feature simple, narrow-range melodies, particularly in the verses. It is one of the musical features that ties together the disparate rhythmic styles of the album. Melodically, "Gett Off," for the most part, consists of repetitions of short phrases that descend stepwise the narrow interval of a minor third. Prince has used brief descending phrases as the basis of the verses of his songs throughout his career. In this respect, "Gett Off" is tied to the melodic approach of a song such as "Sign o' the Times." The arrangement includes a flute lick played by Eric Leeds that suggests the 1971–1975 work of the band War, particularly on songs such as "The Cisco Kid." With such lyrics as "23 positions in a one-night stand" and all the locations around the house (the bedroom, pantry, on the pool table, etc.) where Prince's character would like to have sex with the object of his desires, this is clearly one of Prince's infamous, sexually oriented songs. However, in contrast to some of his earlier sexually explicit songs—"Darling Nikki," perhaps most notoriously—Prince refers to sex obliquely enough in "Gett Off" that the album did not merit a parental advisory, nor was the single release of "Gett Off" kept out of the pop Top 40 because of censorship or lack of airplay.[4]

The song "Walk Don't Walk" uses the metaphor of the familiar urban Walk/Don't Walk sign as a means of delving into the question of whether one should (a) give in to one's fears and prejudices, or (b) follow one's heart and natural inclinations as one goes through life. Clearly, Prince picks the latter, but tells the listener that mainstream society is all too inclined to encourage the former. With its easygoing, vaguely island-ish beat and melodic feel (the instrumentation does not include steel drums, but they would have fit in quite well) the music is disarming, and because of its melodic and harmonic simplicity, never does it draw attention to itself. The lyrical message, therefore, clearly comes through.

In complete contrast, "Jughead" is a hip-hop dance piece, mostly about being out on the dance floor. Although Prince's bandmates provide more stereotypical so-called authentic-sounding raps than the rap that Prince delivers, his is notable for its explicit sexuality: he talks about masturbating in the corner of the dance club. The last 45 seconds or so of the song feature interplay between the New Power Generation's lead rapper Tony M. and a purported manager. This interchange, in which Tony talks about how artists are exploited in the music industry, is especially telling, since Prince's relationship with Warner Bros. was heating up to a breaking point that would be reached in just a few years.

The song "Money Don't Matter 2 Night" finds Prince adopting a relaxed, understated (and somewhat undersupported) voice. The character he observes in the third person has never had success with money; more precisely, he has never had money. He concludes that "money didn't matter yesterday," and therefore, "it sure don't matter 2 night." As he looks around, the man sees that having one's soul is more important to happiness than money. Prince's music is laidback, repetitious, and includes minimal accompaniment (at least within the context of the New Power Generation, a fairly big band). The repetition and the musical texture suggest both the constancy of the character's financial state and the sense of ease he feels with his situation. The piece is so understated that it is easy to overlook; however, it is a match of mood, music, and lyrics that shows Prince's continuing development as a songwriter.

On the surface, the song "Push" revisits the dance focus of "Jughead." Yes, the introduction sends the listener out to "the dance floor"; however, the lyrics here are more obviously supposed to be meaningful than those of the earlier dance piece. The theme here is that despite the tendency of people and society in general to "pull you down," the thing that one needs to do is to "push—until U get 2 the higher ground." Prince includes some synthesized string writing that ventures away from traditional tonality. This suggests the tendency to stray from a focus on one's soul that is the lyrical theme of the song. Structurally, too, Prince and the New Power Generation play on the dichotomy between pushing up and being pulled down by allowing the piece to stray toward the realm of pure, physical dance music a little more than 3 minutes into the nearly 6-minute piece. So, compositionally it is interesting. If the listener is expecting a focused expression of the need to reach for the "higher ground," such as one finds in Stevie Wonder's classic hit "Higher Ground," however, one is likely to be disappointed with "Push." The listener needs to keep in mind that Prince's aim seems to be to focus on the complexity of the interplay between the pushing and the pulling; he shows the listener the shades of gray that exist in life.

Prince and the New Power Generation explore the complex relationships between the physical and the spiritual further in the album's next song,

"Insatiable." Taken by itself—out of the album context, that is—this song is completely focused on Prince's character's "jones," or insatiable desire for sex with the woman to whom he sings. Since the song follows "Push," and precedes the love (on several levels)-focused song "Live 4 Love," "Insatiable" becomes part of the complex continuum that represents *Diamonds and Pearls*. What makes the song especially interesting is the fact that musically it is a slow romantic ballad. The disconnection between a musical style that is most commonly associated with expressions of romantic love and lyrics that focus almost entirely on the physical is interesting and a little disconcerting to consider. Prince forces his listener to consider to what extent emotional romance is tied to the visceral pleasures of sexual teasing and intercourse. "Insatiable" would have the listener believe that the two cannot be separated.

In the hard rock song "Live 4 Love (Last Words from the Cockpit)," Prince portrays a military pilot who manages to complete his assignment of dropping two strategically important bombs despite having been hit and seeing his buddy die. The lyrics indicate that the military was a way out of the ghetto for Prince's character. Now that his plane is going down, he concludes that love is the only thing worth living for. Here, Prince uses the word *love* in a more universal way than anywhere else on *Diamonds and Pearls*. For example, in previous songs, "love" represented God ("Thunder"), emotional attachment/romance ("Diamonds and Pearls"), carnal desire ("Insatiable"), and so forth. In "Live 4 Love," the word represents a broader concept, more in keeping with platonic, or agape, love. Musically, "Live 4 Love" is complex fusion music with unusual phrase lengths and unexpected rhythmic shifts. Although Prince stays within the bounds of conventional tonality, the melody is unpredictable. The vocal lines shift abruptly from solo singing, to vocal chorus, to electronically processed spoken text. All of this suggests the young airman's life flashing before his eyes, the swirl of images that bring him his revelation as he approaches his doom.

Diamonds and Pearls was an auspicious beginning to Prince's association with the New Power Generation. There is little to the packaging of the collection to suggest that it is meant to be a unified, concept album. However, it all fits together—lyrically and musically—very well. The obvious "tribute" songs, "Daddy Pop" and "Cream," sound like their sources of inspiration, but are strong, commercially viable songs in their own rights; Prince explores various meanings of the word *love* using some intriguing deliberate musical-lyrical disconnections, and the singers, rappers, and instrumentalists of Prince's new band establish a musical identity. Some of the individual strengths of this musical identity would emerge even more strongly on the band's next album.

Interestingly, *Diamonds and Pearls* is one of the few Prince albums that has generated serious academic study by several scholars. Stan Hawkins's 1992 University of Oslo dissertation, "Stylistic Diversification in Prince of the Nineties," focuses in part on the album, while Anne Danielsen's 1993 University of Oslo dissertation, " 'My Name Is Prince': en studie i *Diamonds and Pearls*," covers the entire album. In addition, Danielsen's 1998 article in the journal *Popular Music*, "His Name Was Prince: A Study of *Diamonds and Pearls*," uses the album in a discussion of postmodernism and the contrast between using various methodologies as approaches to this work of Prince. I believe that this interest was generated by the complexity of the album, both in its lyrical explorations and in its exhibition of a wide range of musical styles. While the album may or may not be Prince's best, or most important, work of his career, or even of the 1990s, it tends to stand out in fairly sharp relief to his other albums because of the stylistic break it represents from his work with the Revolution and his post–Revolution, pre–New Power Generation recordings.

⚥ ("The Love Symbol Album")

Although the 1990 soundtrack album *Graffiti Bridge* contained an early incarnation of Prince's so-called love symbol in the album artwork—that curious combination of the male and female symbols that eventually would became Prince's name in the mid-1990s—here the symbol is used as the title of an album attributed to Prince and the New Power Generation. Because of the fact that the symbol can only be approximated using standard ASCII characters, this 1992 opus generally has come to be known as "The Love Symbol Album." The album brings to fruition the wide musical possibilities promised by the New Power Generation, although Prince himself plays a less prominent role as an instrumentalist than he would on later projects, such as *The Gold Experience*. Although Prince and his collaborators explore several subthemes on "The Love Symbol Album," perhaps one of the more enlightening ways to experience the work is to focus on the way in which they develop and contrast different characters and character types: this is an album that is principally about identity.

The album kicks off with "My Name Is Prince," a send-up of the rappers and hip-hop DJs of the era. It is as if Prince instantly gained 100 pounds and traded the skin-tight outfits and ruffled shirts of his past for a sports jersey, an oversized baseball cap (with the bill at exactly the right curve and tipped at exactly the *au courant* angle), baggy pants, and a jewelry store's worth of gold chains. What else could explain the normally very religiously reverent Prince rapping a line such as "In the beginning God made the sea, but on the seventh day he made me," or his use of such deliberately trite lines as "My name is Prince, and I am funky" and "When it comes to funk, I am the junkie?" One of the other things that makes the song so entertaining as a parody is that the bulk of the rap on "My Name Is Prince" is so square compared with the raps that the NPG's Tony M. lends throughout the album. The strength of the track can be found in the fact that even after it ceases to be funny as a parody (maybe the fourth or fifth time one hears the song), it is still danceable and catchy. In my mind I can still see tricked-out Cadillacs bouncing up and down in rhythm to the song.

There are several especially notable features of the lyrics of "My Name Is Prince." First of all, Prince's reference to God creating him "on the seventh day" places him (Prince) one step above ordinary human beings. The fact that he (an artist who routinely dedicates his work to the glory of God) is endowing himself with near god-like qualities suggests that the "Prince" of this part of the song is in part his public rock star side. The "Prince" of this part of the song is also a parody of mono-maniacal hip-hop stars of the period. Eventually, however, Prince speaks more in line with his long-established spirituality. First, he intimates to listeners that he tries to draw them into his message by giving them danceable, funky music, but that his ultimate goal is to give listeners a serious message. In the next stanza, he raps that he does not want to be a king, because although the joys of being a king might bring immediate pleasure, they cannot "save your soul." He then more specifically tells listeners that his true role is to help save their souls. Unfortunately, the serious part of the Prince's message—that one's soul is more important than possessions, fame, money, and power—tends to create confusion because the shift is a little too abrupt. Ultimately, the listener could be left wondering if the song is about Prince balancing his egotistic and spiritual tendencies, if the song is a parody of hip-hop artists that turns on a dime and does an about-face, or if Prince just uses the humor of the first half as a hook to pull the listener into the really important message of the second half. However—and it is a big "however"—even if the piece can be a bit confusing and does not wear as well as some of the other tracks on the album, "My Name Is Prince" establishes the hip-hop credentials of Prince's new band, and it provides fascinating insight into Prince and the possible motivation behind some of his controversial combinations of what some might label the sacred and the profane.

While much of "My Name Is Prince" is somewhat one dimensional musically as a hip-hop genre piece, and a little bit confusing from a rhetorical standpoint, "Sexy M.F." is a rich combination of parody, serious exploration of the late twentieth-century incarnation of an old African storytelling tradition, hip-hop, and jazz. The fact that the song's refrain consists solely of the phrase, "You sexy motherfucker" guarantees that this is one Prince track that the listener is unlikely to hear in its original form on radio or television. It is, however, a masterful song, and one that demonstrates Prince's range as a writer and arranger. As Prince spins his tale of how he is going to make love to the woman he addresses, he uses the art of creative exaggeration, combined with a feel that he, the man, is in control. He is (to use the colloquial expression) the badass dude who is descended from the exaggerated and glorified villain of west African storytelling tradition. Another way to look at the character, at least the way in which he is developed in the first half of the song, is that he is sort of a 1990s version of the 1970s character Shaft. He makes it clear that he is after the woman's mind, as opposed to her body. The unwritten implication is that if one gets the mind, one also gets the body and a whole lot more. Prince is the epitome of cool in his approach.

In the middle section, Prince invites the horn section to stand and play their chorus, and he invites Levi Speacer to play a guitar solo. He controls the scene much like a 1990s hip-hop version of James Brown and other R&B bandleaders. It should be noted that the brass and saxophone section, the organ solo, and especially Speacer's guitar solo, exhibit the strong jazz chops of the New Power Generation. Speacer's presence in the band is particularly important because his approach to the guitar contrasts so much with Prince's guitar work, which tends toward funk, hard rock, and heavy metal.

A very important subtext carries through the first part of the song and the instrumental section. While Prince's character clearly sees himself and would expect others to see him as the epitome of cool sophistication, a little dig below the surface shows that he is egocentric and manipulative, and is recognized as being so by those around him. Clearly, the Sexy M.F. is trying to control the woman he addresses in the first part of the song, and he also clearly puts himself above her. His need to control also emerges as he directs the horn section and the soloists. It is easy to miss, but the character's need for gratification also comes through in his spoken response to the horn section: "I like it; I like it." The subtext is that it is important that the horn section pleases him.

After the organ and guitar solos, the mood changes, as the backing musicians begin chanting, "Sexy motherfucker shakin' that ass" over and over. Gradually the chant turns into a simple, jazz-oriented singsong tune, which makes it sound more and more derisive. This creates the image of the supposedly ultracool dude exposed as the laughable character he ultimately is, as he is seen dancing, apparently in a decidedly uncool manner. Since the Sexy M.F. plays the role of bandleader through the instrumental sections, this derisive singing exposes the way his fellow band members really feel about him, his need for self-gratification and control; they mock him. In this way, "Sexy M.F." follows in the continuum of Prince songs, albums, and films that explore the complex relationships between members of bands, especially between the leader and his supporting musicians. Because of the strength of the jazz inclinations of the piece, and the character development, "Sexy M.F." remains one of Prince's best compositions and performances.

The album's next track also features a clear change of mood. "Love 2 the 9's" begins as a moderately fast ballad in which Prince tells a young woman not to use the word *love* unless she loves him "2 the 9's" (to the nines). His mellow-voiced character, singing in falsetto, sounds like a sensitive man, who wants commitment before he is willing to let the relationship progress any farther. Suddenly, however, the scene changes to a club, where "the band play[s] new power soul." Now the male character is looking for a woman whose "booty" turns him on. Singer Mayte portrays a young (her age is described as "jailbait") woman named Arabia who steps onto the dance floor to show off her booty. Apparently, Prince's character is favorably impressed, because he asks her if she could be the one to love him "2 the 9's." She replies in the affirmative. So, the listener hears a move from the romantic and emotional to the physical, and back again to the romantic, albeit a romantic encounter with an underage partner. The final section, however, is decidedly more sexually charged than the opening falsetto romantic section. What really captures the listener's attention is the jazz style and the instrumental and vocal arrangement, which is complex and ever-evolving. The arrangement tends to overshadow the lyrics and the evolving mood.

In "The Morning Papers," Prince plays a third-person observer of a relationship between an older man and a younger woman. Prince observes the man taking things slowly in the relationship because of the young woman's lack of experience—her naïveté. Prince uses the metaphor of "the morning papers" in several ways that effectively tie the images of the couple together. The music is a hybrid R&B/rock power ballad that features a strong, heavy metal guitar solo *obligato* from the composer. Prince sets the verses, which include images of what the couple might be doing were the man not so hesitant and questions about age and its role in a relationship, to a melody that generally trends downward at the start of each phrase, and then moves back upward at the end of the phrase. Although this may be a highly personal interpretation, to me this suggests the dichotomy between the man's hesitance and the wonderful experiences the couple could be having were age not an issue. Ultimately, it is a hopeful song, and the most haunting song on the album.

The next song, "The Max," starts out with long synthesizer tones that closely resemble those of some of the Moody Blues' songs on their 1980s and 1990s albums. It also calls to mind "My Name Is Prince," which started out with a similar introduction. In the case of "The Max," instead of this slow, mysterious opening being followed by a mellow Justin Hayward singing "Once upon a time, once when you were mine . . .," the listener is greeted by Prince as a character who goes "2 the max" whenever his back is against the wall, and who "put[s] on crooked shoes" when he is asked to "walk a straight line." In other words, his character is a fiercely independent nonconformist. It seems highly possible after one listens to the first several songs on "The Love Symbol Album," including "The Max," to get the idea that the theme that links these songs together is identity. The song "My Name Is Prince" is the most obvious example: Prince describes himself as the sort of superman of funk, yet acknowledges at the end of the song that his main purpose in life is to help bring people to God. But, "Sexy M.F." is also about identity: in this case, a man who believes that he is one thing but is exposed as something else. "Love 2 the 9's" is somewhat more oblique, but the basic theme that runs through the song is that the man defines his lover's identity by how she feels about him. In "The Morning Papers," the male character defines the relationship by the difference in age between himself and his potential life partner. And, here in "The Max," Prince sets up another character type. The song includes a narrow-range melody consisting of short phrases, in some respects a slightly more minimal version of the melodic structure of "Sign o' the Times." This song, however, is not as memorable as "Sign o' the Times," primarily because it does not exhibit the musical development nor the lyrical impact of the earlier song.

"The Max" is followed by a 21-second piece called "Segue." This is an *audio verité*-type recording that purports to be of Prince hanging up on a reporter (played by Kirstie Alley) who has called to interview him. Other than providing a little comic relief and playing on Prince's reputation for avoiding the press, the piece is not significant in the Prince canon.

Prince and the New Power Generation turn to reggae style for the song "Blue Light." This is notable because, of the more prominent styles in American pop and R&B music of the late 1960s through the time of "The Love Symbol Album," reggae was conspicuous by its absence from Prince's compositional vocabulary. In the hands of earlier major figures in the genre, such as Bob Marley, reggae songs dealt with a disparate set of subjects, notably sex, social issues, and politics. American musicians who turned to the music of Jamaica seemed to find one of these genre-defining lyrical focal points in their reggae-style songs. Stevie Wonder, for example, incorporated a wink-wink, nudge-nudge naughtiness in his incorporation of mild sexual references in his "Boogie On, Reggae Woman." Wonder turned to social issues (Pan-Africanism) in his other reggae song, "Master Blaster (Jammin')," which was a tribute to Bob Marley. The song "Blue Light" finds Prince's character asking his lover to "turn on a blue light" to get the couple in the mood for making love. What makes the lyrics especially interesting is the conflict between Prince's character and the object of his desires: she says "not in public," but he wants to make love in the backseat of the car; she wants to make love in the dark, but he wants the blue light to be on, and so on.

The funk-style song "I [Eye] Wanna Melt with U"[5] steps well beyond "Blue Light" in its sexual explicitness. Prince's character seduces and beds a woman who implicitly was a virgin, because he observes that their sexual intercourse causes her to bleed. Yes, it is graphic; and, no, it is not a pretty picture of sex. It is sex without romance or much of anything beyond bringing physical pleasure to Prince's character. This is the kind of song that seems to cause some listeners to conclude that Prince's music is misogynistic; however, the range of male-female relationships and (especially) the range of characters he develops throughout the album suggest that he is not supporting this particular character's treatment of women. Rather, it would seem that the male character of "I [Eye] Wanna Melt with U" just represents an extreme character type—Prince gives the listener the freedom to decide the character's value (or lack thereof) as a role model. Prince, in essence, simply exposes male roles in the society of his day.

The album's next track, "Sweet Baby," finds Prince portraying an entirely different character. In this case, he is a man providing encouragement to a female friend whose heart has been broken. He tells her that she is not alone, and he encourages her to avoid the "bad boys" on the rebound, because she will soon find "better days." The musical setting is gentle, easygoing, and rich with jazz-inspired seventh chords. And, while this may not be Prince's easiest-to-remember music, "Sweet Baby" works well as a mood piece. Its placement on "The Love Symbol Album" is significant because it cuts through the emotional bankruptcy of the male character of the previous song.

One of the most noticeable attributes of Prince's albums, particularly some of his longer albums of the late 1980s and through the 1990s, is the constant push and pull of characterizations and musical styles. It is not that he was writing and producing in a fundamentally different way than he had done even on his earliest albums, but here Prince expands the range and creates a more polarizing, ping-pong effect. Such is the case when he pulls the listener from "I [Eye] Wanna Melt with U" to "Sweet Baby," and then to "The Continental." Here, Prince portrays a man who tries to pick up a woman he sees on the dance floor. His character, Continental, displays some of the egotism of the Sexy M.F. of the second song on the album. He is frank in his come-on to the object of his desires, with such choice lines as "pull me down on top of u and grind really fast" and "I want all of your germs." The musical setting is dramatic in its combination of hard rock–style guitar chords, Sly Stone–style vocals, big band horn section, and hip-hop DJ scratching effects. Perhaps more than "Sexy M.F." and "Love 2 the 9's," "The Continental" illustrates the point of how important the arrangement is to the overall meaning of a pop song. The melody, harmony, and lyrics by themselves are not nearly as memorable or descriptive of Prince's character as is the musical setting, which captures the character's ego, the character's emphasis on the physical side of relationships, the ties between the motions of dancing in a club and the motions of sex, and the glitziness of the dance club setting. Despite the relative lack of importance of harmony *per se* in the piece, it is interesting to note Prince's heavy use of the tonic (I) and subtonic (bVII) chords throughout the piece. The subtonic chord, which is built on the flatted seventh scale-degree, is not a Prince exclusive by any means—one hears it used, for example, in the mid-1960s British bands of the so-called Mod school, such as the Who—however, it is important to note that it is associated with the Mixolydian mode, a scale Prince turned to in earlier compositions, such as "The Cross" and "Around the World in a Day."

The song "Damn U," a love ballad, reflects back to the lyrics of earlier Tin Pan Alley songs, perhaps most notably, Betty Comden's lyrics for "You're Awful," from the 1949 Leonard Bernstein musical *On the Town*. In the Bernstein-Comden song, the title line is sung by the sailor Chip, which causes the character Hildy initially to recoil. The line proves, however, to be only a partial thought, as Chip continues, "you're awful nice to be around." Similarly, the title line in "Damn U" is quickly followed by the clincher, "u're so fine." Of course, the Prince song does not enjoy the benefit of the film/theatrical context that the Bernstein-Comden song enjoys, so the impact is not quite as strong as it is when Frank Sinatra sings to Betty Garrett in the movie *On the Town*. "Damn U" does, though, very much follow in the tradition. Musically, "Damn U" is a slow ballad with a lilting triplet feel that feels very much like "Still Waiting," a ballad from Prince's self-titled second album. The lyrical sentiments and the musical setting would not be out of place in the adult contemporary genre. This is worth noting, because the song contrasts so thoroughly with all the previous tracks on "The Love Symbol Album."

Prince turns to more directly and obviously autobiographical material for "Arrogance," a brief 1 ½-minute song that deals in part with questions about his motivation and religious beliefs from a reporter with unveiled pre-conceived notions. The lyrics represent Prince's question-based answers to the reporter. Prince's circular responses—in real life and in the song—cause the reporter palpable frustration. It is a clear connection to the earlier piece "Segue." Prince includes samples of tracks by the C.F.M. Band ("Jazz It Up [Jazz Mix]"), Eric B & Rakim ("I Know You Got Soul"), and N.W.A. ("Nig-gaz 4 Life"). Although that might sound like an awful lot for such a short song, Prince weaves it all together seamlessly, showing the compositional approach he takes as a producer. Prince collaborated with the New Power Generation's lead rapper Tony M. in the writing of "The Flow." Like "Arro-gance," this one deals with a would-be biographer with whom Prince is less than fully impressed. And, like "Arrogance," this song shows off his work as an arranger and hip-hop producer. "The Flow" is also a piece that is relatively brief, as are all of the vignette-sized antipress pieces on the album.

The song "7," written by Prince, with samples of material written by Low-ell Fulsom and Jimmy McCrackin, seems to be a Book of Revelation and Book of Ezekiel–style reaction to the kind of press mistreatment that formed the heart of the previous two songs. That is, in the context of the album "7" functions that way. Taken out of context, the song is a mixture of gos-pel, alternative, and Quiet Storm that seems somewhat like a 1990s version of Queen's "We Are the Champions." In this case, an angel descends to Prince's maligned character and brings with it the destruction of the "seven" enemies, the ultrasophisticates who can only elevate themselves by knocking down others. Prince offers the promise of a brighter future in the heaven that will follow "a plague and a river of blood." Prince's arrangement includes the sound of the sitar, which he had used in the past in songs with a reli-gious message. The chorus melody is especially easy to remember—haunting even—with its distinctive use of Mixolydian mode (another feature of more than one Prince song with religious connotations) and its motivic shape. This shape includes a skip from scale-step five to scale-step three, and then a generally falling line from scale-step four to the flatted seventh, followed by a resolution on tonic.

While the next track, "And God Created Woman," continues some of the religious imagery of "7," its focus on the female of the human species also links it to the song it precedes, "3 Chains of Gold." Princes tells the famous story of the creation of woman from Adam's rib from the Old Testament Book of Genesis. The clincher is that he tells it from the viewpoint of Adam ("In a deep sleep I [eye] fell . . . "). Part of the focus of the song is the fact that Adam and Eve's fall from grace was precipitated by Eve giving in to the serpent. The subject of women yielding to temptation links "And God Created Woman" to other Prince songs. For example, "I Could Never Take the Place of Your Man" and "Sweet Baby" both are based on the stereotype that women are easily tempted, especially on the rebound. In fact, "I Could Never Take the Place of Your Man" is especially notable, because it finds the jilted woman tempting Prince's character—the rhetorical connection to Eve first yielding to temptation and then tempting Adam is easy to see. Prince's character, though, proves to possess a stronger will than the biblical Adam. While some listeners might interpret this as a sexist trait in his writing, listeners familiar with earlier Prince songs, notably "Delirious," will note that some of Prince's male characters are also susceptible to temptation, particularly on the rebound. Musically, "And God Created Woman" is a moderately bright-tempo R&B/adult contemporary ballad with stylistic connections to the earlier track "Sweet Baby"; because the song shows off the lighter side of Prince's composing and arranging, it provides strong contrast with the heavier funk and hip-hop tracks on the album.

The next song, "3 Chains of Gold," is one of the most complex of Prince's entire career. Musically, Prince combines elements of Quiet Storm ballad, power-pop, and jazz, with shifting rhythmic, tempo, and metrical feels. The melody abruptly shifts several times from being clearly diatonic (within a single major scale) and based on sequence (short melodic figures that begin on successively higher or lower scale-steps), to chromatic, dissonant, and unpredictable. And, what is the reason for this apparently conflicted music? It provides a fascinating setting for lyrics that represent a wash of emotions and imagery that comes from a relationship that has just ended. The first verse, for example, finds Prince telling the listener that if he does not think about the fact that his lover left him, that she accused him of blasphemy, that he finds no inspiration from heaven, and that if he ignores the fact that he is crying, "this is the best day of my life." If one reads the text in the album booklet, one might assume that Prince's statement must be meant to be ironic, or even sarcastic. The gently swaying musical setting of this verse, though, contradicts this. The musical setting—including Prince's falsetto singing style—suggests that he is truly relieved that the relationship is over. Later, however, he focuses on the regret he feels for the break-up. Still later, he refers to his former lover as "evil girl" and tells her that if one of them "has a date with the undertaker," he hopes that it is her. The three chains of gold that Prince's character wears "are the nucleus of [his] soul." Whether he refers to the Holy Trinity, three life tenets that define his soul, or something else, he does not tell us. With its wish for death for the woman that jilted him and the religious imagery of the number three, though, it is clear that "3 Chains of Gold" brings back the Ezekiel-like wrath of the earlier song "7."

With "3 Chains of Gold" Prince moves away from the simple structures of much pop and R&B music. Rhythmic changes, texture changes, moves away from conventional tonality, and the intensely conflicting emotions make this an art piece. While this makes for fascinating listening, it is not nearly as direct as, say, the 1986 Elvis Costello song "I Hope You're Happy Now." While Costello also expresses some conflicting emotions about a broken relationship, he comes down more clearly on the side of spite, in large part because the music setting he creates with his band, the Attractions, is so powerfully unrelenting. The Costello performance is also more typical of pop song treatment of complex emotions because Costello's lyrics keep coming back to spite, and he emphasizes this by spitting out the lyrics. By contrast, in "3 Chains of Gold" Prince mostly forces the listener to feel his character's anger by really listening to the actual text (as opposed to the singing style) of the lyrics.

Because "The Love Symbol Album" began with vivid character studies ("My Name Is Prince" and "Sexy M.F."), it is fitting that it concludes the same way. After another Prince-reporter "Seque," the album's final song, "The Sacrifice of Victor," begins. Musically, this piece combines elements of hip-hop, gospel, and jazz. Prince includes clear musical ties to the song "My Name Is Prince"; the pickup note rhythm of the repeated phrase sung by the chorus (which consists of the Steeles, Prince, and the members of the New Power Generation) is the same three pickup eighth notes that lead into a downbeat on the line "My name is Prince," in the album's opening song.

While one listens to "The Love Symbol Album" it is sometimes unclear what the overriding theme is supposed to be: at the start it seems to be the development of vivid male characters who run the gamut from good to bad, caring to emotionless, and so on; however, the little vignette dialogues and songs seem to be focused on Prince's real-life relationship with the press. "The Sacrifice of Victor" serves an important structural function, because it ties everything together. The basic lyrical theme is that those who sacrifice eventually will become the victors. Since religious imagery fills a few of the other songs on the album, it is easy to hear "The Sacrifice of Victor" as a combination of (1) the Ezekiel "And they shall know my vengeance" sentiments of a couple of the other songs with (2) the Jesus' parable in Matthew 20, which ends, "So the last will be first, and the first last." Although "The Sacrifice of Victor" deals specifically with the plight of blacks, it can be read to be more generally about any oppressed group or individual. In the context of the various black male characters Prince develops throughout the album,

"The Sacrifice of Victor" says that it does not matter how good or bad, caring or shallow these characters might seem to be, they all deserve to be treated with respect, because they are all human beings. However, more to the point, Prince tells the listener in no uncertain terms on this song—as well as on "7" and "3 Chains of Gold"—that Old Testament wrath and retribution awaits those who deny basic human dignity to another person or group. More obliquely, "Sexy M.F." illustrates the same premise: the Sexy M.F. initially controls his would-be lover and the members of his band, but later in the song his fellow band members deride him.

Prince's use of primarily Old Testament imagery on several songs on "The Love Symbol Album" brings up one of the great ironies inherent in his work: the fact that he is so selective when it comes to his biblical use. For example, throughout this album Prince turns to the sort of Old Testament wrath found most famously in Ezekiel (although it can found in numerous Old Testament books); however, in song after song throughout his career Prince discusses, describes, and even simulates on recordings some of the sexual activities (oral sex, in particular) that the books of Ezekiel and Leviticus label as blasphemous. And, it is this apparent conflict and selective use of biblical reference and adherence that makes Prince's canon of works particularly interesting: by placing these apparent contradictions right in the face of the listener, he forces his audience to grapple with their own beliefs.

"The Love Symbol Album" is quite a full package, with 18 compositions (including the brief segues) that represent nearly an hour-and-a-quarter of music, and none of it based on extended instrumental groove sections. In other words, on the nonsegue pieces—the "real" songs—everything is musically and lyrically important. And, Prince and the New Power Generation gel as a band. Still, the characters Prince develops are so thoroughly disparate, and the musical styles so wide-ranging, that it is a challenge for the listener to make sense of it all.

COME

Members of the music and popular press, the same people that Prince took to task on the short, vignette-style pieces on "The Love Symbol Album," found much to write about Prince in the period 1992–1995. In 1992, Prince signed a $100 million multialbum deal with Warner Bros., a deal that gave him a seat on the company's board; however, by 1993 and 1994, he announced his retirement, announced that he was changing his name to the famous "love symbol" because Warner Bros. had enslaved "Prince." Then, Warner Bros. pulled the plug on Prince's Paisley Park label. Although this was also the period in which the ballet *Billboards*—with music by Prince—appeared, thereby providing more evidence of the pop culture iconic status of his work, most of the press coverage of Prince was negative. He was also widely lampooned by late-night television hosts and other comedians for his claims of enslavement (under a huge, multimillion-dollar contract) and his new moniker. It was in this circus-like atmosphere that the 1994 album *Come* was released.

"The Love Symbol Album," which immediately preceded *Come,* was conceived as an album, and in fact, can seem like a pretty grand artistic statement. *Come* was not nearly as formidable, nor was it as successful. The reviews were not as favorable as they had been for "The Love Symbol Album," nor as they would be for the album that followed *Come* (*The Gold Experience*). Tom Moon's review in *Rolling Stone,* for example, was decidedly lukewarm.[6] While *Come* made it to No. 2 on the R&B/Hip-Hop charts, it only made it to No. 15 on the *Billboard* pop album charts. While the success on the R&B/Hip-Hop charts is notable, Prince had been, for the biggest part of his career, an artist who defied stylistic categorization. The albums on either side of *Come,* "The Love Symbol Album" and *The Gold Experience,* while not the sales smashes of several of Prince's 1980s albums, both reached the Top 10 on both the pop and R&B charts. In other words, they exhibited more universal appeal than did *Come.*

The album's title track begins with a brief wash of white noise that sounds like breaking ocean waves, something that links songs throughout *Come.* The song "Come" is one of the most graphic of Prince's career, it takes to an extreme his sometimes disconcerting combination of religiosity/spirituality and the physical gratification of explicitly described sex acts, and it is a rich example of Prince's jazz writing. It is also one of Prince's lengthiest compositions, clocking in at just more than 11 minutes.

At the beginning of the song, Prince combines two meanings of the word *come,* inviting someone (1) to arrive somewhere, and (2) to reach sexual orgasm, that mixes religiosity (washing the soul) and graphic sexuality. As the song progresses the religious references vanish. Prince makes increasingly graphic references to the oral sex he would like to enjoy with his lover. Clearly, Prince wants his lover to be pure of soul and open to sexual activity that goes beyond conventional intercourse. Without saying so in as many words, the implication is that sex (conventional or oral) between two consenting adults (married or unmarried) is not sinful. Rather, it is something to be celebrated.

The minimal liner notes for *Come* do not include lyrics, and even the lyrics of the oft-repeated chorus of the title track are not easy to remember. To a large extent, however, that does not make a great deal of difference. The impact of "Come" comes from the sexual references in the verses and, especially, from the musical setting. Prince's melodic phrases are simple, with narrow-pitch range, and with easily remembered pitch and rhythmic motives. The arrangement of the song, with its horn section and combination jazz and hip-hop rhythmic feel, includes nice tone color touches, such as the use of muted trumpets, and contrasting countermelody and chordal brass writing. Ultimately, this proves to be a thoroughly disarming style: it implies romance in the face of the graphic physicality of the lyrics. "Come" is, however, a very long piece. While the instrumental solos, and especially the Middle Eastern scale references in the soprano saxophone solo, are musically satisfying, it seems as though it would be easy for the listener to zone out after a while. The entire album is less than 50 minutes long, a good 20 minutes shorter than "The Love Symbol Album," and "Come" is not the only song that includes fairly long instrumental sections.

In the album's second song, "Space," Prince explores the metaphor of space flight with getting high on love and sexual fantasy. Although Prince does not explicitly go in this direction, it is fairly easy for the listener to assume that he intends a connection between the simulated Mission Control/spacecraft radio chatter that leads up to liftoff and the liftoff of erection, or perhaps the liftoff of orgasm. The nature of the song (love and sexual fantasy) is just too convenient for the listener not to interpret the liftoff of a rocket this way. The song is tuneful and features Prince taking on a thoroughly romantic voice. It should be noted that the song is slow to build: Prince does not enter with the lead vocals until 50 seconds of the 4 ½-minute song have gone by. The gradual addition of instrumental accompaniment figures makes this time pass pretty quickly; however, listeners who are more accustomed to Prince hitting the ground running are apt to ask the question, "Why does the song start out this way?" A range of possibilities presents itself. Perhaps, it is because, as *All Music Guide*'s Stephen Thomas Erlewine suggests, *Come* is "a record fulfilling a contract, nothing more and nothing less."[7] Perhaps, though, it is to make a longer transition between the launching pad chatter and the theme of sexual desire, or perhaps the gradual, subtle building of instrumental resources somehow corresponds to the anatomical swelling that Prince enjoys later in the song as he fantasizes about the woman he sees "on the ceiling."

How likely is it that the word *pheromone*—a natural chemical that elicits automatic behavior—would ever find its way in a pop song, let alone a title? Well, if the songwriter is Prince and he is constructing an entire album that revolves around sexual attraction, the answer is, "it's a natural." After the same wave-breaking white noise that opened the song "Come," "Pheromone" begins. It starts off with Prince speaking the line "Come, lay down beneath my shadow." As this God-like invitation proceeds, it becomes clearer and clearer that is an invitation to recline in a love embrace. When Prince begins singing, he calls upon the pheromone of the song's title to come upon him and stimulate his sexual interest. It is not a particularly strong piece, but the melodic writing of the verses—which features an emphasis on and repeated descent from the dissonant flatted fifth scale—tends to stick in one's head long after the strangeness (there is no other way to refer to a song to a naturally occurring chemical substance) of the lyrics is forgotten.

In "Loose!," a song with an interesting electronic arrangement, Prince calls upon the proverbial wallflower to get up on the floor and dance. The call to the dance—a dance, by the way, of sexual frenzy—and the funky musical setting suggests Prince's work on *The Black Album*. Here, however, the listener tends to get the feeling that Prince is coasting artistically. On the earlier *Black Album*, the hard-core R&B sound was so new for Prince that it sounded more innovative and vital.

The relatively brief song "Papa" is a fascinating and touching exploration of domestic violence and suicide. The song features sharp contrast between quiet minimalism and hard rock. In the first section, Prince recites the tale of the fictional "Papa" who abuses him as a four-year-old child, screams at the heavens about the complete lack of emotional attachment he feels for his woman, and proceeds to commit suicide with a gun. In the louder, hard-rock section, Prince sings of hope, of the "rainbow at the end of every rain." The high degree of stylistic contrast suggests the influence of the grunge and alternative styles, which were very much in the air at the time. The rapid-fire sixteenth notes in the drums and the warning about the gun-related violence would seem to come from the influence of the Jimi Hendrix composition "Machine Gun." In fact, some of the near-psychedelic imagery in the last part of the lyrics sounds pretty close to the aesthetic of Hendrix as a lyricist in some of his 1968 work. While "Papa" might not have had the exposure of some of Prince's other overtly socially conscious works—such as "Sign o' the Times"—it is a haunting piece and very effective. The theme of social consciousness continues in "Race," a rejection of racism. Prince's music combines the rap and beat of hip-hop with a chorus, lead instrumental line, and horn section arrangement that recalls the work of funk pioneers such as Sly Stone and George Clinton in the late 1960s and early 1970s. Because of the musical resemblance to music of a couple of decades earlier, and because the rap is less intense than that associated with early 1990s gangsta rap, the piece does not immediately grab hold of the listener the way some of Prince's overtly innovative-sounding pieces do; however, it is effective in its soft-sell approach. As is customary with Prince's work, the arrangement and production are absolutely first rate.

The song "Dark" finds Prince taking on a more gospel-oriented approach; his singing and the arrangement even conjuring up the sound of Al Green at times. The song connects with several others from Prince's huge canon of works, because here he plays the role of the jilted lover. Clearly, he just plain feels hurt (in his words, he's been "left in the dark"). There is, however, little of the sense of Old Testament retribution that permeated the jilted-lover songs on "The Love Symbol Album." He does sing that he never knew "a bitch so mean," but the lyrical focus is not on hate or any harm he hopes will come to her (as had been the case on "The Love Symbol Album" tracks).

A very different song of loss, "Solo," features a good bit of *a cappella* singing from Prince. The melody includes wide difficult-to-sing intervals, touches of jazz, little hints of unaccompanied black songs of sorrow in the nineteenth-century spiritual tradition, and blues. The sense of loss here goes well beyond the self-pity of "Dark." In "Solo," Prince sounds like the loss is profound: perhaps his lover has not jilted him; perhaps she has died. While

Prince sometimes takes a somewhat emotionally detached approach in his songs, "Solo" is pure, heartfelt loss.

In the context of Prince's name change, the battles that he was already having with Warner Bros., and his decision (thankfully reversed) to retire as a recording artist, the song "Letitgo" makes for fascinating study. On the surface—that is, in the context of *Come*, with its focus (mostly) on love and sex—"Letitgo" appears to be about maturing. Prince's character has had numerous sexual relationships—sown his wild oats, as it were—but now he realizes that he has to grow up and make a commitment to a different lifestyle. However, the lyrics include enough signifiers that paint it as an autobiographical testimony about the music industry (he refers to musicians and to being involved in this lifestyle for 14 years—the length of time Prince had been a recording artist) that it is easy to see hints of the business problems, feelings of enslavement, and so forth. The long and the short of it is that Prince's character is burnt-out and in need of a lifestyle change. Because some of Prince's work on *Come* and on the past couple of albums with the New Power Generation had incorporated elements of hip-hop, including rap, Prince did not consistently emphasize melody to the extent that he had earlier in his career as a composer. "Letitgo" stands out because of its old-school soul melodic approach. The verses feature a distinctive long-range descending melody that contrasts with the more wave-like melodic shape of the chorus.

The final track on *Come*, "Orgasm," is just that: over Prince's experimental avant-garde electric guitar playing (think of Jimi Hendrix's live version of "The Star-Spangled Banner" from the 1969 Woodstock Music and Art Fair) an unidentified woman works closer and closer to sexual ecstasy. While it may fit the theme of *Come*, it is not really anything new, it's even on album tracks by other artists. Witness, for example, Ray Manzarek's 1974 song "Perfumed Garden" (from the former Doors keyboardist's album *The Whole Thing Started with Rock and Roll Now It's Out of Control*) or Yoko Ono's 1980 song "Kiss Kiss Kiss" (from the John Lennon–Yoko Ono album *Double Fantasy*).

Generally, critics were not kind to *Come*. The listener who is accustomed to Prince breaking musical and lyrical boundaries and writing strongly melodic material that sticks in the head could be left with the sense that this album is (as *All Music Guide*'s Stephen Thomas Erlewine suggests) a case of Prince going through the motions in order to fulfill a contract.[8] But, it would be wrong to dismiss the entire album as such. *Come* contains several effective songs, and—as is customary throughout the entire Prince catalog—the performances and production are strong. In particular, "Papa," "Letitgo," and "Dark" each, in their individual ways, are strong pieces.

THE GOLD EXPERIENCE

Prince, working with the New Power Generation and several other accompanying musicians, wrote and recorded the music of *The Gold Experience* for intended release in 1994. Warner Bros. refused to release the album in such close proximity to the relatively commercially unsuccessful *Come*. Finally, in 1995, after Prince had "officially" declared himself to be a slave to the record company, the album saw the light of day. Despite the fact that 1994 was the low point in Prince's relationship with Warner Bros., *The Gold Experience* is an extremely strong album. Prince revisits the structure of "The Love Symbol Album" by means of thematic connections between the songs and by means of brief vignettes that form an overarching storyline. Music critic Jim Walsh provided extensive liner notes for the album. Walsh explains Prince's reasons behind dropping his given name (Prince) and using the love symbol as his new moniker. According to Walsh, Prince's name change finds the artist effectively breaking with the triumphs of his past and setting his sights on new musical promise for the future.[9] While one needs to be leery of liner notes that tout the product—after all, the writer was chosen by the artist and/or the record company, and the artist, producer, and/or record company executives approved the blurb—Walsh's assessment of the future promise represented by Prince's name change and the music of *The Gold Experience* is not just hyperbole. The writing, arranging, and musicianship of *The Gold Experience* are strong—stronger than any previous Prince album since perhaps *Sign o' the Times*—and the thematic focus is easier to follow than that of "The Love Symbol Album."

Although the CD booklet and CD itself give the title as "P Control," what Prince really sings in the album's opening song is "pussy control." And, yes, as one might expect, he refers not to a cat, but to the sexually graphic, slang use of the term *pussy*. The story is somewhat obtuse. Prince uses *pussy control* to refer to what the female character needs to exercise so that she avoids getting into fights (sort of the female equivalent of a man, in the vernacular, avoiding having "too many balls"). In addition, though, *pussy control* is something that she exerts over various men (she controls them with her sexuality), and the term also refers to the control she has over her own sexuality (she controls her own *pussy*). The language is vulgar and decidedly "street," and it is easy to miss the complex implications of Prince's lyrics. In fact, it is very easy to hear the song as a sexist putdown of the song's female character. Yes, there is an element of that in the lyrics, but the lyrics also speak of her (in not so many words) empowerment. The listener may sense that Prince's character does not think much of the sexual empowerment she possesses, but he acknowledges that it exists. He raps more sympathetically, though, about the way in which the woman—when she was a young girl—made up her mind to stand up to the mean girls at her school. There is a taste of the Old Testament retribution that had been the focus of several songs on "The Love Symbol Album," although here it is in muted form. Perhaps, though, the most important thing about hearing and interpreting the lyrics is not to try to determine to what extent they may be sexist, or reflective of empowerment. Perhaps the most important thing that Prince provides the listener is a rap that is just vague enough in intent that it stimulates thought and discussion.

One of the other interesting touches on the recording finds Prince delivering a joke about his new "name" when he introduces himself as "your captain with no name." A song is much more than lyrics, however. One thing that probably strikes the listener is that the musical setting of "P Control," as well as the other songs of *The Gold Experience,* is stronger, more upfront, and more of an equal hybrid combination of R&B and hard rock than any recent Prince music.

The principal songs of *The Gold Experience* are separated by brief interludes, each of which is entitled "NPG Operator" on the album track list. To an even greater extent than the brief segues of "The Love Symbol Album," these interludes lend a sense of structural cohesiveness to the album. The fact that they are so pervasive makes them work better in my opinion, because the segues of "The Love Symbol Album" were so sporadic that they tend to confuse the album's structure. Not all critics agree: *All Music Guide*'s Stephen Thomas Erlewine writes that they "end up interrupting the flow of the music."[10] To me, the "Operator" segments function very much like the *faux* radio commercial interludes on the Who's album *The Who Sell Out:* they link the songs in such a way that they all seem to be part of a bigger conceptual piece, the album. The "NPG Operator" track that follows "P Control" serves as an introduction to "Endorphinmachine." The operator mentions that the New Power Generation offers a large number of pleasurable experiences to the listener, and "here is an example." At that point, "Endorphinmachine" begins.

The title, "Endorphinmachine," probably first suggests that the song is an outtake from *Come,* since it is so closely related to the title "Pheromone." To make that assumption, however, would be to do a great injustice to "Endorphinmachine." First of all, the concept of a pleasure machine that releases endorphins conjures up images of some sort of future world in which all human needs are met by machines. Such a world could very well be the stuff of a dark sci-fi film, or it could be the stuff of a Woody Allen film. In fact, absent the song's context, the pure concept of an endorphin-releasing machine might stir up memories of the hilarious orgasmatron from Allen's *Sleeper* (1973). It turns out that this is not exactly what Prince has in store for the listener to "Endorphinmachine." The endorphinmachine is, in fact, Prince's character's car; he invites a woman to whom he is sexually attracted for a ride in the backseat of it.

Musically, "Endorphinmachine" combines elements of R&B with a strong dose of the organ and distorted guitar heavy sound reminiscent of the British band Deep Purple. In fact, the guitar riff in "Endorphinmachine," as well as the song's entire hard rock feel, suggests that Prince was not entirely unfamiliar with the song "Woman from Tokyo." That Deep Purple's album release a year previous to the song "Woman from Tokyo" was *Machine Head* (boldface print mine) might not be coincidental with regard to the Prince song. Despite the many positive attributes of the New Power Generation lineups of *Diamonds and Pearls,* "The Love Symbol Album," and *Come,* the revamped lineup of *The Gold Experience* provides Prince with more possibilities on the rock side of his musical repertoire: "Endorphinmachine" is not the only song on the album to showcase this more equal balance of R&B and hard rock.

The next song on *The Gold Experience* is entitled "Shhh." Without making too much of the connections between this album and the work of Deep Purple, it is interesting to note the resemblance of the title of this song to that of "Hush," a 1968 hit for the British band. Indeed, the song's opening instrumental section—which recurs later on as an interlude—suggests the energy of "Hush," as well as the organ-heavy tone color of some Deep Purple recordings. Michael Bland's drum figures in the opening of "Shhh," with their moves into and out of a triplet feel, come right out of the early 1970s heavy metal stylebook of bands such as Deep Purple and Black Sabbath. This heavy metal opening, however, contrasts with the bulk of the song, in which the tempo is halved and the style is closer to a bluesy, gospel-esque ballad. It is not, however, a conventional love ballad. Prince's lyrics are a sexually charged come-on to a woman he would rather "do" "after school, like some homework." Or, as he says at the end of the song, "Sex is not all I think about; it's just all that I think about u." "Shhh" is a particularly effective musical setting, as the slow, bluesy material captures the emotional need for intimacy and the powerful hard rock instrumental material captures the physical side of the sex act.

Prince and Nona Gaye collaborated in writing "We March." The song is a cry against racism and against all of the economic inequalities caused by racism in the United States. Prince and Gaye's lyrics include a secondary theme of the evils of sexism, as they take some male members of the black community to task for their disrespect for women. One of the masterful aspects of the song is how it links the spirit of black empowerment of the late 1960s and early 1970s with the movement for black empowerment of the hip-hop age. Perhaps the most obvious connection is the fact that here Prince is collaborating with Nona Gaye, the daughter of soul legend Marvin Gaye. Nona Gaye had a brief—albeit not particularly commercially successful—career as an urban contemporary singer just prior to her work with Prince on this song. Her father, of course, dealt with urban poverty, racism, environmental degradation, and the Vietnam War on his masterful album *What's Going On,* back in 1971. "We March" uses the double-time rhythmic feel of early 1990s hip-hop; however, the catchy hook-laden melodic writing connects the song to early 1970s R&B songs of social consciousness such as Stevie Wonder's "Living for the City," and the music of Sly Stone.

The obvious main lyrical theme of "We March"—racism, and taking an activist stance against racism—seemingly makes the song stand apart from the rest of *The Gold Experience.* In some circumstances, that might be heard as a structural weakness of the album. The interesting thing here, though, is that the song's secondary theme of sexism seems to link the song to some of the others on the album ("P Control" and "Billy Jack Bitch," most notably). Plus, the feeling of connection that the song has with music of the early 1970s integrates "We March" musically into the entire package.

The "NPG Operator" segment that follows "We March" informs the listener that he or she has accessed "the beautiful experience" portion of the programming, which will focus on "courtship, sex, commitment, fetishes, loneliness, vindication, love, and hate." At first consideration, some of these topics might seem contradictory to one's definition of "the beautiful experience." The listener eventually figures out, however, that "the beautiful experience" is the sex/love part, and that the loneliness, vindication, and hate come about because of the loss of love.

"The beautiful experience" suite of songs begins with "The Most Beautiful Girl in the World." The song is a rare Prince love ballad free of explicit sexual overtones. It also fits firmly in the tried-and-true soul ballad tradition. In other words, even though it sounds contemporary and resonated with mid-1990s audiences (it reached the *Billboard* pop Top 10), there is nothing in the musical or lyrical style that would have sounded greatly out of place in the 1960s. Listeners who prefer the edgier side of Prince's music and lyrics might consider the song a bit on the sappy side, but its presence on *The Gold Experience* gives the album a wider emotional and musical range. Because the connecting theme of the album is the portrayal of a wide range of life possibilities—sort of a satellite radio (as opposed to the more limited AM or FM radio) variety of entertainment and pleasure experiences—the inclusion of this ballad is important. The listener who wants to explore the song beyond its simple proclamation of love might be interested in considering the melodic construction of the chorus. The overarching principal melodic phrase is as follows: F#, G#, A#, F#, G#, A#, B, A#, G#, F#, G#, A#. If we consider the pitches F#, G#, A# as one self-contained melodic motive,[11] then we can see this chorus phrase as an organic whole. The phrase begins with the three notes (F#, G#, A#), moves to an extension of the motive (F#, G#, A#, B, A#, G#), and then reiterates the motive (F#, G#, A#). In other words, it is entirely organic from a structural standpoint (ABA), just like Prince's declaration of love is entirely organic.

Although it might not be one of Prince's best-known songs, "Dolphin" is an interesting, multilayered song that shows the extent to which Prince had grown as a sophisticated composer of both music and lyrics by the time of *The Gold Experience*. In this song Prince portrays a man who has been rejected in love, or possibly in friendship. He asks the person who rejected him if that person would welcome him into his or her life if he came back as a dolphin. To the extent that one can view a dolphin as (1) perhaps the one mammal that unconditionally accepts human beings, (2) a mammal that is no threat to people, and (3) an animal that is perhaps universally loved, then Prince's question can be taken as a suggestion of just how icy cold the person to whom he sings really is. If that person could not accept him as a dolphin, swimming free in the ocean, then there is no hope for the relationship.

The musical setting of "Dolphin" is pop rock. The chorus melody is strong in the hook area—it is one of those tunes that just invites singing along. There is more to the musical setting, however, than the chorus tune. For the attentive listener, one of the more interesting points of "Dolphin" might be Prince's instrumental use of a fully diminished-seventh chord in the song's bridge section. Although this type of harmony is not all that unusual in the classical repertoire, it is more rarely used in late twentieth-century pop music. In fact, the one songwriter of the last several decades who made fairly prominent use of the chord in a number of songs was George Harrison. The arpeggiation of the chord, which occurs at the 2:39 mark of the song, comes immediately after Prince asks his would-be friend to shine a light to guide him. Perhaps I make too much of the George Harrison connection, but I find it significant that this Harrison-esque touch follows the reference to being guided by light. The devout Harrison was widely known for his references to spirituality in his songs. In any case, the chord contrasts with the rest of Prince's harmonic vocabulary in the song to the extent that it cannot help but stand out.

Prince's performance on electric guitar on "Dolphin" also deserves the listener's attention, especially as an example of Prince's increasing musical sophistication. Although the lead guitar is prominent throughout the song, it is particularly in the final half of the song that it becomes a featured solo voice. Since the song's tempo is fairly brisk, it might have been tempting for Prince to use the solo section to show off his technical brilliance as a guitarist. Earlier in his career, especially, this might well have been the case. For example, although the fast runs in his solo on "I Could Never Take the Place of Your Man" are brilliant, the solo does not exactly match the mood of the lyrics. On "Dolphin," however, sheer technique is subservient to mood and context to a greater degree. It is musicality over technique.

The song "Dolphin" is followed by another "NPG Operator" track. Here, the operator tells the listener that he or she has accessed "the now experience." This experience is said to be "great for dancing and for building self-esteem." The dance track that follows, "Now," falls squarely into the hip-hop genre. For the second time on *The Gold Experience*, Prince incorporate a reference to his name change. He raps that the "freaks on the [dance] floor don't worry about [his] name." In other words, Prince's music speaks for itself; his choice of moniker makes no difference, if his music is right. Although much of Prince's rap ostensibly has to do with encouraging the "freaks on the floor" to express their total freedom through their dancing, it is fairly easy to read the piece as a call for freedom on a much broader level. Prince does not hit the listener over the head with the concept, but he drops enough clues about the broader meaning of the composition that they would be hard to miss. For one thing, he begins with the reference to his new name. Clearly, he has exercised the freedom to change his name to a symbol. As would become apparent in the liner art to his next album, and as he made abundantly clear through his public statements, he felt that Warner Bros. had enslaved the "Prince" name: breaking the bonds of corporate slavery was his motivation in rejecting the name "Prince" for his professional work. But, that is not the only clue; some are much more to the point, such as Prince's references to how much better it is to "ride up front" than in the back. He doesn't say "in the back of the bus," but it is easy to hear the text in the context of the struggle for racial equality. "Now," however, is a rich piece of rap-based poetry, with multiple possible readings. Perhaps, Prince appreciates "the ride up front" better now that he, as a music industry superstar, has ridden in the back of the limousine. In other words, perhaps Prince is telling the listener that it is better to be a regular person than to be a star. Admittedly, there is not a whole lot to support such a reading of his text in the piece itself. In retrospect, however, if one knows that the liner notes for Prince's next album, *Chaos and Disorder,* would proclaim that album as his last recorded work and would reveal that he had retired from the music industry (short-lived as that retirement would turn out to be), it is an interpretation that can make sense.

The next "NPG Operator" segment finds the electronic operator machinery apparently malfunctioning and getting stuck. The female voice introduces the listener to "the beautiful experience" once again; however, she then says that this experience includes "sex, commitment, commitment, commitment . . ." The listener's first introduction to "the beautiful experience" also included a number of other possibilities, including fetishes. Despite the fact that operator gets stuck on "commitment," Prince in fact turns to fetish for the next song, "319." In this piece, he plays the role of a photographer who is excited by the sexually explicit photographs or movies that he is about to take of his female model, in room 319. The sex in this song is all about voyeurism, pornography, and physicality. While the scene is seedy, it does not approach the implied rape of Prince's earlier song "Lady Cab Driver." Musically, "319" combines aspects of techno, jungle, hard rock, and funk.

Over the years, there have been a number of things about Prince's career, public persona, music, and lyrics that have created controversy. Certainly, the overtly sexual nature of his songs has generated the greatest amount of this controversy. Additionally, the tendency of his songs to look at sex from a variety of male perspectives has led to accusations that he encourages the use of women as sex objects. Certainly, some of his characters do objectify women in such a way. Such is the case with the character Prince portrays in "319." However, it is not necessary to read Prince as a writer who encourages misogyny or objectification because of his lyrics. Because of the fact that his male characters exhibit such a high degree of contrast in their relationships with women, it seems more logical to read songs such as "319" (or "Lady Cab Driver," or others) as representing part of the contemporary spectrum of male attitudes in Western society. Prince typically does not take an overt stance on whether he finds the actions and attitudes of some of his characters desirable or undesirable, and perhaps that is part of the reason that he has been characterized as a misogynist. Ultimately, it seems that what Prince does by looking at sex from the viewpoint of the photographer/voyeur/pornographer is to expose something that is real—something that is part of society, whether one likes it or not.

In the song "Shy," Prince focuses on violent urban relationships. In reality, the outwardly "shy" man and woman are anything but shy: he roams the streets of Los Angeles looking for material "for a poem," and she kills in retaliation. The man gets material from the woman's story. Although framed as a song about the artistic muse, the deeper messages here are that (1) looks can be deceiving, and (2) survival is the only rule of the urban jungle.

The disarming, pop-oriented melody, rhythmic feel, and orchestration of "Shy" stand in stark contrast to the harsh reality of the urban situation Prince sets up. In this respect, the song calls to mind the early 1970s pop hit "Something in the Air," by the British band Thunderclap Newman. That song bathed what could be interpreted as a call to revolution in lushly orchestrated, moderate-tempo, pop-rock music. Prince's "Shy" presents the listener with a similar deliberate lyrical/musical disconnection. It is still easy to hear the harsh reality of contemporary urban life in the text itself, but the musical setting suggests that we hear it filtered through the eyes of the poet (the male character in Prince's story). The setting also supports the fact that there is a secondary filtering—this is a story that Prince tells as an outside observer.

Prince's "Billy Jack Bitch" is based in part on samples of Fishbone's "Lyin' Ass Bitch," which Prince incorporates into his song. Prince's title calls to mind the 1971 film *Billy Jack*, in which Tom Laughlin portrayed the Native American title character, a man who went on a vengeful killing streak to make up for wrongs that white townspeople had committed against his people. Prince's character asks the woman who mistreats him and calls him names how she would feel if he called her names, such as "Billy Jack Bitch." He tries to turn the tables on the person he addresses to force her to walk in his shoes, as it were. The song is tuneful and includes a catchy instrumental hook. The whole that Prince creates by this combination of lyrics and almost playful music is that his character is hurt by the woman's mean-spirited words, but that he would not really refer to her as a "Billy Jack Bitch," except as a means of showing her what it feels like to be on the receiving end of verbal abuse. Yes, the "bitch" reference is sexist and petty, but it is there solely to make a point. The extended fadeout features some strong horn section writing and a reappearance of the NPG Operator. This time she announces that the listener has selected the hate experience and encourages the listener to select another experience instead. This provides a thematic segue into "I [Eye] Hate U."

Prince explores the complex intersection of love and hate that occurs when his character finds out that his lover has given her "body 2 another in the name of fun." The romantic R&B ballad style of the musical setting, as well as Prince's falsetto singing, suggests that the hate Prince's character expresses really is still mixed with love. His character is truly conflicted because of the experience of having discovered betrayal.

The last "NPG Operator" track recaps and overlaps the previous iterations. Prince uses electronically processed pitch changes on the operator's voice so that it becomes unclear whether what at first had appeared to be a female voice really was one after all. The feeling of ambiguity that this introduces into the operator's identity is a nice touch, because it supports the ambiguity and strange intersections of emotional states that the songs themselves explore. The final experience that the operator introduces is the "gold experience." The fact that snippets from the previous experiences were woven together just prior to this introduction suggests that this final experience is somehow going to wrap everything together—that the "gold experience" will be a summation.

The promised "gold experience" arrives in the form of the song "Gold." Here, Prince returns to the spirituality that was found in some of the other songs on the album. The difference is that spirituality is the focus on this, the album's concluding song. The gist of Prince's lyrics is that money is good for nothing if it is not used for good, and that living a good life, dying, and coming to rebirth in heaven should be each person's goal. The music falls squarely into the pop rock genre; it is bright, both in its delightful tunes, but also in Prince's use of higher-pitch registers in the piano and synthesizers, as well as in the bright tone colors of the instruments. This gives the musical setting a thoroughly optimistic sound. Prince also provides a scorching electric guitar solo in the last 2 minutes of the nearly 7 ½-minute song that also comes across with a feeling of triumph. As the song fades out, the NPG Operator announces that the listener is "now an official member of the New Power Generation." The listener is welcomed "to the dawn." Although a written description of the song is apt to make it sound a little corny, listening to the song with the aim of hearing how Prince develops his message through the musical setting (including melody, harmony, arrangement, performance, and recording production) of the lyrics reveals it to be a well-unified piece of music. Without saying so in so many words, he tells the listener that all the foibles of human relationships—especially the sexual ones, since those receive most of the focus on the other songs—ultimately will not mean anything in the hereafter.

The Gold Experience is an amazing album, especially considering the turmoil that was taking place in Prince's recording career at the time of its recording and its release. Musically, Prince retreats from the focus on jazz, R&B, and hip-hop that marked the New Power Generation's first two albums. longtime Prince fans might actually be left with the feeling that *The Gold Experience* finds Prince rediscovering the heavy-duty eclecticism of the early part of his career as a composer and performer.

CHAOS AND DISORDER

If one believes the liner notes, *Chaos and Disorder* was supposed to be the last recording of new original material by the artist formerly known as Prince for Warner Bros. Records. He had changed his name to a symbol, and had been laughed at; he had declared himself a slave, and had been jeered in the press; he had seen one of his better albums withheld by his record company; and now, he was fed up. Because of the amount of press coverage of the mid-1990s travails of Prince, and the liner notes themselves, it is difficult not to come into listening to *Chaos and Disorder* as a final artistic testament. Of course, Prince broke away from Warner Bros., and continues to write, perform, and record right up to the present. No one who listened to *Chaos and Disorder* when it was released in 1996 could have known that, though. Once one actually sits down and listens to the album, it quickly becomes clear that it is not a grand artistic statement that is meant to bring closure to a major artist's career: it sounds more like Prince, the New Power Generation, and some other musicians recording live in the Paisley Park studio for their own enjoyment. It should be noted that the entire package looks to be a calculated attempt to look homegrown and like a bootleg recording. Since this approach has been used so many times before, it looks an awful lot like a highly stylized extension of the punk sensitivities of the Sex Pistols' 1977 album *Never Mind the Bullocks*—in other words, it looks coldly calculated, almost as though the Brothers Warner were cashing in on Prince's discontent. Be that as it may, *Chaos and Disorder* finds Prince fulfilling a contractual obligation in a totally different way than on *Come*. Here, he rocks out. The packaging may look like a conscious attempt to look bootleg-punk, but the music sounds like honest rock jamming—musicians playing for musicians.

The album's title track, "Chaos and Disorder," establishes a clear connection with the rock/funk hybrid songs of Sly and the Family Stone. This includes everything from simple, concise melodic phrases of the type that Sly Stone used in "Dance to the Music," to the distorted guitar and the distinctive late 1960s organ tone color. Prince plays the role of social observer (again, much like Sly Stone did right around 1970). He contrasts, among other things, the old meaning of *gay* (happy) with the unhappiness of gays in the mid-1990s (AIDS, discrimination, etc.). He mentions the devastation caused by drugs and violence. The character Prince portrays—the "reporter"—clearly sees the urban situation of the mid-1990s as the flip side of the proverbial good old days. The reporter observes an end-of-the-millennium nightmare that has come to life. Although Prince did not explore the end-of-the-millennium *angst* to the extent that some other artists did—David Bowie, for example, devoted several 1990s albums to the theme—it is easy to hear the song

"Chaos and Disorder" as a logical follow-up to "1999." This song says in not so many words that the purple skies foretold in Prince's "1999" might well be upon us as that fateful date approaches.

The song "I Like It There" combines the musical sensibilities of early-1980s new wave (the steady eighth-note rhythm guitar figures in the verses) and 1990s grunge (the extreme dynamic and texture contrasts). The lyrics speak of Prince's sexual desire: "On your heavenly body, I like it there"; "My emotions ejaculate on the floor," and so on. It may not be profound, but it is a strong driving rock song that works on a visceral musical level.

The next song, "Dinner with Delores," features hazy, impressionistic lyrics of the kind for which Prince was more known on *Around the World in a Day*. The "Delores" of the song's title is an insatiable woman who seems to be too much for Prince's character to handle. He sees that her desires stem in part from a lack of self-respect and urges her to metaphorically and literally get off her knees. In a sense, Delores is a reincarnation of Darling Nikki. The difference is that while Prince betrayed an almost voyeuristic fascination with the earlier character, he is torn between fascination and near-disgust with Delores. With the exception of Prince's guitar solo, which practically screams, "this is the 1990s," the tone colors, subtly shifting chords, and impressionistic lyrics would not have been out of character in the psychedelic 1960s. In fact, the tone color and chording style in the rhythm guitar part are not all that far removed from the 1967 Youngbloods recording of the song "Get Together."[12] The real genius of the song is found in Prince's unlikely combination of this pseudo–late 1960s folk-rock with a frank 1990s approach to sexuality. The sense of disjuncture caused by this combination is haunting.

The next song, "The Same December," features more obvious record production than some of the material on *Chaos and Disorder*, including more variety of instrumentation and more studio effects. The metrical changes and sophisticated use of metric modulation in order to change tempo show that this is no jam, but a fully composed, arranged, and produced composition. Prince uses the metaphor of a ball that is half black and half white (and one side doesn't understand the other) to illustrate the reluctance that some people have to understanding or empathizing with others. He sings that when people understand that "we all come from the same December," and that "in the end, that's where we'll go," we will finally enjoy peace and understanding. In other words, we have to recognize, accept, and celebrate our shared humanity in order to improve the world. Or, in a more religious context, we have to believe that we are all God's children in order to improve the world. The abrupt rhythmic and metrical shifts suggest the diversity of people, some who would buy into Prince's vision and some who would not. The great diversity of musical styles allows Prince to send his message to a wide rock audience, but it is also dizzying. Ultimately, the listener tends to be drawn to the musical virtuosity at the expense of the message.

"Right the Wrong" is another track that exhibits more orchestrational and production attention than one might expect from material originally "intended 4 private use only." The tempo changes and horn arrangement go well beyond the level, say, of a demo record. The musical style of the song fits squarely in the black gospel tradition. Although the songs only share superficial stylistic cues, think of a song such as "Movin' on Up," the theme from the 1975–1985 sitcom *The Jeffersons*. Prince begins his text by telling the story of a Native American woman who buries her grandfather in the hills that were stolen from her people. He then moves into the tale of an urban youth who was given a harsh sentence for a petty crime. The last victim of society's wrongs is an artist who "died when he wanted 2"—the implication being that he took his own life. Because Prince provides just a snippet of the story behind each of the three victims, and because they range from fairly specific personalities (the Native American woman) to almost faceless characters, the song is not as focused as Prince's best works of social commentary.

For "Zannalee" Prince turns to traditional blues-rock structure. The style is hard driving blues rock that sounds like the old Leiber and Stoller composition "Riot in Cell Block #9" meeting George Thorogood's "I Drink Alone" and "Bad to the Bone" in a dark alley. This is one of the most obvious Prince-having-fun-in-the-studio songs on *Chaos and Disorder*. He sings of a girl named Zannalee and her sister, Fendi, with whom he enjoys a *ménage à trois* of oral sex. Prince lets the listener in on the exact nature of the threesome's escapades by using some wink-wink-nudge-nudge, dirty joke references that are probably best left untouched in print. Anyway, because of reports of a disturbance, the police are called out. The responding officer sees the threesome through the window and reports back to his superior that they had best just let the matter drop. The musical style supports the frat boy, dirty joke humor of the lyrics, and although it is a trifle in the Prince catalog, to the extent that one enjoys the style and a "good" dirty joke, it is a fun piece.

The next song, "I Rock, Therefore I Am," is more substantial. It also represents a return to the R&B focus of Prince's first two albums with the New Power Generation. Prince's message is that money, power—in short, none of the trappings or "bullshit" (to quote the lyrics) of the world—do not matter to him. One of the more interesting features of the song is that the "I rock, therefore I am" message can easily be heard even more specifically as a dismissal of Prince's critics in the media. To wit, Prince tells the listener that he doesn't need to hear anyone tell him that he is right or wrong because he is "in the band." Admittedly, it is easier to hear the lyrics in this light because of Prince's more direct criticism of the media on some of the songs and in the between-song transitions on "The Love Symbol Album."

Prince also includes references specific to the recording industry, which can be understood on several levels. He writes, for example, of selling "CDs for a dollar," in such a way that he could be referring either (1) to artists and record companies that are only concerned with profits (as opposed to art), or (2) to the underground, bootleg record industry. Certainly, Prince had reason to complain about both in his own career. For example, he had waged highly publicized battles with Warner Bros. about the timing and number of his releases, and some of his unreleased work—notably material from the long-delayed *Black Album*—was so well distributed in bootleg form that when the official releases finally came, sales lagged because a number of fans already owned the recordings illegally. The writing, performance, and production all represent meticulous R&B funk. As such, it sounds more like a New Power Generation track than some of the more rock-oriented work on *Chaos and Disorder.*

To the extent that *Chaos and Disorder* is supposed to represent the, well, the chaos and disorder of earthly life, the album's next song, "Into the Light," might seem a little misplaced. Here, Prince concludes that after all the travails of life, "every soul must return into the light." Whether one understands that as meaning reaching nirvana, going to heaven, and so on, it is clearly about reaching a better life after death. As I will discuss later, this song shares musical and lyrical ties with "I Will," which follows it. Because of the meaning behind the two songs, it would have been interesting to conclude the album with them. But, then, that might have left the listener with too much hopefulness. As it stands, *Chaos and Disorder* is more about the ongoing difficulties, bickering, and messiness of life than about their resolution.

After a slow, piano-based introduction that exhibits some ties with the late twentieth-century classic style known as minimalism, "Into the Light" turns into more of a power ballad, with heavy metal guitar underpinnings. The rhythmic transitions of the piece make it musically interesting, but the relationship of Prince's melodic writing and the lyrics is the real highlight of the song. The verses, which deal with the earthly life, feature short phrases—really, more like rhythmic motives with a handful of syllables. These include mostly repeated pitches. Once Prince reaches the chorus, however, with its promise of journeying "into the light," the phrases become less truncated feeling and the melodic motion becomes more expansive. Prince thereby contrasts the troubles and grayness of earthly life with the glories of the afterlife.

The instrumental introduction to the song "I Will" shares a descending pitch motive with the introduction to "Into the Light." The resemblance is so close that musicians will probably notice it right away, and the attentive nonmusician listener probably will not have a great deal of difficulty feeling the ties between the songs. Prince sings that he "will walk this road," despite the dangers he sees. In the context of the album, it is easy to understand the lyrics as a reference to the troubles of life. This reading comes especially easily when the listener thinks of "Into the Light" and "I Will" as a little miniature suite of pieces on *Chaos and Disorder.*

The song "Dig U Better Dead" signals the return of New Power Generation–style funk. The lyrics create a wide range of impressions. One might feel a certain amount of disdain for critics and rabid fans that dig musicians more after they die than when they were alive. The image of artists such as Janis Joplin, Jim Morrison, Kurt Cobain, Gram Parsons, and others that jumped from notoriety to near-cult status after their early demises comes to mind.

"Had U"—a brief, minute-and-a-half song—features a lyric that consists entirely of two-word phrases (such as the title). Taken together the 20 phrases chronicle a relationship that turned sour. The way in which Prince is able to document the relationship (as well as his character's emotional transformation) from a telephone call to a sexual encounter to a breakup over the course of the 20 phrases is masterful. He sets each two-word phrase to a two-note descending melodic motive. He then combines several of the motives in descending sequences. This recursive (the same basic shape [a short melodic descent] on several levels of structure) treatment of the descending motive gives the piece a sense of organic wholeness. Although the piece is not a widely known Prince composition, it shows the higher level of sophistication that was coming into his work in the mid-1990s—to a greater degree than at any previous time in his career he was able to get the most out of a minimal amount of material. Prince also provides a few tasty Jimi Hendrix–like blues-rock guitar licks in the piece.

The album's liner notes suggest that *Chaos and Disorder* represents a bunch of tracks that were not necessarily intended to appear together. More to the point, the notes clearly claim that they were not even intended for public release. While a title such as *Chaos and Disorder* might suggest a collection of widely disparate tracks, and while the liner notes might characterize the material as such, the fact is that every song on the album can be interpreted as some sort of chronicle of, or reaction to, the chaos and disorder of life, and especially the pop life. In other words, *Chaos and Disorder* becomes a concept album almost in spite of itself. None of the tracks contain the kinds of lyrical or musical hooks that helped to make Prince's most popular songs so successful in the commercial arena; however, like the songs of *The Gold Experience*, there is evidence on several songs on this album that Prince was continuing to mature as a writer. And, as is customary on his albums, the attention to detail in the production is top-notch.

Prince became a pop culture icon in the early 1980s. This 1979 photograph finds him on the verge of stardom. Courtesy of Photofest.

Prince starred as lounge pianist Chris-topher Tracy in the 1986 Warner Bros. film *Under the Cherry Moon*. Copyright Warner Brothers. Courtesy of Photofest.

Acknowledged as an exciting live performer, here Prince performs in the 1987 concert film *Sign o' the Times*. Copyright Cineplex-Odean Films. Photo by Jeff Katz. Courtesy of Photofest.

An artist whose music has included hip-hop, funk, heavy metal, Quiet Storm, jazz, and pop, Prince here captures the fashion of 1980s new wave. Courtesy of Photofest.

Prince wearing his famous "Love Symbol" at the time of *Rave Un2 the Joy Fantastic* (1999). Courtesy of Photofest.

In the 1990s, Prince changed his name to a symbol that appeared to be a stylized version of a combined male and female symbol. Here, Prince performs next to the so-called "Love Symbol." Courtesy of Photofest.

The Approach of 1999

"Free at last!" Prince's work for Capital-EMI beginning in 1996 practically screamed this phrase. His first album of the 1996–1999 period, *Emancipation*, was a mammoth three-CD set that can only be characterized as Prince's declaration of artistic freedom. This period also saw him issuing the equally huge set *Crystal Ball,* a collection of new material, outtakes, and alternative versions that covers the period from *Sign o' the Times* into the late 1990s. Perhaps because these two mega-albums were not entirely successful with fans, they were followed by *New Power Soul,* an album that sounds like a calculated move toward commercial appeal. Although Prince and the Brothers Warner had parted ways, Warner still retained the rights to some of Prince's material, and so they released *The Vault: Old Friends 4 Sale.* This period ended with Prince seemingly trying to regain some of his lost commercial appeal with the 1999 album *Rave Un2 the Joy Fantastic.*

EMANCIPATION

Prince had declared himself a slave to Warner Bros. despite a financially enormous contract. Because of his declaration, he incurred the wrath of music critics in the mid-1990s. For example, Melinda Newman of *Billboard* wrote in October 1994 in reaction to Prince's assertion, "Well, all we can say is that for $100,000,000, we'd walk barefoot across hot coals singing 'Raspberry Beret' in Swahili. Or maybe we'd realize we were getting paid way more than we ever deserved and graciously shut up and cash the check."[1] The triple-disc set *Emancipation* represented, well, Prince's emancipation from Warner Bros. Some critics claim that each of the three CDs has a musical and lyrical personality all its own. It is true that there are three main lyrical foci (sex, love, and God) and three main musical genres (mainstream R&B, hip-hop, and rock) that Prince explores; however, songs that mix all three lyrical and musical styles can be found on every disc. Add to that the fact that some of the songs deal with dancing, partying, warnings against drug abuse, and some other topics, and it is difficult to hear *Emancipation* as a set of three distinctly focused discs. This having been said, there is a general sense of progression throughout the album, with the songs of disc 1 generally dealing with courting, breakups, falling in love, and some of the songs of disc 2 focusing on marriage and children. However, the pattern does not continue nearly as clearly on disc 3. Clearly, some of these songs on all three discs rank with the most autobiographical material Prince has written—the liner notes tell the listener as much—however, Prince makes the references universal enough that it is easy (in most cases) for the listener to project his or her own experience onto the lyrics. One of the more telling features of the album is the fact that it includes several cover recordings—truly rare for a Prince album. The most interesting thing that is revealed by comparing the covers (two of which are famous Philly soul standards) with Prince's compositions is the extent to which Prince's writing stands up to, and in some cases, surpasses the popular standards. The other interesting feature of *Emancipation* that comes out of Prince's unusual use of cover material is the extent to which a few of his own compositions completely capture the musical style and lyrical feel of earlier soul compositions without sounding derivative.

Emancipation begins with "Jam of the Year," a song that finds Prince revisiting the combination of falsetto singing, disarming approach to sexual frankness, and commercially accessible, hook-filled dance-oriented R&B that had in part defined his two pre-1980 albums. The focus is on music and dancing, but the sexual overtones are clear, as is common in most of Prince's songs that are ostensibly about dancing. The recording includes jazz-inspired inflections in the horn solos, as well as in Prince's keyboard and guitar playing.

"Right Back Here in My Arms" finds Prince portraying a character whose lover needs "some time out." He, however, cannot wait until she is "right back here in [his] arms again." This comes closer to a conventional R&B love song than the vast majority of Prince songs, both lyrically and musically. Musically, it combines old-school R&B sensibilities with a touch of hip-hop rhythm and sampling of the work of Poet 99.

The song "Somebody's Somebody" finds Prince collaborating as a writer with Brenda Lee Eager and Hilliard Wilson. It is another easygoing R&B ballad that leans ever more in the direction of old-school, radio-friendly soul than "Right Back Here in My Arms." In particular, Prince's use of a sitar-guitar sound in the lead instrumental line suggests any one of a number of late 1960s/early 1970s soul classics, including, for example, Stevie Wonder's "Signed, Sealed, Delivered (I'm Yours)" and the Stylistics' "You Are Everything." Given the slow tempo, the song most resembles the work of the

Stylistics with producer-songwriter Thom Bell. Prince's incorporation of the feel of Bell's popular style of Philly soul works well, particularly because Prince covers two of Bell's compositions on the album.

While the greater emphasis on Ebonics in "Get Yo Groove On" moves the song farther away from the style of old-school 1960s and 1970s pop soul Prince explored on the previous two songs, there are still plenty of links to the past. In particular, the stamp of Smoky Robinson's vulnerable falsetto vocal style is all over this song. Unlike many of Prince's time-to-party-and-dance songs of the past, here he eschews in-your-face sexual explicitness. This provides another clear tie to the work of Motown artists such as Robinson and non-Motown soul artists of the 1960s whose work easily fared as well on the pop charts as on the R&B charts. Curiously, like the previous two songs—which also exhibit clear ties to Prince's predecessors—"Get Yo Groove On" is thoroughly listenable, radio-friendly, but is not as strong in the melodic, instrumental, or lyrical hook departments as Prince's earlier classics. By absorbing the past so thoroughly, these songs lose some distinctiveness.

The next track, "Courtin' Time," is just quirky enough that it rates higher in the distinctiveness area. Here, Prince brings back big band swing. Well, sort of. Actually, what Prince does is to take the listener back to the mid-twentieth century with a highly stylized version of swing. Like Stevie Wonder had done back in the mid-1970s on the hit song "Sir Duke," Prince provides clear swing signifiers while studiously avoiding writing what one might term "the real thing." While it might be overstating it to call this a clear stroke of pure genius, it is nevertheless important that Prince took this route. Writing something too close to "authentic" swing-style jazz would open the composer up to the possibility of his song being felt as an example of mere musical imitation or mere nostalgia. It would also open up the song to questions of authenticity and to possibly unflattering comparisons to the work of the Duke Ellingtons, Ella Fitzgeralds, and Benny Goodmans. Prince's tactic artfully conjures up images of the earlier era, while always making it clear that he knows that he is writing a highly stylized, 1990s version of swing music. That being said, his vocal phrasing shows that he clearly understands jazz vocal style, even though he has so rarely used straight-ahead jazz style in his previous—or later—vocal work. The lyrics of the song present Prince as a character who has grown tired of being lonely; he has decided that it is finally "courtin' time."

Philadelphia producer and songwriter Thom Bell provided several vocal groups, most notably the Delfonics and the Stylistics, with light soul hits in the late 1960s and early 1970s. Among these standards was the 1971–1972 Stylistics hit "Betcha By Golly Wow!" The Stylistics' single release of the song reached No. 3 on the *Billboard* pop chart and No. 2 on *Billboard* Black Singles chart. If one interprets disc 1 of Prince's *Emancipation* album as following a loose program of boy loses girl, boy decides to find new girl, boy finds new girl, then "Betcha By Golly Wow!" signifies that the "courtin'" he described in the previous song has paid off in a solid love relationship. Even if the programmatic content of the disc is fairly loose, this soul standard is still a great choice for Prince: he has the vocal technique to soar on the falsetto solo line, and the instrumental, arranging, and production chops to create something that stands up against the original version. Prince's NPG Records released this track as a single, and it made several of *Billboard*'s singles charts. Although Prince's version of the song did not enjoy the same degree of success as the Stylistics' recording of more than two decades earlier, it was the most successful of the surprisingly small number of singles Prince released off of *Emancipation*.

So, this is the point where the so-called program of the previous two songs on *Emancipation* falls apart.... "We Gets Up" is a dance number that finds Prince bragging about the power of his "band" and about the power of their "new power soul." It is, therefore, very much the kind of song that was found on his earlier albums with the New Power Generation. Here, though, it's almost entirely a Prince solo effort, with instrumental support from bassist Rhonda S. (Rhonda Smith), and overdubbed horns by Eric Leeds and Brian Lynch. Because of the lyrical content and the early 1990s funk style, it would seem to be a song that was intended to be a New Power Generation track. And, that is one of the things that makes *Emancipation* so interesting. It is not an album that follows a strict program. Certainly, there are elements of a program (quite probably related to Prince's marriage) that seem to trace a relationship from meeting through courtship and physical intimacy to commitment, but there are breaks, such as that provided by "We Gets Up," that at times get to be part of the core problem Prince had with Warner Bros.: too many songs, and not enough willingness from the company to allow Prince to release them all.

The centerfold of the elaborate *Emancipation* booklet shows Prince standing in front of an amazingly grandiose white mansion, with a white grand piano, and a white BMW sports car. The listener might ask, "Is this what represents 'emancipation' to Prince? Is it all just about material wealth?" The song "White Mansion" finds Prince's character wishing for just that kind of material wealth. He sings of the "big white mansion" he dreams of owning and all the "latest fashions" he hopes to wear, for example, Gucci and Versace. The lyrics confirm that for some people, this is exactly what emancipation means. At this point on the album, he still leaves open the possibility that material things can bring true happiness. He does, however, leave a small chink in the armor of material wealth. At the end of the song, his character snaps back to reality when he sees the attractive posterior of a young lady who is walking by. This provides a touch of somewhat sexist humor in the song, but it also suggests that true happiness on earth might better be found in one-on-one sexual relationships than in idle dreams of possessing material goods. Musically, "White Mansion" is a Quiet Storm–ish hip-hop era ballad that references the old 1970s hits of Barry White and his Love Unlimited Orchestra in its string arrangement. The melody basically is monothematic, and is not liable to hold the listener's interest to the extent that most of Prince's songs do.

If there is one song on *Emancipation* that could cause the listener to question why Prince has shied away from the piano as an instrumentalist (and there are several songs on the album that show off Prince's piano work to good effect), then "Damned If I [Eye] Do" would be that song. Certainly, much of the piano comping[2] up to approximately the last 2 minutes of the song is mixed into the background of the texture and takes a backseat to Prince's more demonstrative guitar playing. However, the Latin-style piano work in the last 2 minutes of the song suggests a song such as Stevie Wonder's "Don't You Worry 'bout a Thing," with its incorporation of the technically demanding piano *ostinato* sound of Latin American salsa. Prince does not go out in featuring the piano here (so the listener will not hear the kind of focus on the instrument that saturates the Stevie Wonder song), but a close listening to the background keyboard work is well worth the effort.

Musically, "Damned If I [Eye] Do" stands apart from much of the material on disc 1 of *Emancipation*. It is the one piece on the disc that fit squarely into the pop-rock genre of the day. Here, Prince's character addresses a woman with whom he is in love. She refuses to consummate their physical relationship, apparently deriving more pleasure from a bottle of vermouth than from the advances of Prince's character. Since Prince's character is tired of his would-be lover's alcohol-driven passive-aggressive nature, he tells her that he is through with the relationship. The attitude portrayed in his words seems to be stronger than that provided by the radio-friendly pop-rock musical setting. The music, in fact, is so hook-laden that it stands up well against radio favorites of the mid-1990s, such as Hootie & the Blowfish.

The song "I Can't Make You Love Me" was recorded by a wide variety of artists in the 1990s; however, the best-known version is probably the 1991 recording by Bonnie Raitt. This collaborative composition of James Allen Shamblin II and Michael Barry Reid is not exactly an old-school soul standard—it's too new for that designation—but Prince's arrangement on *Emancipation* brings back the Thom Bell early-1970s Philly soul sound. Mostly because the melody of the song tends to meander a bit, and because the sentiments are for the most part covered elsewhere on *Emancipation,* it is not the most essential part of the album.

With its dance groove, lyrical focus on dancing and sex, and its secondary focus on defining a distinctive lead character, "Mr. Happy" calls to mind some of the songs of the New Power Generation's "The Love Symbol Album." The lead character here, though, is not as vivid as, say, the lead characters of "My Name Is Prince" or "Sexy M.F." Musically, too, "Mr. Happy" does not stand out from other mid-1990s R&B the way that Prince's most successful songs do from the prevailing music of their eras.

The last song on disc 1, "In This Bed I [Eye] Scream," is more successful. Here, Prince combines the spirit of popular 1960s R&B singer-songwriters such as Smoky Robinson and Marvin Gaye—including an engaging melody, distinctive vocal harmonies, and an easy-to-remember instrumental hook—with the rhythms of 1990s R&B. Like, say, a Smoky Robinson, Prince's singing about his sense of loss over a relationship that has gone sour evokes sadness and vulnerability. It is not a gut-wrenching approach to emotionalizing by any stretch of the imagination; there is very little overt acting. However, that is what makes it seem honest.

Musically, too, "In This Bed I [Eye] Scream" ratchets up the distinctiveness factor quite a bit over Prince's own "Mr. Happy" and the Shamblin/ Reid cover "I Can't Make You Love Me." The chorus, with its A-B-A-B melodic structure sets the lyrics in such a way as to heighten their meaning. For example, the "A" phrase, which is in the higher pitch range, consists of the song's title line; the "B" phrase finds Prince asking how he is going to get by, now that his relationship is over. The "screaming" A is carefully balanced, then, by the "pleading" B. Because the vocal harmony includes a fair number of open intervals (e.g., perfect fourths—C and the F above—and perfect fifths—C and the G above), it gives the listener the sense that something is missing (standard vocal harmony would more frequently feature the intervals of thirds and sixths, or complete chords in which the open fourth or fifth would be accompanied by another note)—an altogether appropriate musical feeling, given the state in which Prince's character finds himself.

Emancipation's second CD begins with "Sex in the Summer." It is easy to miss some of subtlety of the song, in particular its deeper meaning, if the listener focuses in on the chorus and pays less attention to the verses. On the most obvious level, Prince's lyrics pay homage to the young bikini-clad women, handsome young men, and the promise of sexual pleasure that brings them together. Prince describes sex as pleasure in its own right, and as something that transcends the poverty, police brutality, and other horrors of black urban life. As Prince later turns his attention to listening to "Mahalia's greatest," however, the lyrics start to take on a religious tone. To the extent that the listener makes the connection with the great gospel singer Mahalia Jackson, he or she will understand that the spirit of Prince's character is not driven entirely by the earthly physical pleasure of "sex in the summer." Other religious references give the song even more character. On one hand, it brings to mind the linking of sex and spirituality that dates back to some of Prince's work of the late 1970s and early 1980s: the gist of which is that there is spirituality in sex—or, to put it another way, God never would have given humans the gift of sexual pleasure if he had not intended for us to enjoy it. Interestingly, though, the music here is rather laid-back R&B. It does not exhibit the rhythmic drive that some of Prince's New Power Generation sex-related songs exhibit. There is not quite a sense of sadness, but clearly a sense of understatement. Because of the mood of his music, I believe that it is also possible to read the combination of lyrics about 24/7 sex in the summer and spirituality in another way. The endless sex in the summer could be understood as a metaphor for heaven. In this reading, heaven represents an endless supply of what to Prince's character is the most joyous, satisfying earthly pleasure that can be shared by two people. The linkage between sexuality and spirituality is undeniably there in "Sex in the Summer"; however, Prince is just cryptic enough that he allows for a range of interpretations as to exactly how they are linked. Prince further links sex with the transcendent by including as part of the track "the ultrasound heartbeat of the 1st conceived 2 ♀."[3]

The album's next two tracks, "One Kiss at a Time" and "Soul Sanctuary," get into the heart of the purely romantic side of *Emancipation,* the side that critics have linked with Prince's marriage. "One Kiss at a Time" includes jazz-inspired rhythmic touches. The most interesting feature of the song, however, is probably its overall structure. The first half of the 4:41 song has the effect of a strophic song with no chorus section. The almost tick-tock–like rhythmic feel in the instruments, as well as the high degree of repetition in the vocal melody, give the listener the feeling of time progressing through eternity. It is a musical recreation of the slow lovemaking Prince describes in the lyrics. A new section begins at exactly the mid-point of the song, with another new section starting at the 3-minute mark. This section is marked by a pregnant pause in the song (a complete break with approximately a second of silence). The silence and melodic contrast makes this a major focal point. It just so happens that this focal point is very, very close to the exact point that the Golden Mean would dictate, thus giving the piece a classical sort of background structure.

The next song, "Soul Sanctuary," has a more conventional pop song structure than "One Kiss at a Time," and it is more immediately melodically appealing. Prince makes the sexual references more oblique and metaphorical—it is more of an emotional (as opposed to physical) song than "One Kiss at a Time." Even though Prince sings both songs in falsetto, "Soul Sanctuary" is by far the most gender-neutral in its lyrical content. There is nothing necessarily stereotypically male or female about the lyrics, which incidentally are co-written by Prince and Sandra St. Victor. Therefore, one could understand "One Kiss at a Time" and "Soul Sanctuary" as a dialog between a male character ("One Kiss at a Time") and his female lover ("Soul Sanctuary").

Another slow ballad song, "Emale," incorporates more of the double-time rhythms and deep bass of hip-hop music than the previous songs on disc 2 of *Emancipation.* Perhaps a bit too obviously, the title is a play on the word *email.* It is a tale of a male/female couple that apparently "meet" electronically. Prince never specifies the exact nature of how or why the woman received the email—for example, if it was the result of a visit to a dating Web site—however, he allows that a certain sadistic streak might run through both characters. Much of the lyrical content is somewhat disconnected and obscure, but Prince provides hints that this relationship goes into a dark, sinister area of sex: perhaps the world of sexual predators. The music is seductive and nothing about it suggests the over-the-top world of fetishes hinted at in the lyrics. This disjuncture makes for a haunting, disturbing look at a side of sex that Prince had explored a few times earlier in his career. Unlike a song such as "Lady Cab Driver," which seems like a look at the dark world of male fetish fantasy, here both characters seem to be on the prowl for the extremes of sex.

One of the shorter songs on *Emancipation*, "Curious Child" is an almost Renaissance-styled love ballad (musically, at least). Prince's poem consists of three stanzas, and his musical setting is strophic, with an instrumental introduction, an instrumental interlude between verses two and three, and an instrumental coda. In the world of late twentieth-century pop songs, or rock songs, or R&B songs, such a straightforward strophic form is rare: most pop songs of the era include a chorus section and often also include a bridge. The strophic structure, simple tune (in which each verse has an AAAB phrase structure), and instrumental focus on the guitar suggest a late twentieth-century version of the Renaissance song with lute accompaniment. A wash of synthesizer in the background enhances the reference point of the lyrics: a man who is looking back at his first encounter with his lover, whom he meets in a room filled with "harlots and fantasy." The reference to "harlots and fantasy," the seamy side of sex, links the song to the electronic fantasy world of sex chat rooms suggested by "Emale." Here, however, Prince's character and his lover stand clearly outside the others in the room—they are the two innocents who find a love that goes beyond physical fulfillment or the selling of sex.

In the next song, "Dreamin' about U," Prince portrays a man obsessed with a woman. Taken out of their musical context, the lyrics basically find Prince's character telling the woman that wherever he is and whatever he is doing, as long as she is not with him, he is dreaming about her. The steady tick-tock of the musical accompaniment, the fact that the lyrics make so many references to Prince's character at home, and the short, clipped melodic phrases all combine to create the image of a man truly obsessed. He lies on his bed all day just thinking about the woman he apparently can't have. Prince's liner notes for the song, which read simply "Addictions R many,"[4] supports this reading. In fact, if one were, say, to write a contemporary pop opera about a sexual predator/stalker, this song would establish the obsession that could send a character over the top quite effectively.

At nearly 8 minutes in length, "Joint 2 Joint" is the longest piece on *Emancipation*. As suggested by Prince's liner notes, "Wear a condom. SAFE!,"[5] this is one of his sex-related songs. However, it is a great disservice to this piece to think of it as "just another Prince song about sex": the piece is far too interesting and sophisticated. First of all, the lyrics include spoken portions (rap) and sung portions. The lyrics include signifiers that make it clear that the piece deals with the physical actions of intercourse and oral sex, as well as sexually transmitted disease, but they are couched in such a way as to maintain a distinctly impressionistic air. There are so many lyrical twists and turns that it becomes a wash of double entendre imagery.

The most interesting feature of "Joint 2 Joint," however, is the overall construction. Prince avoids the conventional song structures of the past, such as simple strophic form; the AABA form that is so typical of Tin Pan Alley standards; the verse, chorus, and middle eight form that pervades pop music of the rock era; and so forth. He uses something that, structurally, at least, is more in keeping with instrumental compositions. The first large section (A) lasts up to the 2:02 point. It consists of two distinct subsections with a brief introduction: (subsection "a" lasts from approximately 0:06 to 1:09, and subsection "b" lasts from 1:09 to 2:02). While lyrically the two subsections can be understood as two verses, and are linked with the same background riff in the keyboard and the same stationary harmony, they are sung to two contrasting melodies. The large section (B) is in a contrasting tonality, and finds Prince introducing new material, including new keyboard riffs, rap by Poet 99, new scratches by Michael Mac, and a tap performance by Savion Glover. Prince also includes references to his vegetarianism in rap, a subsection defined by the slap-bass sound of 1970s funk, and highly contrasting densities of material, especially in the last minute of the piece. With all of this development and avoidance of obviously unifying textures and instrumental figures, the B section is far grander in scope than the opening section, and rather than maintaining the feel of easily definable, distinct subsections of A, it moves in the direction of through-composed fantasia.

The next song, "The Holy River," is about as complete a contrast with "Joint 2 Joint" as one could imagine. First of all, Prince returns to conventional pop song structure, with verses, chorus, and bridge—or middle eight—sections. The verses use conventional rhyme schemes, although Prince tends to mix rather freely hard rhymes and soft rhymes throughout the song. The three musical phrases that make up each verse use a fairly standard a-a-a^1 structure. The texture, too, is quite even throughout and is largely acoustic rhythm guitar–based. The lyrics find Prince addressing a person who has seen his or her share of trials throughout life and who manages to face life with "another glass of port." Prince suggests that the person puts his or her trust in Jesus in order to find true deliverance at "the Holy River." Taken as a standalone song, "The Holy River" is a believer's statement of faith that "if we drown [in this life] then we'll be delivered [in the next life]." It is clear that this Christian statement of faith is to Prince one form of emancipation; the song clearly fits the context of the album. What is startling, though, is to hear the song within the album's playing order. Structurally, texturally, and lyrically, it represents a complete break from "Joint 2 Joint." By setting "The Holy River" up with a physical, sexually oriented song, Prince snaps the listener to attention.

The next song, "Let's Have a Baby," also takes on added meaning when it is considered in the context of *Emancipation*'s running order. While "Joint 2 Joint" focuses exclusively on sex as physical pleasure, and on some of the not-so-pleasant possible outcomes of sex without love, and "The Holy River" focuses exclusively on deliverance through faith in God, Prince tells the listener in "Let's Have a Baby" that sex as a combination of love and procreation is a form of spirituality and part of God's plan. This is a rarity in Prince's output and can best be understood as his reaction to the birth of his first child. Earlier Prince songs that linked sex and spirituality suggest that sexuality is a gift from God to be enjoyed by humans—for the physical pleasure it brings. Now that Prince is a husband and father, he takes one more step and acknowledges that not only is the physical pleasure part of the gift, but that the ability to perpetuate the human species is also part of the gift. There are some notable compositional touches that add to the effectiveness of the piece. "Let's Have a Baby" begins with a tick-tock rhythm in the percussion and keyboard parts. This immediately precedes the first line, which states, "I can't wait no more." While the musical mimicry of a ticking clock marking the passing of time might seem rather clichéd, there is really more to it than that. The *ostinato* figure in the keyboard in this introduction bears a strong surface resemblance to the theme music of Rod Serling's 1950s and 1960s television program *The Twilight Zone*. Regardless of whether the musical connection is intentional, if the listener picks up on it, it is easy to imagine Prince's character and/or his character's wife finding themselves in something of a *Twilight Zone* situation. Perhaps earlier in their relationship they thought of sex solely in the context of physical pleasure; now they see it in an entirely different light. Prince sings the song using falsetto and an almost Al Green–inspired style.

The song "Saviour"[6] resumes the clear influence of 1960s and early 1970s soul ballads on Prince's work on *Emancipation*. The main distinction between the impact of this song and some of the early tracks on disc 1 of the collection is that this one has more in the way of stick-in-your-head hooks. The entire arrangement, which includes the traditional instruments of a soul group (electric guitar, bass, drums), as well as strings and brass, is lush without turning schmaltzy. Prince's lyrics find him telling his lover that—to paraphrase—"she is the only saviour he will ever need." This presents the listener with yet another variant on the theme of just what brings true "emancipation." In contrast to "Joint 2 Joint," in which the physical pleasure of sex brings emancipation, "The Holy River," in which purely religious faith brings emancipation, and "Let's Have a Baby," in which one finds emancipation through bringing the next generation into the world, here Prince suggests that a liberating religious spirituality can be found in the emotion of romantic love.

Prince brings these various liberators together more cohesively in the last track on disc 2 of *Emancipation:* "Friend, Lover, Sister, Mother/Wife."

Here, he revisits a theme he had explored earlier in his career in songs such as "I Wanna Be Your Lover" and "If I Was Your Girlfriend." While those earlier songs found Prince blurring gender boundaries, the gist of the *Emancipation* track is that in a truly loving, lasting relationship, a man will find his partner to be everything (friend, lover, sister, mother, wife, etc.). The song, which Prince showcased at his wedding reception,[7] is a beautiful restatement of the biblical theme that the two (male and female) shall become one in marriage. The piece is tuneful and perhaps the best pure love ballad Prince has written to date.

The third disc of *Emancipation* begins with "Slave," a highly stylized version of the sorrow songs of nineteenth-century African American slave experience. Prince sings his elaborately harmonized and heavily multitracked lament over a rock steady drumbeat. The combination of blues-inflected melodic line, complex and sometimes highly dissonant vocal harmony, and heavy percussion beat fully integrates the styles of the sorrow songs, nineteenth-century spirituals, twentieth-century art music, and hip-hop. It is an effective piece in showing that slavery can exist on many levels. More to the point, the combination of musical influences illustrates the continuity of lamentations and protest about unequal treatment on the basis of race from the days of slavery in the nineteenth century to the 1990s. Unfortunately, however, it is difficult to divorce the song completely from Prince's assertion that his $100 million contract with Warner Bros. was tantamount to institutional enslavement. The context of Prince's pronouncement of his personal slavery to Warner Bros. cheapens the impact of the song somewhat, although the musical setting is so captivating that it mostly overcomes what has come to be seen as one of the low points in Prince's public image.

In the song "New World," Prince paints the picture of a futuristic world in which various pills cure all sorts of major and minor ills, but humankind still stands on the brink of "obliteration." He concludes that the only way "to make it in this brave new world" is to "love one another." The lyrical sentiments, the upbeat funky musical style, and the multirange lead vocals have a clear lineage in the 1969–1970 work of Sly and the Family Stone. While Prince had turned to Sly Stone's aesthetics in a fair number of earlier songs, "New World" is an especially effective piece. Not only is it tuneful and immediately accessible lyrically, the piece also integrates well into the overall feel of *Emancipation* because of the presence of so many cover songs from the late 1960s and early 1970s and other deliberately slightly retro-feeling new compositions by Prince.

Prince incorporates aspects of electronic dance music—with some assistance from programmers Cesar Sogbe and Joe Galdo—in the song "The Human Body." The various dance riffs have a distinctively 1980s feel to them, and the lyrics—one of the shorter poems Prince has set to music for commercial release—find Prince asking his lover to "freak him dirty all night long" and alternately praising God for the gift of "the human body" and the sexual pleasure humans can enjoy. Lyrically, it is succinct in espousing Prince's philosophy of sexuality as spirituality; however, the main interest in the song comes from the various rhythmic *ostinati* that give the song its dance groove.

The song "Face Down" brings the listener back into the world of 1990s hip-hop. Prince raps about the mistreatment he has received at the hands of the press, including charges—which he denies in the most vehement terms—that he is only in the music business for the money. The composition is also a warning to celebrities that end up living for the fame, stardom, and wealth that celebrity can bring. Included in this is the spoken refrain, "Dead like Elvis." Here, Prince refers to Elvis Presley, perhaps one of the best-known examples of a musician who became caught up in his celebrity and ended up dying in part because of the excess that seems sometimes to come with celebrity. Prince's citation of Elvis is interesting on more than the obvious (Presley's death in 1977) level. After his groundbreaking work in the late 1950s, Presley had died artistically by catering to the mainstream in the 1960s. Prince clearly lets his listeners, as well as the "motherfuckers" who unjustly criticize him, know that he will not end up "face down" and "dead like Elvis." Clearly, the piece presents the flip side of the liner booklet's centerfold photograph of Prince in front of a mansion with a sleek BMW sports car. One of the most interesting side features of the piece is that the rhythmic groove—whether intentionally or unintentionally—resembles (at least a little bit) the feel of the David Bowie, John Lennon, and Carlos Alomar composition "Fame," the most famous song of the 1970s that deals with the hidden price of celebrity. The use of rap, the emphasis on identity, and the way in which Prince calls on the horn section, the bass guitar, and eventually the (synthesized) orchestra to play their licks are all reminiscent of Prince's earlier New Power Generation work, particularly on songs such as "My Name Is Prince" and "Sexy M.F." Taken as a standalone piece, "Face Down" is a powerful statement about personal priorities and a testament to the fact that Prince had received an awful lot of negative press in the mid-1990s. It is, however, a problematic piece in the context of all the peace, love, and understanding-type material of *Emancipation*. The level of invective on "Face Down" far exceeds anything else in this 3-hour collection of music.

Because he is such a prolific writer, Prince has rarely recorded cover songs. While each of the covers on *Emancipation* is well crafted from a production standpoint and meticulously sung by Prince, the Thom Bell and William Hart composition "La, La, La (Means I Love You)" is especially notable for the incredible technical range that Prince brings to his multitracked singing. From a thematic standpoint, the song would seem to fit better with the love- and marriage-related material of disc 2 rather than here on disc 3 of the album, particularly as it directly follows the anger of "Face Down." However, be that as it may, this cover shows that despite the fact that his own compositions tend to avoid the blushingly, overtly romantic, Prince the performer fully understands the style.

Prince returns to the issues of image and personal priorities that marked the earlier song "Face Down" in the song that follows his Delfonics cover: "Style." This song again brings the listener back to the centerfold photo of Prince, apparently living in the lap of luxury. Although the BMW logo in the photograph is prominently, and apparently very purposefully, displayed, this song dismisses logo wear and other accoutrements of current must-have, peer pressure–driven fashion. As Prince raps and states in the liner notes, "style is a second cousin 2 class."[8] He seeks to redefine style as something that reflects self-worth and classiness. The music features a light hip-hop beat and jazzy horn lines. As Prince had done in "Sexy M.F." and in "Face Down," he calls out section changes in the song, in this case introducing the bridge of the song. But, then, Prince had done this occasionally even in his early work. The technique has perhaps its clearest precedent in the work of James Brown, although examples can be found scattered through R&B of the 1960s. In any case, this technique, as well as the sense of cool that pervades the track and the use of a soft-sell approach to making a rhetorical point all come together to link "Style" with the better-known song "Sexy M.F."

Emancipation's next track, "Sleep Around," not only contains a section taken directly from Tower of Power's "Squibcakes," it maintains a connection to 1970s dance music throughout. Prince integrates the hook-laden melodicism, the style of horn lines and synthesized string lines, and the rhythmic feel of 1970s disco into his vocabulary. In fact, the music more closely resembles commercial disco than the funkier, more horn-oriented music of the Tower of Power. The melody of the verses, which focuses on the half-step intervals found in the B-flat minor scale, is particularly memorable. The generally upward motion (with a slight fall at the end) of each phrase lends a sense of urgency to the instructions found in the lyrics. In these lyrics, Prince tells a man—who represents all men in general—to treat "their baby right," so that she doesn't want to "sleep around." The message seems pretty universal: treat your lover right so that she remains true. Countless other pop songs deliver exactly the same message; however, the way in which Prince phrases it—treat her right "so she don't wanna sleep around"—is just quirky enough that the song stands out from others that use more clichéd phrases, for example, "so she stays true." Although this is really the only song on *Emancipation* that comes close to the prevailing disco style of the 1970s, it feels like it fits completely with the other love-related songs. Just the generally retro feel of the song is enough to make it at least a dance-oriented second cousin to the Delfonics and Stylistics covers.

Prince enlists the assistance of rapper Scrap D and drummer, associate producer, and arranger Kirk A. Johnson (Mr. KA'J) for "Da, Da, Da," a hip-hop piece that explores the feelings and experiences of young black men who cannot find work in the ghetto. Gang violence, individual violence, intergenerational conflict, and broken love relationships all emerge as the real-life results of poverty and racial intolerance. Although this theme might sound pretty much like standard fare for a whole host of rap compositions that preceded this work, "Da, Da, Da" is a striking piece. Prince's (and Mr. KA'J's) musical setting, with its singsong "Da, da, da, da, da, da, da" refrain, juxtaposes the hopelessness and anger of the rap with a thoroughly disarming tune. This combination of happy-go-lucky refrain and thorough alienation in the rap is more disquieting than a composition in which the anger of the lyrics is merely mimicked in the musical setting. The effect is somewhat akin to the early twentieth-century composer Gustav Mahler's settings of texts concerning death to child-like tunes. Despite the difference in genres, Prince's piece is eerie in the same way.

One of the great debates about vocal music concerns the extent to which the lyrics themselves or the musical setting determine the listener's sense of the true meaning of the song. And, this is not just a debate of the rock era. For example, composer Franz Schubert's setting of Goethe's "Der Erlkönig" for solo voice and piano reportedly was ill received by the poet because he felt that Schubert's music forced the listener to interpret the action and emotions of the poem in one particular way. Apparently, Goethe preferred contemporary strophic settings in which the music did not portray the dramatic action of the poem. Rock critics, perhaps most notably Greil Marcus in *Rock and Roll Will Stand*,[9] also deal with the so-called true rhetorical meaning of songs. In his book, Marcus discusses a number of songs of the late 1960s in which the lyrical sentiments and the musical setting were completely at odds. Perhaps one of the best-known examples of such a song is the Beatles' 1968 single version of "Revolution," a recording in which distorted, high-energy rock music is used to set lyrics that dismiss violent revolution out of hand. Just as that version of "Revolution," which was the B-side of "Hey Jude," the Beatles' biggest-selling single, forces the listener to grapple with just what message John Lennon (the lead singer and principal songwriter of the piece) and his bandmates are *really* trying to deliver, Prince's "Da, Da, Da" does the same thing.

Prince includes electronic sound effects, including spacey synthesizer sounds and the familiar "You've got mail" message associated with America Online, on the next track, "My Computer." With the assistance of guest vocalist Kate Bush, Prince portrays a character who, lonely on a Saturday night, surfs the Internet looking for an interesting Web site or for someone with whom to chat. Interestingly, Prince's production on the piece includes the use of artificial static and surface noise that one used to hear back in the days of vinyl records. The combination of stereotypically computer-oriented sounds with the old-school noise of predigital sound recordings seems to suggest he is somewhat out of touch and ill at ease with the digital world. He seems, in fact, to be a desperate man, caught between the dating and courtship rituals of the past and the rituals of the late 1990s. Although "My Computer" is not necessarily framed as a message song, at least on the surface, it takes on the air of a message song in the context of *Emancipation*. For one thing, Prince's character seems to be a failure at using the computer to emancipate himself from his loneliness. Secondly, the other love-related songs on the album deal with one-on-one relationships in which the characters—who are successful in love—are in the same place at the same time. The unspoken message would seem to be that old-school courting wins out over habituating dating Web sites.

For the most part, *Emancipation* is not a particularly guitar-focused album. Therefore, Prince's electric guitar work on Eric Bazilian's song "One of Us" (best known through Joan Osborne's hugely successful 1995 recording) is most welcome as the album gets closer and closer to coming to a conclusion. The song is not, however, merely a vehicle for Prince's guitar virtuosity. Prince writes in the liner notes that Bazilian's lyrics are "an important statement 4 all of us...every one of us."[10] These lyrics ask what we would do "if God was one of us," rephrasing Jesus' words in Matthew 25:40, "And the King will answer them, 'Truly, I say to you, as you did it to one of the least of these my brethren, you did it unto me.'"[11] In the overall context of the album, it is no mistake that Prince begins to narrow his focus with this, the third-to-last song. It anticipates the way in which he will define true emancipation on the album's final track.

Written for "a lost friend,"[12] Prince's composition "The Love We Make" urges the listener to turn to God to deal with the problems of life, and to avoid turning to deadly addictive drugs ("Put down the needle; put down the spoon"). It is essentially his late twentieth-century adaptation of Jesus' "Beatitudes," as found in Matthew 5. Prince uses the short harmonic pattern F major, C major, G major throughout most of the phrases of the verses. This triadic harmonic lends a hymn-like or anthem-like quality to the piece, as does the slow tempo. The descending fourth sequence of major triads (C is the interval of a perfect fourth lower than F; G is a perfect fourth lower than C) is found in countless late 1960s rock songs. Therefore, even though the song is fundamentally different in style than most of the rest of the songs on *Emancipation* (which lean in the direction of R&B), it shares a retro feel with many of the album's songs. The melodic phrases are simple and most feature short descending lines. Prince's arrangement and production makes use of electric guitar, keyboards, and strings, all of which play occasional responses to the vocal melody. These unpredictable instrumental answers give the piece an ever-evolving feel, despite the fact that the harmony and melody are so full of internal repetition. In short, "The Love We Make" shares big rock ballad attributes with such earlier well-known anthem-like hits as the Beatles' "Hey Jude," Foreigner's "I Want to Know What Love Is," and Prince's own "Purple Rain." Since "The Love We Make" was not released as a single, it is not nearly as well known as those earlier hits. And, because the late 1960s musical style might have seemed dated, there is no guarantee that the song would have been successful had it been featured as a single. It does, however, stand as one of Prince's best rock ballads and is one of his few songs to so clearly tie together his religious faith and social concerns.

The album's closer, "Emancipation," is a straightforward R&B-style song that delivers (in different words) the message contained in the liner notes for the song, "True freedom takes place in the spirit." Unfortunately, the music is not as memorable as Prince's best work, causing the album to end musically a bit on a down note.

Emancipation presents the listener with much to consider. Prince explores sexuality, relationships, spirituality, friendship, the effects of technology on interpersonal relationships, all mixed in with some dance tracks, and meticulous covers of songs that had been hits for others. Clearly, Prince felt emancipated by means of his newfound control over his career: he could record and release what he wanted, and as many songs as he wanted. But, that is part of the challenge for the listener: *Emancipation* contains nearly 3 hours of music, exploring several lyrical themes, and sometimes jumping abruptly from one theme and musical style to another. As a collection of new compositions and covers, the listener who is most interested in individual songs will find much in *Emancipation* that stands up well to repeated hearings. As a concept album, *Emancipation* is a challenge, mostly because it makes sense once one puts the whole thing together; it's just that there is so much material. The listener that takes the time to listen to the entire album and really think about what it all means probably will conclude that Prince spends two-thirds of the time exploring different ideas about what might constitute "emancipation." These include some that he will eventually dismiss, but he gives each consideration, because they are all part of contemporary society. Sexuality for its own sake, material wealth, love, friendship, pursuing celebrity, partying, and giving oneself over to God are all means that Prince sees people around him turning to for emancipation. The theme of romantic love and all that comes with it (e.g., sexuality and procreation) gets a lot of attention, so the message seems to be that God is found through these kinds of human relationships. Prince never counters this. He does, however, eventually reject the idea of the accumulation of material wealth and power for its own sake as a form of fulfillment/salvation/emancipation. He does the same, albeit less emphatically, with reliance on technology. The last three songs on the album, though, find Prince concluding that ultimately it is one's faith in and relationship with God that brings fulfillment/salvation/ emancipation. It takes a long time for that conclusion to emerge, and *Emancipation* is not a linear path—given the juxtaposition of divergent musical styles and lyrical themes—by any means. It is a journey that is worth taking, although it is easy to image that many listeners will be more likely to pick and chose individual songs that they like from the album.

CRYSTAL BALL

Releasing one triple-CD album is unusual enough in the recording industry. To follow such a collection up with a quadruple-CD set was unprecedented when Prince's *Crystal Ball* appeared in 1998. Actually, the four-disc set really consists of a three-CD collection of previously unreleased songs and alternative versions/outtakes of songs that did make it onto Prince's albums (*Crystal Ball*), and a one-disc set of new material (*The Truth...*). This all makes for some confusion, since the whole set of four discs is packaged together with no reference to a distinction between the three-disc set and the one-disc set on the outer labeling of the package's box. At the risk of adding to the confusion, in the discussion that follows, I will refer to the three-CD set as *Crystal Ball* and to the one-CD set as *The Truth...*, as though it constitutes a separate album. Since *The Truth...* is packaged along with *Crystal Ball*, I have not included a separate entry for it in the discography at the end of this book. Compounding the confusion about exactly how the listener is supposed to deal with more than 3 hours worth of material on four compact discs, Prince labels each of the discs of the *Crystal Ball* part of the package as "bootlegs." Actually, maybe that clears things up a bit: one might best understand *Crystal Ball* (the three-disc collection, remember) as a new version of *The Black Album;* that is, a collection of material some of which had already been circulating on bootlegs that was now receiving its official release. Indeed, some of these tracks had been around on the musical black market for years. Because Prince treats the two collections differently—*Crystal Ball* is the casual collection that is not necessarily meant to hang together as a single artist statement, which *The Truth...* is—I will treat them differently in the following discussion, examining the "official" material of *The Truth...* in more detail than the "bootleg" material of *Crystal Ball.*

Considering that some fans anticipated that *Crystal Ball* would somehow represent Prince's great "lost album": the legendary three-disc set that was shortened to produce *Sign o' the Times,* it is surprising that so much of the *Crystal Ball* that Prince released in 1998 was devoted to New Power Generation–style hardcore funk and hip-hop. Such is not the case with the title track, which leads off the album. The song "Crystal Ball" includes elements of avant-garde electronica, contemporary jazz, rock, R&B, lots of tempo and metrical changes. By combining these disparate styles, and by sometimes smoothly connecting them and sometimes abruptly cutting from one style to another, Prince creates an aural image of the swirling, nonlinear images that the seer perceives in his or her crystal ball. It is one of Prince's most complex single compositions to have seen commercial release, albeit in the context of this official so-called bootleg.

Several of the selections that Prince chose to include on *Crystal Ball* are clearly pieces that were discarded in favor of the compositions that did make it onto his albums of the late 1980s through the mid-1990s. "Dream Factory" is one such piece. Others, such as "Acknowledge Me," are more successful—because they incorporate more interesting music and arrangements and more focused lyrics. "Acknowledge Me," in fact, probably would have fit in well with Prince's songs of identity on "The Love Symbol Album."

In the present song, he asks a woman who won't give him the time of day to at least acknowledge him, but the sense of recognition that Prince demands aligns with the recognition of self of his early work with the New Power Generation. The heavy use of hip-hop style in the piece, in fact, practically screams "New Power Generation."

Another particularly interesting piece, "What's My Name," sounds—at least from its title—as though it should follow in the "Acknowledge Me," "My Name Is Prince" identity mold. And, to some extent it does. Prince speaks—not raps—all the vocal lines. His lyrics are somewhat hazy, impressionistic, and open to some interpretation, but basically he encounters a person who is completely fixated on name as image. The premise behind the piece is that someone's name is not necessarily the essence of who the person is, and that our prejudices can cloud our view of the reality of someone's true identity on a human level. Because of the focus on identity, the composition would have fit in nicely with "My Name Is Prince," "Sexy M.F.," and the other songs of identity of "The Love Symbol Album." It also functions as a sort of why-I-did-it piece that explains Prince's need to change his name to a symbol. As significant as the piece may be as a semiautobiographical statement, though, the real interest is in the musical combination of hard rock and R&B. The hard-edged musical setting is as no-frills/minimalistic as the lyrics. The combination of Prince's quiet, well-back-in-the-mix speaking, hard minimalistic (almost punk) rock with a few hip-hop rhythmic touches creates a truly raw, visceral, from-the-guts atmosphere. "What's My Name," although quite different in character from "Sexual Suicide," is one of the lost classics from the late 1980s through mid-1990s period that deserves to be better known.

Perhaps because of the fact that Prince is so prolific as a songwriter, most of the songs on *Crystal Ball* fall into the previously unreleased—the one notable example of an alternate version of a previously issued song is "P Control." It is most interesting to compare the version of the song that had been released in 1995 on *The Gold Experience* with *Crystal Ball*'s alternate version. First of all, the two represent pretty much exactly the same piece, at least from the standpoint of music and lyrics. The contrast between the two versions comes from the different vocal approaches and from the different arrangements and production. While the contrast is not necessarily huge—at least from the standpoint of individual components—the effect of the two pieces is entirely different.

The Gold Experience version of "P Control" combines elements of a sexist putdown of women who use their sexuality to control men with an acknowledgement of female empowerment. The overall feel of the song is that Prince (or his character) sees pros and cons from this empowerment. It is a complex mix, and decidedly not one-sided. The *Crystal Ball* version of "P Control" sounds more like either a sexist, almost misogynistic, putdown of female empowerment, or a parody of hip-hop style—it feels decidedly less balanced than the other version. The vocals sound nastier, partly because of performance (the touch of humor in Prince's inflection is missing) and partly because of the production mix (the mix is not as clear and clean on *Crystal Ball*). The *Crystal Ball* instrumentation is more minimalistic (less pop-ish, if you will), with stronger, more bass drum–oriented percussion, fewer pop-sounding synthesizer lines. Prince's *Crystal Ball* mix also includes some decidedly over-the-top scratching effects. These effects are so exaggerated that the piece becomes almost a parody of some of the stereotypical elements of hip-hop, including turntable playing (scratching) and misogynistic lyrics. This rendition of "P Control," then, does not feel as much like a mix of complex, real emotions that a man might feel as it feels like either a hopelessly anti-empowerment putdown or an over-the-top parody of hip-hop. In either case, it as not as interesting or rich in meaning as the "P Control" of *The Gold Experience*.

One of the more noteworthy songs on *Crystal Ball* is "Sexual Suicide," a piece that had achieved something of a legendary lost classic status among some Prince fans. The song finds Prince addressing a lover who has "taken a walk" away from Prince's character—she has left him—which causes him to decide that he is going to "take a sexual suicide." Ultimately, though, at the very end of the song, Prince concludes "you take a walk; we can talk." This suggests that rather than write off the relationship completely ("take a sexual suicide"), he has taken her rather pointed hint to heart and now is willing to discuss and compromise. What really drives this composition, however, and what makes it a Prince classic, is the music. The upbeat, funky setting suggests absolutely none of the angst (and if Prince's character *really* is considering literally committing suicide, he must feel *some* angst about the state of the relationship) expressed in the lyrics. The upbeat feel to the music, in fact, makes the lyrical sentiments sound like unbelievable hyperbole, at least until the listener focuses in on the details of Prince's arrangement. The brief, dissonant descending figures in the synthesizers hint at the character's angst; however, the horn fills and dance-oriented rhythmic syncopation suggest hope. Prince's multitracked vocals, his use of unusual tone colors in the synthesizers, and the unexpected background instrumental figures make it a highly effective piece for the listener that is attracted to sonic variety.

Generally Prince's *The Truth*…is the closest thing that he has released to an acoustic, or unplugged-style, album. None of the songs fully reach the level of sounding like live, nonoverdubbed recordings, but the production is remarkably spare for a Prince album. The contrast with the full hip-hop thump and scratching of *Crystal Ball*'s New Power Generation pieces, as well as with the complexities, expansive nature, and lyrical ambiguities of pieces such as "Crystal Ball" and "Cloreen Bacon Skin" is stark. It is easy for the listener to get the sense that either Prince has entered a new stylistic period, or at the very least, that he must take the message of the songs of *The Truth*…very seriously to create arrangements and production that focuses like none of Prince's previous recordings of the 1990s. So, the entire four-disc package includes the extremes: one tightly focused album that found Prince continuing to more precisely define his mature philosophy of life, and one massive outpouring of songs. Although there was no way for fans to know it in 1998, the focus that Prince took with *The Truth*...did indeed define a new approach; each of his subsequent albums, right up to the 2007 release *Planet Earth,* have been single-disc collections. That *The Truth*...is as acoustically based as it is quite noteworthy. There have been relatively few live Prince recordings available legitimately, and Prince is so highly skilled as a producer and so adept at using drum machines, sequencers, and multitrack recording that it is easy to lose sight of his abilities as an instrumentalist and singer. Certainly, his work is not all about skillful use of the technological resources of the recording studio, but it is very easy to misperceive his music that way. The available live recordings (such as "Purple Rain" on the *Purple Rain* soundtrack album) and his work in a (for want of a better word) "thinner" context such as that of *The Truth*...shows him to be a sensitive, technically skilled, multifaceted musician, and not just a skillful user of the studio.

Many of the songs of this album within an album deal with real human emotions and the quest for the meaning of life in a more serious tone than any of Prince's previous songs. The opening track, "The Truth," for example, finds Prince searching for the meaning of life and concluding that the ultimate question that will determine how one's life is assessed is if one gives more than one takes. The texture consists entirely of Prince and his guitar: no studio gimmickry, no extensive overdubbing, and minimal effects and other production ambience. This gives the piece a very personal feel. In fact, one of the criticisms that can be leveled at some of Prince's later serious religious music—such as the songs of *The Rainbow Children*—is that they exist too much in a pop music world that conflicts too greatly with the significance of the words. That does not happen in "The Truth." Prince uses a modified version of standard blues form. The texture and the casual approach to the form connects clearly to the rural blues of pioneering artists such as Robert Johnson. The synthesizer effects—especially those that Prince incorporates at the end of the song—are eerie and add to the apocalyptical, St. Peter-at-the-pearly-gates feel of the piece; however, they are totally unnecessary. This is a piece that fits perfectly within the blues/folk conception of the solo singer-songwriter accompanied solely by a guitar.

In "The Truth" and in many of the other songs in this set Prince does not deliver a radically different message than in his previous religious songs, at least in lyrics alone. What he does is to change the entire *gestalt* of the message by setting it to this more deeply personal-sounding music. It is almost as though a song such as "The Truth" is the embodiment of what Prince alluded to back in his early 1990s song "My Name Is Prince," in which he told the listener in no uncertain terms that he uses rhythmic dance music to pull the listener into serious messages. As an aside, this is akin to what the theologian Martin Luther advocated when he adopted popular melodies of his day—including such things as drinking songs—for the basis of the early Lutheran chorales. What Prince has done in "The Truth" is to cut the ties to rhythmic dance music. It is as though he now expects the listener to accept the religious/philosophical message more on its own terms and not because one can dance to it. On a personal level, I feel that it works effectively. One issue that some listeners, myself included, have with contemporary Christian music, and especially hard rock and punk rock that delivers a message of faith, is that the combination of the visceral and the spiritual, the sacred and the profane—pick your metaphor—can confuse the true meaning of the song. The academic discipline of rhetoric informs us that this true meaning comes from studying the author, the audience, and the text itself. In the case of song, the "text" would include not just the lyrics, but also the musical setting, instrumentation, style, and so on. If one further defines the piece as a specific recording of a song, one would need to take into consideration the recording mix, studio effects, perhaps even the album artwork to contextualize the piece and determine its meaning. "The Truth" finds Prince aligning words, music, tempo, texture, performance style, and production more closely than in just about any of his earlier religiously based work; therefore, the so-called true meaning is easier to determine.

The next song, "Don't Play Me," has an autobiographical, confessional feel. Again with minimal accompaniment, singer-songwriter Prince identifies himself as an over-thirty abstainer from drugs. Perhaps it is a minor point, but if he were to be entirely autobiographically accurate, he would need to bump his age up a tad. In any case, he tells the woman he addresses not to "play him." Prince allows the phrase to emerge in a triple meaning: don't play his music (if just to criticize it), don't try to fool him, and don't try to get him interested in sex. He also suggests that some people might not accept him because he plays the guitar and that his only competition as a guitarist was long ago. While this may be vague enough to apply possibly to any number of dead electric guitarists, it is very easy for the listener to read Jimi Hendrix into this reference. Like Hendrix, Prince has confounded critics and those in the white and in the black communities who would try to pigeonhole musicians into what some suggest are appropriate race-based musical genres. Hendrix and Prince are the clearest examples of guitar virtuosi who bridged the gap between so-called black music (R&B) and so-called white music (rock). In other words, the song is a putdown of critics, groupies, hangers-on—in short, anyone who will not accept Prince for who and what he is. Like "The Truth," "Don't Play Me" steers clear of pop music's commercial hooks and dance rhythms. The absence of attention-grabbing hooks in the arrangement, too, serves to give the lyrics an air of more importance in the overall *gestalt* of the piece, as well as allowing those lyrics to always be the listener's focus. Also, like successful songs of the urban folk tradition (Bob

Dylan through Richie Havens in the 1960s, and the early 1970s proponents of the singer-songwriter movement), the melody has a natural, easy-to-remember flow.

The song "Circle of Amour" moves a little further from the rural folk ("The Truth") and urban folk ("Don't Play Me") traditions, but finds Prince maintaining the primarily acoustic feel of the album's first two tracks. Because of Prince's use of added note chords and harmonic suspensions there is a richer harmonic feel to the track than what one might ordinarily expect to find in folk music. There is a stronger jazz and pop basis to this song, compared with the first couple of tracks of the collection. The lyrics, too, find Prince moving away from the expression of his feelings and autobiography to playing the role of observer. To the light jazzy accompaniment he recounts the story of four high school girls—Mary, Claire, Denise, and Belle—who form the Circle of Amour of the song's title. This high school "gang of four" becomes involved with sexual experimentation and use of the drug Ecstasy. Prince's character remembers the group fondly all these years after tenth grade; however, there is a hint of the tragic in his account of the girls. He suggests that the "vicious race to maturity" made them losers "at the circle game."

Prince begins the song "3rd Eye" with a guitar solo that, while it does not quite stretch the bounds of traditional tonality, includes some biting dissonance. This is notable because, as experimental as Prince has been with musical form, lyrical content, and mixing of genres, he typically has followed in the traditions of the R&B, rock, hip-hop, and pop harmonic vocabulary of the past. Even his instrumental, more jazz-oriented compositions and performances general eschew more than occasional use of biting harmonic dissonance. When Prince does use dissonance to create harmonic tension, he usually uses it to tie in with the lyrics. Such is the case with "3rd Eye." Here, Prince tells the Book of Genesis story of the fall of Adam and Eve, comparing it with the situation in which his character finds himself—a woman is trying to lead him astray. Prince concludes that, ultimately, each person is responsible to save himself or herself, because "God is inside and for that God you will do whatever it takes." After the dissonant, stylistically vague introduction, the rest of the song is harmonically static on the tonic chord and reflects touches of the rural blues that Prince had used at the opening of *The Truth*...

The song "Dionne" clearly draws upon the long tradition of the rhythmic, harmonic, and melodic influence of music of the Caribbean and South America on music in the United States. In particular, the jazz-inspired added-note chords, the mix of harmonic *ostinato* with sophisticated chromatic harmony, and the extensive use of the upper notes of the harmonies for primary melodic notes all suggest that the piece falls in the continuum from the 1950s and 1960s *bossa nova* of Antonio Carlos Jobim, to the slightly later work of Gaetano Veloso, and other Brazilian musicians. There are clear links to the Caribbean, too: in particular, the synthesized steel drum effects in the first verse. Despite the outward links to Caribbean and Brazilian music, however, Prince's character sings to a woman, Dionne, that he loved from afar, never tried to become closer to, and as a result, lost. While the piece is not one of Prince's strongest musical compositions (his best pieces tend to have at least one particularly strong—often idiosyncratic—musical or lyrical hook, and "Dionne" sounds like it could have been written by any one of a host of composers), it finds him portraying a character with a sexual innocence and vulnerability that pretty much fell out of Prince's repertoire in the 1980s. As such, "Dionne" allows the listener to decompress, as it provides contrast with the blues-inspired and rhetorically more forceful religious songs on *The Truth*....

"Man in a Uniform" also is not as successful as the best pieces on *The Truth*...; however, it finds Prince moving into a fundamentally different direction with regard to his treatment of sex. The story concerns Prince's character and his lover, who has a fetish about men in uniform. She tells Prince's character that his clothes just do not excite her as much. She wants, however, to make love with him with the same intensity that she would reserve for a man in uniform. Prince includes some fairly obvious code for some of the specific sex acts (cunnilingus, most obviously) in which the woman would like to engage. Regardless of how one feels about oral sex, the way in which the woman refers to it here makes it particularly unappealing. While some of Prince's earlier songs had revolved around oral sex and around fetishes, never before in his output had sex for physical pleasure left a character (Prince's) so torn between excitement and repulsion. It is almost as though the focus on sex as lovemaking and sex as procreation on *Emancipation*—possibly as well as Prince's own marriage—had rendered the concept of sex as a legitimate expression and result of mere physical lust obsolete. Prince's character has encountered a woman who proposes sex that comes off as sleazy and utterly distasteful. Unfortunately, the composition is not one of Prince's most memorable pieces of music, and the metrically off-kilter synthesizer references to the bugle tune "Charge" are such a stereotypical musical caricature of a "man in a uniform" as to be rendered ineffective. The synthesizer's tone color is pretty cheesy sounding, to boot. That not withstanding, it is important for the student of Prince's progression as a lyricist to note the fundamental change that this song represents in Prince's approach to sex. This change, as well as the very title of this album within an album, suggests that the ultimate importance of *Crystal Ball* is that it finds Prince tying up loose ends from the first part of his career (discs 1–3) and showing his fans that he had made a commitment to delivering a message to which only some of his early work had fully realized.

The ambient white noise and extended synthesizer tones that introduce "Animal Kingdom" provide a sense of foreboding and expectation. The song itself features Prince utilizing a vocal harmonizer in the verses. The resulting harsh, machine-like tone color contrasts with the unmanipulated vocal setting of the chorus. And, this all serves a rhetorical purpose. "Animal Kingdom" is Prince's first obviously vegetarian-related song. In the verses, where his voice sounds very deliberately unnatural, Prince deliberates about why people eat animals, drink animal milk, and eat dairy products. In the chorus, he concludes that "no member of the animal kingdom nurses past maturity" and that he has no reason to do harm to any animal, because no animal has ever done harm to him. So, the tone color of the voice illustrates what for Prince is the contrast between the unnaturalness of humans as carnivore with the naturalness of the life in the animal kingdom. It is a little too contrived sounding to be truly effective as a way of encouraging Prince's carnivorous listeners to reevaluate their relationship with animals and their role in the food chain.

Prince turns to the familiar topics of love and passion in "The Other Side of the Pillow." He tells his lover that she is "as cool as the other side of the pillow," and "as bad as Bonnie when she ran with Barrow"—a reference to the outlaws Bonnie and Clyde. Interestingly, Prince's description of the intensity of the couple's lovemaking is decidedly more oblique and metaphorical than in his more graphic songs of the 1970s through the mid-1990s. For example, in this song he says that his lover uses "furniture in new ways." The listener may read whatever he or she likes into this phrase, in contrast to the more obvious sexual references in most of his earlier work. This more metaphorical approach matches the musical setting—a combination of shuffle blues and doo wop—beautifully.

Prince has never explored electronic avant-garde music or minimalism to the extent of some other pop musicians, such as Stevie Wonder on *Journey through the Secret Life of Plants* (1979) or David Bowie on *Low* (1977) and "*Heroes*" (1977), but it is interesting to note that several of the songs of *The Truth*...begin with atmospheric electronic introductions. Given the generally acoustical nature of the album, these brief experimental segues stand out. "Fascination" begins with approximately 23 seconds of dissonant, atonal electronic music that suggests an even greater feeling of foreboding than the introduction of "Animal Kingdom." The song's text moves toward impressionism. Prince incorporates disconnected images as he addresses someone who, despite the fact that the person abuses drugs and focuses entirely on the pleasures of the pop life—the very same lifestyle Prince first described in the song "Pop Life"—still fascinates him. This connects "Fascination" with "Man in a Uniform," another track in which Prince explores the yin and yang of fascination and revulsion. His music for the track plays on this dialectic. The piece is a quick tempo, Latin jazz-influenced piece: something that is infinitely danceable. In several sections, however, the mood turns more sinister, as Prince turns from harmonized singing to speaking and the instrumental lines simultaneously move away from the prevailing key area. In some respects—even though the tempo and texture is quite different— "Fascination" is a retelling of Santana's "Black Magic Woman," but with a lot more musical variety that mimics the push and pull of evil. Prince's character toys with the metaphorical devil, rejects the temptation, but still feels it in the back of his mind and heart.

Because of the fact that "One of Your Tears" follows "Fascination" it is tempting to understand the two works as partners. In "Fascination," Prince's character rejects the pop life that someone else (possibly, but not necessarily, his lover) lives, and in "One of Your Tears" he describes the circumstances and feelings that followed the breakup. Apparently, the breakup was not pretty, because all Prince's character received as a firm acknowledgment of its end was a used condom in the mail. His character obviously is heartbroken at the thought of another man making love to the woman and wishes he "could die and come back as one of [her] tears." It is important to note that at the beginning of the song, Prince mentions to his former lover that he is sending his feelings along on a tape. This song very much resembles a taped letter, because it resists feeling like a conventionally structured verse, chorus, middle-eight pop song. It is not completely through composed, but the chorus is little more than a single tag line, and the verses have a meandering melody that suggests off-the-cuff expression of extreme hurt in an unedited letter. The easy paced R&B style of the accompaniment is more commonly associated with songs of a more formulaic structure, so the loose feel of "One of Your Tears" is striking.

The next track, "Comeback," extends the theme of the previous two songs. Now, however, more time apparently has passed, and the mood of Prince's character has turned to sorrow mixed with some nostalgia. The melody of the verses has a singsong quality, which supports the resigned, yet nostalgic feel of the piece. The first two phrases of this melody are based on a descending sequence. The first phrase moves from repetitions of the pitch E, to F-sharp and then D. Prince follows this with repetitions of D, which moves to E and then C-sharp. The problem is that a descending sequence based on a repeated note that moves up a step and then drops the interval of a third is not especially original sounding. For example, it bears more than a passing resemblance to the verse of the Canadian band Klaatu's song "Sub Rosa Subway" (1976), and to the verse of a duet sung by the characters Holling and Shelly Vincouer in an early 1990s episode of the television program *Northern Exposure*. Prince performs the Boyz II Men–ish multitracked vocal harmonies impeccably, so if one does not identify the motive in the verse with Klaatu or with *Northern Exposure,* the song works very well.

The strong sense of song-to-song continuity extends to the album's final track "Welcome 2 the Dawn." In the context of the previous three songs, it is easy to understand the application of Prince's message here to broken relationships. To paraphrase, when all hope is gone, "welcome 2 the dawn." In other words, just when things seem to have gotten as bad as they can, that is when one will feel a divine presence that will bring about the metaphorical *dawn.* Prince's message does not, however, just suggest that the listener rely on prayer and the divine presence in times of trouble. He also tells the listener that sometimes the Almighty will offer other kinds of messages when they are least expected. The lyrical sentiments not only bring the story that seemed to be unfolding over the course of the previous three songs to a conclusion, but they also bring back the theme that Prince established on the album's opening track: that God is the only answer to salvation in this life and in the afterlife. Perhaps it makes *The Truth*...sound too formulaic, but the same kind of connection can be heard between the monologue that precedes "Let's Go Crazy" and the song "Purple Rain" on the *Purple Rain* soundtrack album. And, indeed, "Welcome 2 the Dawn" exhibits some of the anthem-like feel of "Purple Rain." Of course, the song "Purple Rain" is one of Prince's best-known compositions and performances; however, in some respects the (what Prince labels) acoustic version of "Welcome 2 the Dawn" on *The Truth*...is a more effective religious and philosophical statement, mostly because the lyrics are more focused.

The music of "Welcome 2 the Dawn" also lends great strength to the entire feel of the piece. The melody—like that of "Purple Rain"—is easy to sing, easy to remember, with strong hooks. The harmonic progression includes some tasty added-note chords, but stays entirely within the pop harmonic vocabulary. As the song nears its conclusion, Prince references the modal/Hindustani scale material that he had used back in the 1980s on *Around the World in a Day*. To the extent that the listener feels the connection to Hindustani music—and it is nowhere near as obvious as it is in, say, a whole collection of songs by George Harrison—and to the extent that the listener associates Hindustani music with higher-level philosophy, one can feel Prince enforcing his lyrical message with this concluding touch of musical mysticism.

The Truth...arguably is one of the handful of top Prince albums to date. Because of the straightforward nature of much of the writing, arrangements, and production, most of the songs sound personal. While in the past Prince has sometimes effectively used almost a machine-like, deliberately disinterested-sounding approach to snap the listener into putting his or her full attention on the message ("Annie Christian" is the best example), on the songs of *The Truth*...he turns much more to the singer-songwriter, confessional-sounding approach. Perhaps equally important, *The Truth*...contains more song-to-song connections and easily traceable song-by-song progressions of mood than any previous Prince album. Even Prince's best-received albums, *Purple Rain* and *Sign o' the Times*, do not feature album-length shape, progression, and connection nearly to the extent of *The Truth*....The high quality and personal-sounding nature of the album begs the question, "Why bury it within a four-disc set, three-quarters of which consists of outtakes that didn't make the grade the first time around?" While the decision to package *The Truth*...as a bonus disc in the *Crystal Ball* collection may have limited its availability, it does provide the listener with a sense of the four-disc set as a career crossroads: the three official so-called bootleg discs seem to tie up the loose ends of Prince's New Power Generation era, and the bonus *The Truth*…disc suggests a new phase. As mentioned previously, this makes the lyrics of the early 1990s song "My Name Is Prince" sound positively prophetic: he confesses to pull the listener in with his funky dance music and then delivers the serious message that is really his artistic *raison d'etre*. Prince returned to complex musical arrangements and production immediately after *The Truth*…, so the album did not represent the musical turning point that it may have seemed at the time of its release. Prince did, however, continue to explore religion more fully in his post-*Truth* albums than he did in his pre-*Truth* albums. *The Truth*…remains, though, his most concise, focused religious/philosophical album-length statement.

NEW POWER SOUL

Compared with Prince's new, confessional, folk/blues-oriented music on *The Truth*…, *New Power Soul* seems like a backwards step. The album reunites Prince with the New Power Generation. In fact, *New Power Soul* is credited as a New Power Generation album. Interestingly, Prince also alludes in at least one song to his music when he was working with the Revolution in the mid-1980s. On *New Power Soul*, though, Prince and the New Power Generation do not entirely turn back the pages of time to their albums of the early 1990s. Although the themes of dance and sex might bear some surface resemblance to the group's exploration of the themes on *The Gold Experience* and "The Love Symbol Album," there are some important differences here. On *New Power Soul* sex is always carefully linked with love. Sex purely for physical satisfaction, something that Prince and the New Power Generation worked into their earlier songs, has virtually vanished. Musically, all the essential components that made Prince and the New Power Generation's early work succeed are all here: the merger of rock, jazz, R&B, and hip-hop.

A feature of the New Power Generation's early work that is retained is the procedure of introducing the group as a dance music force early on each album. The song "My Name Is Prince," for example, set that tone on "The Love Symbol Album." This album's opener, "New Power Soul," does the same sort of thing. The potential problem with once again extolling the virtues of the band and its brand of music the same way is that it can come off as formulaic. This track is made more interesting than a cookie-cutter formula piece by means of some interesting musical touches, including the horn arrangement and the upward modulation (key change) approximately 3:30 into the recording. It just does not have the energy of the group's earlier dance work.

The next song, "Mad Sex," is one of the *New Power Soul* tracks that, on the surface, appears to represent a clear return to Prince and company's fixation on sex; the title suggests as much. The story, however, runs deeper than some of Prince's earlier sex-focused songs. The real meat of the lyrics lies in the relationship between Prince's character and the beautiful mulatto woman who excites him. It seems that they used to be lovers, and enjoyed "mad sex" quite frequently and in various rooms throughout the house. The relationship has now ended, yet she retains a firm hold on Prince's character's psyche and sexual desires. So, there is a touch of "P Control" here; however, "Mad Sex" is far less likely to be taken as a putdown of empowered women than "P Control." This is more clearly a one-on-one relationship issue song. Musically, "Mad Sex" is perhaps the best song on *New Power Soul*. Prince and the New Power Generation integrate R&B and jazz completely here. The composed horn and keyboard figures (as opposed to the improvisations) fit within the song's tonality, but include a number of disjunct intervals and notes that are deliberately at odds with the key. This matches the conflicted feelings of Prince's character without sounding like mere mimicry.

The next track, "Until U're in My Arms Again," continues the exploration of feelings that follow a broken relationship. This is a slow, soulful ballad in which Prince concludes that his life will never be complete until his beloved is "in [his] arms again." These are age-old sentiments in popular song, so it is possible to hear this piece as either derivative or retro, depending on the extent to which the listener likes the song. The music has a classic pop song structure: the melodic phrases within each verse balance well, with the first two phrases trending downward, and the final phrases moving into a higher range. The melody is easy to remember, and very singable. Prince incorporates several jazz-inspired added note and chromatic chords. These help to move the song away from sounding too much like a rehash of old soul clichés. "Until U're in My Arms Again" would seem to be the perfect soul ballad for other artists to cover. Prince sings it beautifully; however, to the extent that the listener believes that Prince's career has been built around quirky, highly individualistic songs, it does not seem like a Prince song. If one were to hear this performance out of the blue—especially without the context of Prince's exploration of 1960s and 1970s soul on *Emancipation*—one might have a difficult time accepting that something so universal and so traditional in structure and style was coming from Prince. It is an excellent example of Prince's adaptability as a writer and performer, especially his ability to fully integrate various popular music styles into his own compositional voice.

"When U Love Somebody" also has a classic soul feel to it. Prince portrays a character that is in love with a woman who seems not to realize the nature of his feelings. She treats him as a close friend and confidant. All the while she is telling him her tale of woe about another broken relationship, he secretly wishes that he were the one she loved. Like the overarching sentiments of the previous song, there is nothing new here; however, the craftsmanship is greater than in something that would immediately be dismissed as a rehash of older soul repertoire. Curiously, Prince incorporates phrase endings in the verse that come straight out of the verses of "Raspberry Beret." Like his exploration of age-old sentiments, this too is a dangerous move. If one is familiar with the older song from *Around the World in a Day,* it is possible to hear "When U Love Somebody" as a musical rehash of nearly 15-year-old material. I believe, however, that there is another reading of the ties between the two songs.

In the story of "Raspberry Beret," Prince's character becomes aroused by a scantily clad woman who walks "into old man Johnson's store." Clearly, he notices her before she notices him. In fact, it would seem that, because he invited her to go on a ride on his motorcycle, he made the first move, and that this first move allowed the relationship to move forward. In "When U Love Somebody," Prince's character is also the first to feel sexual attraction. In this case, though, he fails to make the first move and the woman never learns that he is attracted to, or in fact in love with, her. Instead, they become longtime friends and confidants, which leaves his character only partially fulfilled. If one views the two songs as companion pieces, "Raspberry Beret" suggests what can happen when one allows one's feelings to be made known after the initial meeting, and "When U Love Somebody" suggests what can happen when one keeps one's feelings hidden.

The next track, "Shoo-Bed-Ooh," is a very different kind of song about sexual relationships. Here, Prince and the NPG address a woman—quite possibly a prostitute—who manages to convince herself that she is happy, despite the fact that her life is defined by a series of sexual encounters that never come close to resembling love. As such, the song continues the theme of good sex being tied to love that Prince began to explore in earnest on *The Truth*...As had been the case in the song "Man in a Uniform," the sex here is so devoid of satisfaction—physical, emotional, or spiritual—that Prince makes it clear to the listener that, unlike his work earlier in the 1990s, he now can only glorify sex that is part of a loving relationship.

"Push It Up" is the kind of dance-oriented hip-hop song that populated *Crystal Ball.* It is not as interesting as the dance pieces on Prince and the New Power Generation's first two albums. This one feels like a rehash of a genre type without the novel feel of the better works in the style.

The song "Freaks on This Side" extols the virtues of the so-called new sound dished out by the New Power Generation. Songs of this type are a staple in R&B music. "Freaks on This Side" does not break any new ground from a writing standpoint within the genre, and the main instrumental riff is not strong enough to carry the song for nearly 6 minutes. The saxophone playing of Eric Leeds, however, is worth several hearings.

With such phrases as "I got the butter for your muffin," and a (for want of a better term) "make out" hip-hop–style tempo, it is clear that "Come On" is another of Prince's songs about sex. Unlike many of his earlier sex-related songs, however, "Come On" betrays a maturity. For one thing, Prince acknowledges that he is older than most of his would-be lover's suitors. For another, he tells the woman of his desires that he wants commitment ("wear my ring") rather than "a mistress." The distinction between sex as emotional commitment and sex as physical pleasure has been expressed more eloquently—and more musically satisfyingly—in earlier songs, such as "I Could Never Take the Place of Your Man." The melody of "Come On" gets a little too repetitious. However, the song is made interesting by the sense of maturity that one feels from the writing and from Prince's vocal performance.

The gentle, romantic ballad "The One" continues the themes of sexual responsibility and maturity. Here, Prince tells his lover in no uncertain terms that he is "not the one" who will leave her in the lurch or use her simply for his own physical pleasure. He tells her, rather, that he is "the one" who will treat her well, love her for who she is, and remain committed to her and her alone. Prince returns to one of his tried-and-true melodic techniques in this song: he follows repetitions of scale-step five with a descent down to the tonic pitch. He had made use of this technique on songs such as "Sign o' the Times." Unlike that earlier piece, here the repeated notes are in a fairly high part of Prince's vocal range, giving the vocal melody a sense of urgency. There is absolutely nothing about the lyrics as words on a page that suggests any sort of urgency; the feeling is generated entirely by the pitch range of the song. It is a case of the whole being greater than the sum of its parts. At a little more than 7 minutes in length, though, "The One" seems more like romantic background music than like a piece that is meant to be listened to in detail.

The album booklet for *New Power Soul* provides credits for just one more song: "(I [Eye] Like) Funky Music." Whatever mood might have been set on the previous couple of songs flies out the window with this up-tempo dance piece. The tune is catchy, the rhythm guitar part grooves with the best of funk guitarists. The concept of the let's-get-out-and-dance-and-get-funky groove piece is nothing new—there are such pieces from James Brown and Sly Stone in the 1960s, George Clinton in the 1970s, and Prince himself in the 1980s. Novelty, however, is not the sole attribute that maketh the successful pop tune. It may be an old-school genre piece, but "I Like Funky Music" shows that the New Power Generation could still establish a dance groove like no other band with which Prince worked.

Curiously, *New Power Soul* ends with an announced bonus track that follows a period of silence. Prince and the New Power Generation accomplish this silence by including several dozen extremely short blank tracks on the CD. Although this seems a little gimmicky, it is a welcome surprise when the bonus track finally sounds from the speakers. Despite its rather dubious unacknowledged status, "Wasted Kisses" adds significantly to the album.

New Power Soul does not seem to intend to deliver any grand messages. In fact, none of the songs seems philosophical at all, in contrast to *The Truth*....If one considers the songs in comparison to the work that Prince and the New Power Generation had done back in the early to mid-1990s, however, it is clear that the developing philosophical/religious outlook of Prince has become integrated into the earlier musical mix of jazz, hip-hop, and R&B that had defined these musicians' first work together. Unfortunately, the end result is a collection that, while fascinating in terms of Prince's evolution as a thematically based lyricist, lacks the cutting-edge feel that made Prince and New Power Generation's first couple of projects together so strong.

THE VAULT: OLD FRIENDS 4 SALE

Prince had stopped using his name after adopting the unpronounceable symbol that looks like a stylized combination of the male and female symbols. His old record label Warner Bros. had a fair number of recordings stored up from Prince's years on the label. In 1999, reportedly with Prince's permission, Warner Bros. released some of Prince's previously unissued material under his presymbol name. The resulting album, *The Vault: Old Friends 4 Sale*, provides a look at some of Prince's work from the 1985–1994 period. While the album contains no megahits, it does show a side of Prince's work not previously exhibited in Prince's self-released official bootlegs, such as the first three discs of *Crystal Ball*. Generally, the recordings of *The Vault* are more fully produced and orchestrated than the outtake material that Prince actually controlled. As a result, the music of *The Vault* seems to represent fully ready-to-go work that did not quite make the final cut on various Prince albums, and it makes collections such as *Crystal Ball* seem more like a collection of material that did not even make it to the ready-to-go stage. While it is not an essential Prince album, *The Vault* contains some music that deserves study and should be more familiar to Prince's fans because of what it suggests about his production and music selection work in putting together the final version of his albums.

As one listens to *The Vault*, it is important to keep in mind that in no way was it Prince's intention that this set of songs go together in one coherent collection. Therefore, any song-to-song connections—musical or thematic—are the result of the work of the compiler(s) at Warner Bros. The album begins with "The Rest of My Life," an under-2-minute song that seems like an experimentation with what a completed track might sound like. What I mean is that Prince includes many more tone colors, instrumental accompaniment figures, improvised solos, and texture changes than what one would usually hear in a 1:40 piece. An added verse, a little more extension to the instrumental solos, and the piece would have made a catchy, commercial album track for a variety of artists shopping around for material. The lyrics find Prince's character standing firm in the face of disappointment. His character decides that he will take life's challenges and disappoints in stride and will make "this day the first day of the rest of [his] life." Given the upbeat music, the song is one-dimensional in its optimism. Facing disappointments solely through one's sheer willpower is not always so easy; therefore, the piece as it stands seems too easy and too one-dimensional. Again, as it stands, all the texture changes in the accompaniment in such a short time make the track seem overproduced.

"It's about That Walk," at 4 ½ minutes, is considerably heftier, in that the song is more fully realized. This piece is upbeat and exhibits the clear influence of Smokey Robinson's writing and falsetto singing style. Robinson's well-known composition "The Way You Do the Things You Do," a song that was taken into the *Billboard* pop Top 40 by the Temptations, Rita Coolidge, Hall and Oates, and UB40, immediately comes to mind. The shuffle rhythm, melodic construction, and the rhetorical style—in which the attributes of the object of Prince's desire are enumerated—all pay more than a passing nod to the Robinson classic. "It's about That Walk" is more retro in nature than much of Prince's work of the late 1980s to early 1990s period—the period covered by *The Vault*. That, and its close connections to the essence of Smokey Robinson's classic, particularly the 1964 Temptations recording of it, probably explains why it remained unreleased. As an example of Prince "doing" Motown—with a little more sexual edge than what would have been found in 1964 Motown—it is a delightful genre study.

The song "She Spoke 2 Me" is one of the more interesting compositions on *The Vault*. Using his late 1970s falsetto, Prince sings about the excitement he feels because the woman to whom he is sexually attracted from afar actually spoke to him. It is a classic high school—or even junior high school—situation: the object of adolescent desire speaks to you, which sends you off into a hormone-surging "wet dream" (to quote the song). The melody, harmonic progression, and (especially) the horn writing are all catchy and hook-laden. The piece turns into an extended jazz-funk fusion piece partway through, which probably partially explains why the nearly 8 ½ minute-long piece was never previously released. The adolescent fantasy nature of the lyrics, too, just seem too far out of reach coming from Prince at this stage of his life. It is a song that would have fit perfectly on one of his first two albums, back in the late 1970s. The instrumentally focused section proves that guitarist Prince and his chosen bandmates were first-rate players, even on the recordings that did not make the final cut.

The next song, "5 Women +," includes many of the same sonic attributes of "She Spoke 2 Me." In particular, the muted trumpets and the horn arrangement suggest that the two songs were probably intended to be companions. Here, Prince sings of a lover he just cannot forget. As he sings, "it took five women to get [her] off [his] mind." Unfortunately for Prince's character, he spotted his former lover again and it only took "five minutes" for the old flame to be rekindled. Prince's character then recounts the details of some of the women that he had (frankly) used to get his former lover out of his mind. Some, he cannot even remember their first names. This is a classic R&B-style tale of the struggle a man goes through to recover from a failed relationship. On one level, it might seem sexist (Prince's character does use the "5+" women), but there is a sadness to the situation that speaks of the profound emptiness that drove him in his ultimately unsuccessful pursuits. Because it is so much a piece about self-definition, explaining a character's state, and trying to justify his choices, lyrically "5 Women +" fits in with the identity songs Prince wrote and recorded with the New Power Generation around the time of his break with Warner Bros.

The music of "5 Women +" makes abundant reference to blues and jazz. Like the arrangement on "She Spoke 2 Me," the mainstream jazz nature of the horn writing is more elaborate, more focused on subtle changes of tone color, and more indebted to past tradition than what one would typically hear in the pop and R&B music of the period. This can make both songs seem either heavy handed, or sophisticated, depending on the level of appreciation the listener has for the subtlety of the writing.

The next track, "When the Lights Go Down," is just over 7 minutes long, and Prince's vocals do not enter until approximately the 2:30 mark. The introduction is an instrumental groove over a minimal *ostinato* harmonic pattern that features some great solo piano licks. Prince contrasts the mating rituals of pickups in bars ("what's your sign") with the lovemaking that "true lovers do" "when the lights go down." The last couple of minutes of the piece features more extended piano and electronic keyboard solos. The emphasis on the instrumentals probably more than anything else explains the song's unreleased status. In addition, the extensive use of harmonic *ostinato,* while common in salsa and other Latin music, gets a little tiresome for the fan of the 3-minute song. This is a composition that seems to be aimed more at the enjoyment of the players and aficionados of instrumental jazz than Prince's traditional fan base.

The song "My Little Pill" weighs in at just longer than 1 minute in length, quite short in the world of post–World War II popular music. Art song composers of the past have written songs of this length, but always as parts of collections that usually were meant to be performed together. This particular piece, however, is little more than a backing track with a heavy lidded recitation of a two-stanza poem over the top. Prince's poem about a pill that makes all of life's difficulties go away is reminiscent of the theme of the Rolling Stones' "Mother's Little Helper." Even more than the first track on *The Vault,* this piece seems like a sketch of an idea that somehow never was completely developed.

The next song, "There Is Lonely," also could be expanded beyond its 2 ½ minutes; however, this is much more like a completed production than "My Little Pill." Prince makes a rare reference to minor key Spanish-influenced music. The melody has a natural-sounding rise and fall within a narrow range, which makes it easy to remember. The lyrics find Prince's character in a profound state of loneliness, remarking that the biblical Cain, when he murdered his brother, was probably the only other human to have ever experienced such loneliness. The hyperbole works pretty well in this case—mostly because the sentiments are so well supported by the music—but the piece probably needed a little more development (such as a middle eight section) in order to be truly complete.

Had a song such as "There Is Lonely" actually made the final cut and appeared on a Prince album, it would have had a natural companion in the form of the song "Old Friends 4 Sale." Here, Prince deals with friendships and love relationships that ended because of lying, cheating, unfaithfulness, and drug addiction. It is natural precursor to "There Is Lonely." Musically, it is one of Prince's more intriguing pieces from the period. He references the jazz standard/torch song tradition and includes a full big band with strings orchestration that would serve as a fitting backdrop for a film or television production of one of Raymond Chandler's short stories and novels of the 1930s and 1940s that starred the hard-nosed detective Philip Marlowe. The orchestration—fittingly for a Marlowe-esque genre piece—is heavy handed. The piece, though, shows Prince's wide musical range and his often hidden ties to mid-twentieth-century jazz. Prince has dealt with the evils of drug abuse and the importance of loyalty in other songs scattered throughout his career; this one is most unique because of the old-school bluesy jazz musical style.

Throughout his career Prince has recorded songs that sound as if they are just examples of him having fun in the studio. For example, on his most recent album, *Planet Earth*, the song "Guitar" is an old-fashioned rock and roll attitude piece that finds the pushing-fifty Prince playing a role probably more likely to be associated with a twenty-something character. The song "Sarah" plays a similar role. This ode to a miniskirted hot babe features similarly hot guitar and horn section licks, as well as a few lyrical jokes. Musically, it is a cross between Rick James's "Super Freak" and old late 1960s James Brown funk. The liner notes to *The Vault* suggest that the recordings therein were made for personal use (of Prince) and never intended for public release. "Sarah" is the one song for which that description seems most appropriate. It is a killer track, but just could not have worked on any of Prince's albums from the period covered by *The Vault*, except maybe for his late 1980s releases.

The Vault concludes with "Extraordinary," a gentle R&B love ballad that is not by any means the strongest song of the set. The short rhyming lines are a little awkward at times and the melody wanders a little more than Prince's tightest, catchiest tunes. For a lesser artist, "Extraordinary" would have made a workable album cut, but for Prince it is an outtake.

So, why would Prince, an artist who waged a very public battle with Warner Bros., claimed that he was a slave to the company, stopped using his name because of what he apparently thought was Warner's ownership of him, allow his estranged former record label to release *The Vault* and credit the album to "Prince"? Perhaps, because the material is so strong—much of it considerably stronger and more diverse in style than the previously unreleased material from the first three discs of *Crystal Ball*. Most interestingly, *The Vault* chronicles a particularly important time in Prince's artistic development. Here, he is heard leaving behind the psychedelia of his Revolution phase and heading into his more R&B, jazz, and hip-hop–oriented New Power Generation phase. From time to time in these songs, there is a strong sense of connection to the work Prince did at the very start of his solo career. All of this suggests a grappling with how Prince is trying to redefine himself as an artist. While *The Vault* is not an essential Prince album for most listeners, hardcore fans probably will find this collection of songs—nearly, if not ready for prime time—fascinating listening. There may be no true blockbusters, but it is anything but an album of dogs. In fact, "There Is Lonely" and "Sarah" are a couple of the best examples ever of Prince having fun and experimenting with arrangements in the studio. And, any fan who doubts Prince's indebtedness to and understanding of jazz will find this album particularly illuminating.

Rave Un2 the Joy Fantastic

When a musician not generally known for bringing in a lot of celebrity guest artists on albums suddenly does so, it can raise suspicions. Prince's 1999 album, *Rave Un2 the Joy Fantastic,* his first on the Arista label, was such an album. Was the inclusion of rapper Chuck D., guitarist Ani Difranco, singer-songwriter Sheryl Crow, and James Brown's ace saxophonist Maceo Parker, and others, a desperation move? It would seem to have been done at the suggestion of Arista boss Clive Davis, the man who had overseen the reemergence of guitarist and Prince influence Carlos Santana. The guest artists seem to have given Prince some sort of inspiration, because generally the album is more focused and listener-friendly than much of what he had recorded since the early 1990s. *Rave Un2 the Joy Fantastic* is not, however, a grand reinvention of Prince as an artist, nor is it a true comeback album in the sense that his later albums *Musicology* and *3121* would be. It is solid, enjoyable, listenable, impeccably produced—just not cutting edge.

The album begins with the title track, "Rave Un2 the Joy Fantastic." The text of this song is a variant on what Prince had written several times during the New Power Generation phase of his career. On the surface, it appears to be a call to come out and dance and party. One must ask, however, exactly what Prince means by the cryptic phrase "rave unto the joy fantastic." While it might be couched in references to dancing, partying, and sex, this "joy fantastic" could just as easily be a religious ecstasy. The references are just impressionistic enough that it makes the listener think and analyze. The music, driven largely by Prince's electric guitar, combines R&B and hard rock, sort of like Sly and the Family Stone's music updated to the end of the millennium. Because the verses and the chorus use the same minimalistic *ostinato* chord progression, it is easy for the listener to zone out somewhat during the song—this despite the fact that the guitar hook is so unique and easily recognizable.

The next song, "Undisputed," also revisits some of Prince and the New Power Generation's work of earlier in the 1990s. Here, Prince at once hypes his "originality" and complains about the sameness of radio playlists and the overcommercialization of the recording industry. The rhythmic stops and starts in the vocal line work effectively to pull the listener in—to focus his or her attention on the message. The message seems to be especially provocative, given Arista's work at reestablishing stars such as Carlos Santana back on the record charts and radio playlists, and given the presence of an unusual (for a Prince album) number of prominent chart-topping guests on *Rave Un2 the Joy Fantastic*. The song, however, does have an experimental, cutting-edge sonic feel, even though Prince had explored the same lyrical theme on *Emancipation* and other albums.

One of the features of *Rave Un2 the Joy Fantastic* that can seem either clever or a real groaner to the listener are the song titles that are plays on popular figures of speech and well-known titles. For example, "The Greatest Romance Ever Sold" is a play on "The Greatest Story Ever Told" and "So Far, So Pleased" would seem to be a play on "so far, so good." Other song titles rely on clichés, including "Strange but True" and "The Sun, the Moon, the Stars." Prince provides little twists on the puns and clichés that let the listener know that, yes, he did mean to use them, but he did this so that he could rework them into something at least partially unexpected.

The first of these, "The Greatest Romance Ever Sold," is a most unusual song of romance and passion. It is possible to read Prince's lyrics as revolving around a couple that has met for the first time; however, Prince includes a few clues that suggest that his character and the woman he addresses are really falling in love all over again after some time apart. What really captures the listener's attention, and what makes the song haunting, is the musical composition. Prince uses an extended phrase structure in the verses, including an extended descending melodic sequence. This creates the impression that Prince is spinning his tale out spontaneously. Of course, if the listener catches the fact that each verse uses pretty much the same melody, then it becomes clear that it is not really spontaneous. This does not detract from the effect of the music. It is so unusual in melodic shape and phrase structure that it keeps the listener focused. Prince adds an interesting touch in the pseudo-Middle Eastern figure he plays on the guitar at the end of each verse. This, and the minor key area, gives the song an exotic, almost fantasy film–like quality.

The next track, "4 Blank Seconds," is just that: four seconds of silence. Had Prince and the New Power Generation not already used a whole bunch of short silent tracks to separate the last two songs on *New Power Soul*, this would not seem so much like a gimmick. Apparently, Prince felt that it was important to put a four-second break between "The Greatest Romance Ever Sold" and "Hot Wit U." Musically, the two songs could not be more different, so the silence is useful for the listener: certainly it helps the stylistic transition, and it works, unless the listener remembers the somewhat pointless way in which the extended period of silence was achieved on *New Power Soul.*

The song "Hot Wit U" turns the romance of "The Greatest Romance Ever Sold" into hot, physical passion. Despite the emphasis on a moderate dance groove, the funky horn section, and the obvious lyrical metaphors for sex, this is a very different animal from Prince's songs of sexual desire of his New Power Generation days. Prince's lead vocals in the verses are harmonized and slightly electronically processed. This gives the song a deliberately machine-like, impersonal feel. Prince contrasts this with an unprocessed vocal tone color in the introduction and chorus, which makes his lewd metaphors of the verses seem even more impersonal. Because the song follows "The Greatest Romance Ever Sold," it would be easy to assume that the passion/lust of "Hot Wit U" would be passion born of love. The vocal setting, though, gives the listener more of a feeling of sex purely for the sake of the physical satisfaction of Prince's character. He might claim in the lyrics to care for his partner, but the recording's arrangement and production suggests otherwise. Rapper Eve's rhyme suggests that her character feels as much lust as Prince's character, and that she is prepared to take him on in erotic fantasyland, despite the fact that she is not the least bit impressed that he is known as "the Artist."

The next song, "Tangerine," lasts for a minute-and-a-half, and consists of two verses separated by the briefest of guitar interludes; there is no chorus, no middle eight. It is a sunny singer-songwriter style piece in which Prince's character describes his unsuccessful attempts to forget the tangerine color of his former lover's nightgown. The upbeat melody and guitar accompaniment is at odds with the lyrics, so while the song primarily serves as a brief divertissement, however, or trifle, it also continues the theme of contradictions that moves through *Rave Un2 the Joy Fantastic.*

"So Far, So Pleased," a play on the phrase "so far, so good," features a guest appearance from Gwen Stefani. With its steady eighth-note electric guitar accompaniment and synthesizer licks the song has a decidedly 1980s new wave feel. Despite the play on words contained in the title line, this is a straightforward love song: not cutting-edge, but solid listenable pop. Prince provides a hot guitar solo, which is a pleasure to hear considering how little he featured his guitar playing on some of his 1990s recordings.

The next song, "The Sun, the Moon and Stars," is another straightforward love ballad built around a cliché. Because Prince is at his best when he is provocative—challenging the listener to deal with his or her own feelings about sexuality, racism, poverty, faith, or whatever issue he raises—this kind of song, while infinitely listenable light R&B, would probably be more effective in the hands of a more conventional R&B singer. Curiously, the opening phrases of the verses bear more than a little melodic and rhythmic resemblance to part of the verse melody of "Sister," the *Dirty Mind* track in which Prince sings of the praises of incest. For the Prince fanatic who is familiar with

"Sister," this adds a touch of wink-wink-nudge-nudge irony to the song that would be utterly lost on some listeners.

If the listener is familiar with the original version of the song, then Prince's cover of Sheryl Crow's "Everyday Is a Winding Road," begs the question, "With *whom* did you hitch a ride?" You see, co-writers Crow, Jeff Trott, and Brian McLeod wrap the original version of the song about Crow's ride with a "vending machine repairman." This allows Crow to explore her feelings about life and its unpredictability. Prince deconstructs not only the singer-songwriter style of the 1996 Crow recording, but also changes the lyrics so that they become much more personal to him and his musical legacy. In Prince's take on the song, he rides with a "Crazyhorse showgirl." In contrast to the mundane, guy-you-see-every-day vending machine repairman of the Crow performance, Prince gives someone much more exotic, much more open to fantastic speculation. There is an air of sexuality in Prince's driver that is entirely absent from the stereotype of Crow's driver. Prince also includes obvious vocal overdubs and production (including funk, dance-based drum machine and synthesizers) that is the antithesis of Crow's more acoustical and rock-based singer-songwriter style. The amazing thing about this is that Prince's version works, if the listener accepts it on its own terms, absent any preconceived notions about the piece based on the original. The song is surprisingly consistent with the types of characters and situations Prince has portrayed and interacted with in the songs he has written, and the heavy use of the studio that typifies him as a recording artist—yet, that separates him from Crow—fits in with the situations and emotions of the song.

Perhaps because the next song proper differs so much from the Crow composition, Prince includes a brief string segue. This is worth noting, because the use of segues really marks Prince's work of the 1990s; his albums of the late 1970s through the 1980s were more known for their jarring juxtapositions of disparate musical styles and lyrical subject matter. The numerous announcements that separate the songs of *The Gold Experience* are a double-edged sword: they fit in with Prince's program for the album; however, they also distract the listener a bit. The "Segue to Man o' War" is helpful in breaking the mood between songs that are radically different in musical style and message.

The song "Man o' War" itself is a slow-tempo R&B ballad that is focused on a dysfunctional relationship. Prince's character asks his lover why she screams at him, breaks a gold necklace he gave her as a gift, because he is "not a man of war." Prince's character is conflicted about the relationship: he is in love, his friends encourage him to patch things up, but he is fed up with the treatment he receives from his "lover." The melody, harmony, and arrangement have strong hooks, which make "Man o' War" one of Prince's better, if underappreciated, ballads.

Sheryl Crow guests on vocals and harmonica for the song "Baby Knows." While Prince has excelled at message songs about contemporary events, faith and religion, and the cutting edge of sexual relationships, he has also written and recorded several highly successful songs that are just plain fun. The song "Guitar" on his most recent album to date, *Planet Earth,* is an example. *Rave Un2 the Joy Fantastic* contains an older brother to "Guitar" in the form of "Baby Knows." The song concerns a "funky joint" in which Prince's character finds all sorts of beautiful desirable women. He observes one woman who particularly interests him with her "long dark legs" and "butt that go 'round." At the end of the song, though, Prince's character is shot down: when he asks the woman for her number, she turns him down. The vocal melody of both the verses and the chorus contains many repeated notes, and basically either up or down a step or two at the end of each phrase. While this may sound tedious, Prince balances the lead vocal with solid rock guitar licks and a catchy, ascending keyboard lick. The song highlights the irony of Prince's songwriting: he has crafted successful pieces in which melodic motives and accompaniment motives are completely in sync, and equally successful songs (such as this one) in which his focus is on contrast between the principal melody and the accompaniment.

It would seem that the title "I [Eye] Love U, But I [Eye] Don't Trust U Anymore" would be particularly apt to give the listener a preconceived notion about the song's subject matter. One might reasonably assume from the title that one character in a relationship has caught his partner cheating. That pretty much sums up the situation as Prince presents it in the lyrics, except that he leaves the listener with a twist, one that turns a mundane, predictable tale into something more interesting. At the end of the song, Prince intimates that, while he loves his partner, but does not trust her anymore, she trusts him, but doesn't love him anymore. Musically, the composition is strong and follows in the classic torch song tradition; however, Prince's moves between natural voice and falsetto veer just a little too close to yodeling for the performance to be as successful as it might have been had he scored the song in a different key. Any casual Prince listener who doubts Prince's ties to the tradition of jazz standards, or his ability to use subtle musical touches to create a mood needs to listen to this song and to pay attention to his piano playing.

Prince continues to explore the theme of the jilted lover on the next song, "Silly Game." Here, though, not only does he suggest that the person with whom his character is still in love cheated on him, he also implies that there were other things that drove a wedge between the two. It is easy to read the culprit as substance abuse. Musically, it is a solid R&B-style ballad, with lovely orchestral string writing by Clare Fisher. Neither thematically nor musically does it break much new ground, though.

In the song "Strange but True," Prince plays the role of the partner who left the relationship. The gist of the story is that he now regrets leaving. Because some of the previous songs of lost love on *Rave Un2 the Joy Fantastic* are overly conventional, Prince's highly experimental approach to hip-hop on

"Strange but True" stands out starkly. The piece begins with Prince speaking over minimal, slow-moving accompaniment. Gradually, a faster, much more energetic instrumental setting emerges, but only over time. Once the ultimate fast tempo is established, Prince accompanies the rap with dissonant synthesizer and percussion figures that musically convey the pain his character feels as he expresses his mixed feelings about the past he physically—but not emotionally—left behind. The tension of the musical setting makes this a challenging piece to listen to; however, if one is attuned to avant-garde experimental music, it makes for fascinating listening. "Strange but True" is not commercial in any sense of the word; it is more a piece of experimental art music that just happens to come from the hip-hop genre.

The song "Wherever U Go, Whatever U Do" represents another side of Prince's study of relationships on *Rave Un2 the Joy Fantastic*. Lyrically, Prince takes on the theme of universal love and acceptance that is at the heart of such early 1970s classics as Paul Simon's composition "Bridge over Troubled Water" (1970) and Carole King's song "You've Got a Friend" (1971). While the Simon and King songs are more open to interpretation concerning the previous relationship of the two characters, Prince leaves hints that his characters were once lovers. Now, though, his character tells his former lover of his undying, eternal friendship and support, in spite of the fact that they are no longer lovers.

The music of "Wherever U Go, Whatever U Do" is especially interesting. The drum track at the very beginning of the song suggests hip-hop; however, the entrance of the electric guitar and bass snaps the listener back to the 1980s and bands such as the Cars and the Police, or even Prince himself on some of the new wave material back in the *Sign o' the Times* era. Prince establishes the 1980s new wave feel primarily through his use of the repeated steady eighth-note bass line, in the manner of, say, the Police's "Every Breath You Take." Like the best of new wave rock, "Wherever U Go, Whatever U Do" is strong in the melodic hook department. The instrumental accompaniment, too, is memorable and engaging.

The specter of the between-song announcements of *The Gold Experience–*era Prince return in the form of the track "Promo to Website." This track, which features Prince in his electronically processed subbass voice, is just what the title says, a "welcome to the dawn," and to Prince's Web site at http://www.love4oneanother.com. The Barry White–esque voice is not bad—certainly not as annoying as it would be on Prince's next album—but the track reeks of shameless merchandising and self-promotion. It wouldn't be so bad if Prince's announcement did not include an invitation to his merchandising site at www.1800newfunk.com. However, it must be said that the announcement and the large-type, all-capitals "WWW.NEWFUNK.COM" printed in the CD's booklet shows the extent to which Prince was taking advantage of the possibilities offered by the Internet at the end of the century. He, in fact, had been utilizing the Internet for several years at this point. The

"Promo to Website" itself, however, just misses the balance between providing information to fans and commercialism.

On the DJ/promotional version of the CD I own, the "Promo to Website" is followed by the bonus track "Pretty Man." The presence of long-time James Brown sideman Maceo Parker on alto saxophone confirms the track's clear ties to the 1960s work of Brown. Tracks such as "Sister Popcorn" and other late 1960s funk grooves by Brown immediately come to mind. As he did on a few selected tracks on his earliest albums of the 1970s, Prince apes the musical and vocal mannerisms of James Brown. So, "Pretty Man" is nothing new in the Prince canon, but the old-school funk groove is solid and Parker faithfully recreates the sort of saxophone licks that helped to define the James Brown sound back in the 1960s.

With a higher proportion of ballads and more songs that explore love and lost love (as opposed to sex and desire for sex) than any other Prince album, *Rave Un2 the Joy Fantastic* stands apart not only from the late 1990s work of Prince, but also from the bulk of his work from any time earlier in his career. While there are some thematic connections between the songs—especially evident when several songs of lost love give way to the undying friendship the former lover expresses in "Wherever U Go, Whatever U Do"—*Rave Un2 the Joy Fantastic* mostly seems like a collection of somewhat disparate songs, some memorable, some more pedestrian. *Rave Un2 the Joy Fantastic* does not rank with Prince's most satisfying albums, but it has moments of brilliance.

The New Millennium

Back in the 1980s, Prince had been one of the first pop musicians who dealt with the possibilities of the new millennium. His song "1999" might have sounded like a song of partying and celebrating on the surface, but the piece was predicated on the biblical prophesy of the end of the world. As the millennium actually approached, Prince found his career and his life at something of a crossroads. The last several years of the twentieth century had seen him issue an enormous collection that consisted of 1990s outtakes and a single disc of personal, philosophical material that musically and lyrically turned its back on much of what Prince had written and recorded in previous years (*Crystal Ball*). He had followed that up with an album that featured his live backing band, the New Power Generation, performing songs that, while they reflected Prince's developing religiosity, returned to some of the musical styles that Prince had used over half a decade earlier (*New Power Soul*). Prince's first record label, Warner Bros., then issued a collection of outtakes to which it held the rights (*The Vault: Old Friends 4 Sale*), and Prince ended the decade with *Rave Un2 the Joy Fantastic,* a collection of songs that included an all-star cast of guest artists. It all seemed as if Prince needed to find a new inspiration, a new style, in order to become once again a cutting-edge musician. His material from the end of the twentieth century was well crafted and meticulously performed and recorded, but packaging issues (three- and four-disc sets are expensive and tend to alienate an audience base), lack of stylistic continuity, and a sense of musically marking time, all contributed to the feeling that Prince's creativity was on the wane.

The new millennium saw Prince become a Jehovah's Witness. Some of the connections he had made between sexuality and spirituality in the past seem to be quite at odds with his newfound faith; however, he clearly had been moving in the direction of changing his previous almost glorification of sex for its own sake for a few years. His conversion led to Prince writing, recording, and issuing *The Rainbow Children,* a truly rare example of Jehovah's Witness faith translated into the language of contemporary pop music. Prince then recorded two albums that seemed to be aimed at bringing him back into mainstream pop and R&B relevance—*Musicology* and *3121*—both of which succeed better than any of his albums going back several years. In the year 2007, Prince issued *Planet Earth,* an album that, while it has not generated as much critical praise as his previous two albums, finds him reaching musical and lyrical balances that were sometimes missing from some of his earlier work.

THE RAINBOW CHILDREN

The subject of religion had previously found its way into a fair number of Prince songs. The 2001 album *The Rainbow Children,* however, found Prince devoting himself completely to songs inspired by his recently becoming a Jehovah's Witness. Presumably because the entire album was purported to be religiously inspired, and because the Jehovah's Witnesses denomination espouses some beliefs that conflict with mainstream Christian denominations, *The Rainbow Children* was widely touted as Prince's most controversial album ever. Given the high level of exploration of alternative beliefs and lifestyles present in popular music, particularly from the 1960s forward, however, examination of the lyrical and musical content of the songs of this album suggests that the "most controversial ever" publicity amounted to little more than sales hype, at least with regard to Prince's focus on religion. What did generate negative critical comment was the disconnection between the lyrical sentiments and the musical styles. In addition, some of the stories Prince tells in the songs can too easily be heard more as B-movie science fiction than as religiously inspired narratives, mostly because of the way in which he presents them.

The album's title song sets the stage for the purpose of *The Rainbow Children.* Prince introduces the piece with an electronically processed, deep sub-bass voice, which represents the narrator of the album. Maybe it shows my own bias against unnecessary electronic gimmickry, but all I can think of when I hear Prince's electronically processed voice are the television commercials Volkswagen was airing in 2006 for its GTI model that featured the "Fast." Prince does not say, "My Fast thinks that delivery is for the weak," and I realize that *The Rainbow Children* precedes the Volkswagen ads by half a decade; however, VW and the advertising firm that produced its ads hit the nail on the head: the ultra low-frequency speaking voice is better suited to humor than to a quasi-imitation of what the Almighty might sound like. Even in the field of R&B music, Stevie Wonder had used a not-all-that-differently processed voice to portray a humorous insect on his *Journey through the Secret Life of Plants* album back in the late 1970s. The problem with Prince's use of the octave transposer here is that what he intends to be a grand pronouncement about the Rainbow Children (Jehovah's Witnesses) being the present-day keepers of the ancient ties to God can just as easily come off as gimmickry.

Prince further complicates the picture by setting the account of the rise of the Rainbow Children to fast-paced post-bop jazz. The music does convey the urgency of Prince's command to the Rainbow Children to rise and bring forth the truth of God; however, it hardly sounds reverent. Despite the apparent conflict between the story and the fast jazz, it must be noted that Prince's bluesy guitar playing—as well as Najee's saxophone work—is a delight. One of the subtle strengths of Prince's playing is his rhythmic approach to jazz. Unlike some post-bop jazz instrumentalists who play behind the beat, Prince takes an R&B and rock approach to the beat, with rhythmically superprecise attacks.

Prince, the arranger and producer, takes an enormous chance by relying so heavily on electronic processing of his voice in the sung passages, too. This lends an otherworldly quality to the 10-minute-plus track, and this is a potential problem for the listener. To the extent that one associates God with the creation of nature—and to the extent that one accepts Prince's account of the fall from grace in Eden—then the obviously synthetic quality of the narrator's voice and some of the sung vocals can seem to run counter to a story about the relationship of God and mankind. The song can too easily come off as a piece of science fiction.

The next track, "Muse 2 the Pharaoh," tells the story of a captive woman—part of the biblical Rainbow Children, God's chosen—who becomes the "muse to the Pharaoh." The moderately slow R&B ballad style works more effectively than the fast jazz of the first piece. The next "chapter" in the story, "Digital Garden," is one of Prince's more intriguing and engaging experimental pieces. Prince utilizes a wide array of musical textures and has his vocals jumping around in the aural space between the speakers. Unfortunately, the octave-lower-than-Barry White, processed voice of the narrator interrupts the song. This brings up the principal challenge of *The Rainbow Children,* and one that reviewers have noted: Prince delivers some of the strongest music he had ever written and recorded and the most thematically cohesive story to run through any of his albums. However, the religious story and the way in which Prince presents it does not fit easily with the music.

It is interesting to consider *The Rainbow Children* in the context of other jazz settings of religious texts. Duke Ellington's late sacred compositions, for example, while they are intriguing to Ellington aficionados, and while they represent some of the most consciously artful of Ellington's compositions, are decidedly not his generally best-known and best-loved works. Similarly, *The Rainbow Children* is a major artistic stretch for Prince; however, the individual songs are so completely integrated into the narrative that they cannot be effectively separated from the whole. For that reason, like Ellington's sacred works, Prince's music on this album is not as likely to remain as well known or as influential as his compositions that can both fit into the album context and successfully exist unto themselves. The irony of the album is that, because of Prince's insistent use of his electronically processed narrator voice and the mood conflicts between the storyline and some of the jazzy musical settings, Prince's standalone religious songs are better able to connect with the listener than the tracks of his focused religious statement, *The Rainbow Children*.

N.E.W.S.

Up to the release of *N.E.W.S.*, Prince had written and recorded songs about sex, songs of faith, songs about the apocalypse, songs ostensibly about dancing, as well as songs in which he used unusual combinations of imagery and reference. In every case, though, Prince was known for songs; that is, for compositions with singing and words. The 2003 album *N.E.W.S.* consists of a suite of four instrumental pieces, "North," "East," "West," and "South" (hence the acronym N.E.W.S.), each of which lasts exactly 14 minutes. What's more, the entire album was recorded in one day. One of the more unusual features of the collection is the tendency of Prince and his fellow musicians to maintain their own individual styles, so that the group always sounds more like a collection of individuals than an ensemble. While one might assume that this is by necessity a negative feature of the four compositions, it actually fits in with the album's philosophical basis. The stylistic and tempo changes of these pieces are also somewhat unusual in the context of instrumental jazz. As I will discuss in reference to some of the specific tracks, the album seems to be aimed at showing the universality of the world's people, regardless of national origin, race, religion, gender, or age. So, the interplay between individuality and universal connection is an important philosophical concern. Prince and his associates play these out in the stylistic approaches of the players, as well as in the stylistic changes within the pieces. The danger of adopting a philosophical stance such as this in instrumental music is that it is more challenging to pull off in instrumental music than in vocal music: there are no lyrics to help. If the listener does not buy into the philosophical approach, or if one experiences one of the tracks out of context—that is, without the album's packaging (which suggests the philosophical reasons the pieces are the way they are)—then the musical changes and the disparate styles of the players can seem fragmented. Let us examine some of the structural and stylistic features of these instrumental compositions.

Although I have pointed out examples of classical Golden-Mean symmetry in several previous Prince songs, the casual listener probably never thinks of Prince as a structuralistic composer. On the surface, he tends to appear to be a rock songwriter, an R&B songwriter, a hip-hop songwriter, and so on, who seems to work pretty much within the structural boundaries of each of those genres. Interestingly—especially in light of the fact that each of the four "movements" of the *N.E.W.S.* suite seems on the surface to be something akin to structured jams—there are some fascinating, subtle long-range structural features of each of the pieces that align with such structuralist concepts as the Golden Mean and traditional narrative curve.

The use of the Golden Mean and the related Fibonacci Series has been well documented in the work of particular composers of the past 100 years, particularly the early/mid-twentieth-century Hungarian composer Béla Bartòk. Because the Golden Mean and the Fibonacci Series are restrictive in that they define proportions with a degree of mathematical precision that would be difficult to achieve in a musical composition (unless one went out of one's way to adhere to the aesthetics of the Golden Mean), some late twentieth-century theorists have suggested that a more general structural aesthetic governs successful musical forms and compositions. Composer and theorist Barney Childs, for example, calls this the musical "narrative curve."[1] As Childs points out, the gradual rise to a high point (be it pitch, dynamics, intensity, tonal tension, etc.), followed by a comparatively rapid "repose" has precedents in drama, literature, and other art forms going back to the Renaissance. Childs, importantly, allows for structural proportions of a wider range than those of the Golden Mean. For example, a musical composition with an important structural boundary 62 percent of the way through (approximately the Golden Mean) would fit the narrative curve, as would a work with an important structural delineation—or high point—say two-thirds to three-quarters of the way through the piece. Commercially and critically successful pop songs or jazz compositions do not necessarily always follow even this more liberal musical narrative curve. The pieces in Prince's *N.E.W.S.* suite, however, do so to a remarkable degree.

The other structural feature of the suite that the listener needs to keep in mind is each piece's relationship to the instrumental jazz and jazz fusion traditions. If we go back to small ensemble pieces from the swing era to the present, we can easily find a whole host of pieces that musicians refer to as "head charts." These are pieces in which the main melodic instruments play the principal theme either in unison or in harmony at the beginning and at the end of the performance. The middle section—which is usually considerably long—features individual improvised solos over the same harmonic pattern as the "head." The head (and subsequent solo choruses) may be in twelve-bar blues form, 32-bar, A-A-B-A song form, or some other form. While head charts enjoyed their greatest popularity during the bebop era, they remain a staple of small-group jazz form into the twenty-first century. Some jazz musicians of the late 1950s and the 1960s, including John Coltrane, Charles Mingus, and Ornette Coleman, began composing pieces that incorporated more evolving, freer forms. Prince's *N.E.W.S.* compositions follow more in the tradition of the three innovators in jazz formal structure than in the head chart tradition. In general, the four movements tend to evolve and some have the obviously composed melodic material (in which two instruments, say, are playing in melodic unison) only emerging well into the performance.

The other particularly interesting feature of the four pieces on *N.E.W.S.* (alluded to earlier) is how they allow each of the players—Prince on guitar; Fender Rhodes on digital keyboards and percussion; Eric Leeds on saxophones; Renato Neto on piano and synthesizers; Rhonda Smith on acoustic and electric bass; and John Blackwell on drums—to emerge as disparate musical personalities. Despite the fact that each of the four pieces falls in different places along the jazz continuum—from so-called light jazz, to funk and rock-influenced jazz—each musician retains discernable elements of his or her unique sense of style. Although it is a bit of an oversimplification of the richness of the playing, Prince's electric guitar comping and soloing, for example, suggests a combination of Carlos Santana, heavy metal, and R&B throughout much of the entire suite, while Renato Neto's piano work tends to lean much more in the jazz direction. Drummer John Blackwell adjusts to, and in fact, often leads the intensity changes and at times plays with such extreme contrasts of dynamics that he suggests 1990s grunge music. That is not to say that any of the musicians are unmoving in their approach; there is plenty of give-and-take between the members of the ensemble. There is, however, a bit of stylistic tension that actually makes these four pieces more interesting than some of the more commercially focused examples of contemporary jazz.

The opening piece, "North," is perhaps the best example of the use of the narrative curve in the suite. Overall, the piece gradually builds up in dynamics, intensity of mood, and texture to and through Prince's Santana- and heavy metal-inspired electric guitar solo. Then, at approximately the 9:08 mark the texture dramatically thins and the dynamic moves down to a hush for Neto's sparse piano solo. This structural break occurs approximately 65 percent of the way through the composition, thereby fitting in quite nicely with the musical narrative curve Barney Childs describes. And, the piece is really more about the overall ebb and flow within this narrative curve than it is about individual solos, scales, harmonic progressions, or any other foreground or background structural feature. In short, this is a big-picture piece and holds up well.

The second piece, "East," finds Prince turning a little more to stereotype—specifically stereotypical licks and scales of Eastern music. This perhaps is most apparent in the opening of the piece, in which a synthesized shawm plays a repeated melodic phrase that is based on a Middle Eastern–sounding scale in which the tonic pitch is approached by both a half-step above and a half-step below. Approximately 1 minute and 30 seconds into the piece John Blackwell begins playing a steady progressive rock-style rhythmic line on the drum set. Interestingly, the pattern seems at first to be of indeterminate meter, but eventually develops into a discernable quadruple meter. After an Eric Leeds jazz-rock saxophone solo, the drumbeat moves into a half-time (twice as slow) feel and references to stereotypically Eastern music return. This time, though, the synthesizer more closely resembles the plucked string instruments of Asian music. In an even more dramatic and unexpected mix of musical cultures, Prince punctuates the synthesizer melody with loud heavy metal-style electric guitar chords. As challenging as it might seem for the listener to perceive instrumental music as projecting a philosophical statement—music with words can make a philosophical, religious, or political statement more easily—I believe that the pieces of *N.E.W.S.*, and especially "East," can be understood on a level apart from that of pure sound. In this 14-minute piece, which includes several diverse rhythmical, metrical, and tempo feels, in addition to the apparently mixed metaphors of musical culture (Middle East, Asia, American jazz-rock, and American/British heavy metal), Prince tells the listener in not so many words that there is plenty of room at life's metaphorical table for everyone. It might seem to be a stretch to interpret the piece (or the pieces) that way, but such a reading is supported by the entire packaging of the album. Let us briefly examine the physical packaging of *N.E.W.S.*

The cardboard foldout packaging of the album is most unusual. Curiously, each of the four cardboard points that stick out when one completely unfolds the package contains a keyword. They are not, however, the *North, East, West,* and *South* that the listener might expect. Instead, Prince highlights the words *Love, Peace, Charity,* and *Faith*. These spiritual attributes do not seem to correspond to specific pieces of music on the album. In other words, the musical selection "North" does not seem necessarily to represent a musical portrayal of any of the four spiritually oriented words. Instead, since each movement of the suite features clear progression of mood and contrasts of intensity, tempo, sometimes meter, dynamics, rhythmic feel, and density of material, the listener might be left with the impression that each of the four musical pieces contains elements of all of the spiritual attributes. The painting of a compass that is found behind the disc itself also suggests connections of each direction through the center. Hence, the packaging and the diversity of music within each of the four pieces can be interpreted on a macro level as a philosophical statement: all humankind is connected through a center (God), regardless of religious belief, culture, gender, race, nationality, age, and so on.

The piece "West" begins in more of a ballad feel and seems at first to function much like the slow movement in a multimovement classical composition. At approximately the 3:58 mark of the piece, however, Prince introduces a moderate tempo R&B/light funk feel with a guitar line. Over the course of the next 10 minutes, "West" includes touches of atonal free jazz, metal power-ballad, and metal-funk. It is perhaps the most diverse and unpredictable of all the movements. Again, if one reads more than sound for the sake of sound into Prince's compositional work on *N.E.W.S.*, this particularly high level of diversity could be taken as a portrait of the multicultural landscape of

America. Admittedly, Prince never specifically tells the listener this; however, the fact that the album's packaging is somewhat cryptic functions to invite interpretation—reading between the musical lines, as it were.

The concluding piece, "South," with its bright tempo and funk-oriented rhythmic feel, functions as a grand finale for *N.E.W.S.* Because it has a short introduction and then a doubled-tracked Eric Leeds saxophone melody, it resembles a head chart more than the other pieces. Still, the piece gradually develops organically along various lines throughout, including coordinated, arranged-sounding sections, individual solos, and so on, so whatever feeling of head chart comes from the saxophone melody near the start of the piece dissolves away. The funk and rock rhythmic styles, synthesizer tone colors, and Prince's hard rock guitar tone color suggest a bunch of disparate predecessors in instrumental jazz and rock, including several of the pieces on Frank Zappa's *Hot Rats* album, the Edgar Winter Group's "Frankenstein," and a healthy dose of the feel of a number of pieces by the band Weather Report. Just as was the case with the other three "movements," the listener probably tends to leave "South" not focusing so much on particular melodies or individual solos, as remembering the overall feel and progression of the piece.

N.E.W.S. is not as groundbreaking, cutting-edge, or as influential as some of the early jazz-rock-world music fusion work of Miles Davis (*Bitches Brew,* 1969), Frank Zappa (*Hot Rats,* 1969), the Mahavishnu Orchestra (*The Inner Mounting Flame,* 1971), but that is because the work of Davis, Zappa, and John McLaughlin (the Mahavishnu Orchestra) made unprecedented inroads across genres and basically defined a new genre (fusion). Working a little more than three decades later, Prince is not defining a totally new genre, but rather, is working largely in a continuum that connects him to the fusion pioneers. But, then fine music does not have to be genre-defining in order to be artistically successful. Prince's *N.E.W.S.* is an underappreciated part of his vast output. The playing is interesting, and the combination of smooth transitions and abrupt stylistic cuts provides the listener with an overarching sense of expecting the unexpected. It is not necessary to buy into what I hear as the philosophical ramifications of the collection—which comes at least in part from the somewhat cryptic packaging—in order to appreciate *N.E.W.S.* as a musical statement. If one does hear the album as a statement about human connections through the center of a Supreme Being, though, I believe that Prince delivers the message well, even through the relatively abstract means of purely instrumental jazz. Prince does not flash his guitar technique on *N.E.W.S.* nearly as much as he does on some of the solos he takes on his songs from the 1970s and 1980s. Instead, he gives every member of the ensemble the chance to stand out; therefore, the listener who expects Prince's sole instrumental album to be his definitive guitar hero album will be disappointed. *N.E.W.S.* is about something more important than guitar technique, and it is an album that perhaps is better appreciated by those who are not overly fanatical about Prince's work as a pop music superstar.

Still, Prince really is at his best when he combines music, arrangement, and production with lyrics.

MUSICOLOGY

On the 2004 album *Musicology* Prince deals with some of the historically important events of the young, new millennium, and expands on his recent forays into jazz by integrating some of the R&B and rock styles that marked his prereligious conversion work. It is one of the artist's more intriguing albums of the twenty-first century. He fully confronts the conflicts and the intersections between the R&B of his youth—represented by James Brown and Sly Stone—and that of the early twenty-first century. Prince includes some of the thematic and musical connections between songs that mark his most cohesive albums, and through it all he remains true to his newly defined view of the universe and mankind's relationship with God.

The album kicks off with the title track, "Musicology." In this song, on which Prince plays all the instruments and sings all the overdubbed vocals, he evokes the specter of James Brown and Brown's pioneering funk work of the late 1960s. Like Brown did on some of his classics, Prince builds the piece on a rhythmically infectious repetitive riff. Also like Brown, who mentioned contemporary dance styles in songs such "Papa's Got a Brand New Bag," Prince drops numerous names of contemporary R&B stars (e.g., Doug E.) who have ties to old-school funk. Prince's brilliance as a composer comes through in the conflict between the older style R&B and twenty-first century hip-hop that he sets up in the piece. Almost exactly halfway through the 4:24 piece, a bass-heavy hip-hop beat (at a slower tempo than the rest of the piece) invades the song. Prince tells it to "get back" and to "get off his stereo," because this is "my record." In doing this, Prince makes his allegiance to the "old skool" funk forebears he mentions in the piece—James Brown and Sly Stone—crystal clear. The academic field of musicology literally is the study of music and its historical context. In his composition of the same name, Prince places the heart of his R&B-style work in its historical context. Of course, longtime Prince fans have known this along: Prince's first two albums back in the late 1970s found him turning back the clock 10 years and making clear compositional, arrangement, and lyrical reference to the riff-oriented music of James Brown over and over.

The song "Musicology" is notable for Prince's work on keyboards, guitar, bass, and drums. Like multi-instrumentalist Stevie Wonder, particularly on his important 1973 album *Innervisions,* Prince plays the instruments brilliantly. Like Wonder, who is primarily a keyboardist, Prince takes a decidedly improvisational approach to the drum set. The percussion work on "Musicology" makes it all too clear that all of Prince's reliance on simplistic, overly repetitive drum machine programs in the 1980s were a tremendous waste of his musical talents. In fact, about the only Prince song that has ever been significantly enhanced by the use of a pedestrian drum machine beat was "Annie Christian," and only then because the song so closely resembled some of the minimalist New York City loft scene avant-garde music of the day.

Throughout his career, Prince has written his fair share of songs with intriguing and even provocative titles. Certainly, "Illusion, Coma, Pimp & Circumstance," with its obvious reference to Sir Edward Elgar's famous *Pomp and Circumstance March No. 1* is one such composition. Musically, the song retains some stylistic links (the background riff, in particular) to James Brown–style funk, but incorporates scratching, rap, and other signifiers of hip-hop. Prince's story concerns a couple—she of upper-class breeding and training (Prince tells us that she knows which fork to use), and he of the streets (he understands the funk). The lyrics are filled with impressionistic images of kinky sex, co-dependency, money valued over real human feeling. Because the lyrics are nonlinear, and because Prince avoids pretty-sounding melodic content and easy pop-oriented hooks, it is not necessarily a piece that will engage the casual listener at first hearing. Prince's sparse, minimal musical setting, though, fits the dysfunctional (except in bed) and emotionally bankrupt nature of the couple's relationship with each other and in their lives in general.

Over the years, Prince has written a number of excellent ballads of lost love and heartache. The best-known example is "Nothing Compares 2 U," on the strength of Sinéad O'Connor's commercially successful and critically acclaimed recording. On Prince's own albums, the slow ballads tend to work most successfully when they contrast with the songs around them. In other words, the relatively large number of ballads on an album such as *Rave Un2 the Joy Fantastic* tends to diminish the distinctiveness of the individual songs. Such is not a problem with the song "A Million Days," because it forms such a strong contrast with the first two songs on *Musicology*.

The song finds Prince addressing a woman who was both his lover and his best friend. As he sings it, she has "only been gone for an hour, but it feels like a million days." Sentiments such as these have been expressed in countless pop songs over the years. Prince includes a few vivid and idiosyncratic references that stand out from the conventional (crawling "on [his] belly" and seeing his ex-lover as "a hero"). The thing that really makes the recording stand out, however, is Prince's blending of R&B and rock, and the move from a slow tempo to a double-time tempo. Prince takes a chance by doubling the tempo: on one hand, it conveys his character's growing sense of emotional urgency; however, on the other hand, the tempo and beat also negate much of the sorrow that is conveyed in the first 1:06 of the 3:50 song. Later, Prince plays with two metrical feels by quickly moving between them. This conveys the swirling emotions of his character.

In "Life 'o' the Party," Prince revisits the hip-hop style of his early New Power Generation albums. The namedropping (Dr. Dre and Eminem) of the song "Musicology" returns. The early 1990s NPG style and the links to "Musicology" combine to make "Life 'o' the Party" seem a little tired stylistically. It is a delight, however, to hear Prince have some fun with his loss of fan base and some of the rumors about his private life that have swirled around him for years: "He don't play the hits no more, plus I thought he was gay."

The song "Call My Name" shares its stylistic heritage with some of the work of Al Green and Marvin Gaye. It is a gentle love ballad, but in it Prince takes on the subject of the war in Iraq. According to Prince, if those fighting the war "had a love as sweet" as that which his character shares with his lover, then they would "forget what they're fighting for." Prince also questions whether the United States truly is the "home of the free." This tying together larger political issues with the varied emotions and reality of day-to-day black urban life within a disarming soul ballad style brings back memories of Marvin Gaye's famous album *What's Going On*, even though Prince's vocal style on this track is much closer to the gospel-inspired work of Al Green.

Prince had turned so fully toward R&B, especially in the 1990s, that it seems strangely easy to forget that back in the 1980s he had written and recorded several new wave rock classics, perhaps most notably, "I Could Never Take the Place of Your Man." Because the new wave style was decidedly old-fashioned in the twenty-first century, and because he had focused so much on R&B—as opposed to rock—the song "Cinnamon Girl" immediately—and strongly—conjures up images of the bygone 1980s. The lyrics, though, speak directly of post-9/11 America. The "Cinnamon Girl" of the song's title is of mixed racial/ethnic heritage and presumably Muslim. Although she did not think much about her heritage before the terrorist attacks of September 11, 2001, she subsequently has endured racial and religious discrimination. Despite the treatment she has received, she continues to pray for an end to war and hostilities based on religion. Prince seems to be telling the listener in not so many words that people of God, whether Christian, Jewish, Muslim, and so on, are connected to each other and to the ways of peace. Although the image of a "cinnamon girl" is vivid and seems designed to refer to a brownish-red skin tone, Prince's name for the character is, however, curious if taken literally. The plant from which the spice comes is native to Sri Lanka and southern India, not the Middle East. Still, Prince leaves so many specifics about the "cinnamon girl" open to speculation that the character can just as easily be a single real person or a metaphor for the bulk of American Muslims who disavow terrorism.

Structurally, "Cinnamon Girl" is also an interesting song. The last verse follows Prince's electric guitar solo and it begins about 64 percent of the way through the 3:56 piece. This places it at approximately the central focal point of the narrative curve mentioned earlier. It is in this last verse that Prince intensifies his focus on the prayer for peace that the "cinnamon girl" offers. This would seem to suggest to the listener that peace can come only through faith.

In comparison with the best songs on *Musicology*, "What Do U Want Me 2 Do?" is a fairly anonymous mid-tempo ballad about a female audience member that captures the attention of a guitar-playing musician (Prince's character). Prince describes his character as "master of the soft, not 2 [too] loud." The music reflects this almost lounge-like sonic image. The next song, "The Marrying Kind," also finds Prince portraying a musician. This time, his piano-playing character tells another man that he is going to win the affections of the woman the other man is preparing to leave, if he goes ahead and leaves her now. The piece is marked by intriguing stop-time rhythmic punctuations and Prince's distorted hard rock guitar sound. The rhythmic punctuations work particularly well at creating an image of Prince's character grabbing his friend and laying the results of the friend's impending actions on the line.

The love song "If I [Eye] Was the Man in Ur Life" is marked by its musical writing and arrangement. Prince juxtaposes rhythmic elements of reggae, hip-hop, modern R&B, and rock. The metrical feel moves back and forth between half-time feel and double-time feel. The horn arrangement emphasizes bright tone colors, and the synthesizer and electric guitar tone colors suggest the sound of heavy metal-influenced power ballads. While this eclecticism might seem like a recipe for structural disaster, Prince integrates the diverse styles and tone colors so that it all works together. In large part, this is because of the convergence of music and lyrics. Prince's lyrics focus on all the various things that his character will provide his lover, "if [he] was the man in [her] life." The music supports the multiplicity of Prince's list of contributions that his character would bring to the relationship.

Prince, as a writer, singer, piano and organ player, moves more fully into the style of black gospel music on the song "On the Couch" than on any other commercially released recording of his career. The soulful style of his writing provides him plenty of room as a singer to plead with his lover not to force him to sleep on the couch, despite the fact that he tried too hard to push her into sex. What makes the track most intriguing, however, is the idiosyncratic approach that Prince takes to gospel. This is stylized gospel in which Prince plays with rhythmic expectations by moving abruptly between long static passages and brass punctuations.

The nearly 45 years between 1960 and the release of *Musicology* have witnessed a number of famous songs of social commentary and protest in prevailing pop styles of their times. Perhaps the best-known collection of such songs in the world of R&B were the songs of Marvin Gaye's album *What's Going On*. On the song "Dear Mr. Man," war, environmental degradation, drug addiction, poverty, and racism are all the subject of a letter from Prince's character to "the man." Like Gaye's work, this social commentary is set to disarming—in fact, infectious—R&B music. Prince also connects the music back to the *What's Going On* era through his use of the wah-wah pedal on his guitar. Prince's musically gentle social statement stands in stark contrast to the sometimes angry feel of hip-hop music, just as Marvin Gaye's protest music stood in contrast with the more militant-sounding music of the late 1960s and early 1970s. This lends the music of both artists a feeling of sadness that tempers the concern and frustration of the lyrics themselves. Just like the work of the legendary Marvin Gaye, "Dear Mr. Man" is a richer experience in social commentary because of the soft-sell approach Prince takes.

Musicology ends with the song "Reflection." If it was not clear to the listener before this track, the song makes it clear that the entire *Musicology* experience is about both the interplay (and sometimes conflict) between the music of the early twenty-first century and the music of Prince's childhood and musical coming-of-age. This song puts it all into focus and lets the listener know that the entire experience is really about aging—hence, such sentiments as "Remember … when we would compare whose Afro was the roundest?" Despite some unnecessary mimicry in the production (such as the stereo panning on the word *stereo*), this is a poignant song that can easily ring true for people of Prince's age. He ends this song—and the album about the conflict between reflection back to the early 1970s and the early twenty-first century—on an unresolved chord.

Prince's previous two albums, *The Rainbow Children* and *N.E.W.S.*, had found him focusing on jazz and on spirituality to a greater extent than on any of his earlier work. *Musicology* was a very different kind of album: jazz references are muted and the spirituality is present, but more subtly integrated into the thematic texture. There are very clear—some might say too obvious—sonic ties between the songs, and between these songs and the work of earlier R&B legends. In particular, Prince's James Brown–like guttural enunciations can clearly be heard near the beginning of nearly every track. *Musicology* is, however, an effective personal testament about reconciling the past with the present. Reviews might call it a comeback album,[2] but *Musicology* is more like a coming-of-age album.

3121

The conventional wisdom about *Musicology* and *3121* is that they were both comeback albums for Prince. They are, however, very different kinds of comebacks. While *Musicology* found Prince dealing with the reality of aging by looking back to the music with which he grew up, *3121* finds him mixing in elements of his early 1990s work with the New Power Generation, as well as making clearer direct musical references to his work of the early 1980s. Perhaps because of the fact that Prince plays most of the instruments on each song of the album, *3121* has a more unified sound than most of his recordings. The album is even more unified feeling because Prince incorporates subtle lyrical ties between some of the songs.

The album begins with its title track, "3121." Here, Prince introduces the location of the ultimate party: 3121. But, does this number refer to a date, or a hotel room number, or is it a metaphor for the spiritual afterlife? The line,

"You can come if u want 2, but u can never leave," may conjure up images of the Eagles song "Hotel California," another place that one "can never leave," however, while the Eagles invest their ultimate destination with both a sense of attraction and foreboding, Prince's ultimate destination—despite his statement "u can never leave"—is largely absent the sense of foreboding of the Eagles' song. Instead, Prince's vocal interpretation suggests a benign inevitability. The place can be understood as an earthly party central, but listeners familiar with Prince's spirituality and religiosity can just as easily hear Prince metaphorically describing the afterlife. Prince's most memorable and popular songs from the 1980s featured melodies that either (1) played on stark contrast between verse and chorus in melodic shape and range, or ironically, (2) were built from a single, easily identifiable motive. The song "3121" is of the first type. Both verse and chorus are catchy and easy to remember—like good pop songs, and the music contains enough of a hip-hop feel that it calls to mind the first collaborations of Prince and the New Power Generation back in the mid-1990s. One of the more intriguing tags that Prince uses in the first two verses that distinguish the poet structure from that of the chorus is the persistent placement of rhythmic accents on weak syllables.

Much earlier in his career, Prince had written and recorded numerous songs about the kinkier side of sex. At that time, a song entitled "Lolita" might well have been about a lurid physical relationship with an underage girl; after all, he did write about incest ("Sister") and sex that verged on the edge of rape ("Lady Cab Driver"). And, Prince did choose to call the song, "Lolita," a name clearly associated with promiscuous underage girls since the 1955 publication of Vladimir Nabokov's novel *Lolita*. Prince, however, does not portray a character that is fixated with the prospect of sex with a willing underage girl. Instead, the Prince of the twenty-first century tells the proverbial Lolita that all he wants to do is dance, despite her assurances that she is willing to do *anything* he wants to do.

The music and performance of "Lolita" is particularly strong. The piece is based on a compact infectious riff in which the first measure is heavily syncopated and the second places the emphasis squarely on the beat. It is effective in the tradition of the distinctive riffs of *Sign o' the Times*-era Prince classics such as "U Got the Look"; however, the dialogues between Lolita (spoken by the female members of Prince's band) and Prince's character and between Prince and the "fellas" in the band follow more in the tradition of his 1990s early work with the New Power Generation. The instrumental work sounds remarkably band-like, despite the fact that Prince plays everything on the track: guitars, bass, drums, and synthesizers. Perhaps most delightful, though, is the genuine dismay that the Lolita character—a self-professed "bad" girl—expresses when Prince tells her that all he wants to do is dance. While the song sounds very much like it is about Prince and the guest vocalists having some fun and creating engaging pop, it is also about Prince defining appropriate and inappropriate sexual activity. He expresses his faith-based sexual attitudes without preaching and without resorting to the science fiction-like world of his grand religious statement: *The Rainbow Children*.

One of the things that ties several of the songs of *3121* together is Prince's exploration of Latino themes and forays into the Spanish language and Latin musical style. The song "Lolita," for example, incorporates touches of Spanish and therefore paints Lolita as Hispanic. The album's next song, "Te Amo Corazón," moves even more obviously into the Latin world. Prince sets his lyrics—one of the purest expressions of complete romantic love—to gentle Latin American–influenced music. In addition to the 3+3+2 subdivision of a common-time measure of music that is commonly found in Latin music, Prince includes instrumental touches that confirm the influence, such as acoustic guitar and Latin percussion instruments such as the guiro. While the piece might not scream "instant classic" like, say, "1999" or "When Doves Cry," "Te Amo Corazón" is well-crafted pop.

Prince revisits the hip-hop–based R&B music of his New Power Generation work of the 1990s in the song "Black Sweat." The sweat of the song's title can be understood as a literal sweat and also as a sexual desire. The song, though, sounds a little listless compared with the rhythmic dance music of sexual desire of a decade before. "Incense and Candles," a much more seductive and romantic song on which Prince duets with singer Támar, is more successful. Prince includes elements of the minor mode Middle Eastern melodic style he first had explored during his early 1980s psychedelic era.

In the next song, "Love," Prince continues to explore the theme of love and desire. Here, however, he and Támar sing in harmony and in essence tell each other that in the future neither will put up with the indiscretions, lies, and two-faced attitudes of the past. At first listen, it seems curious that the two singers—who seem to be portraying the two parties in the relationship— are both expressing the same attitude. Perhaps both characters were guilty in the past and now want to renew their relationship. To the extent that the vast majority of Prince's songs about dysfunctional relationships feature situations in which just one party is in the wrong, the situation suggested by the duet setting is a little confusing. It might have worked better as a solo number. Because the up-tempo piece is riff-based and combines the male and female voice in harmony, it calls to mind Prince's work with the Revolution, and his slightly later work with Sheena Easton.

Prince brings back old-school gospel-based R&B music of seduction in the next track, "Satisfied." Make no mistake about it, however, despite the retro musical setting, "Satisfied" is conspicuously a song of the twenty-first century. What else could explain a couplet such as "time to send your company home, time to turn off your cell phone." The slow, triplet-based setting is not instrumentally nor vocally especially virtuosic, but Prince plays all the instruments (except for the horns), and sings nearly all the vocal lines beautifully. This track proves both that Prince can "do" 1960s R&B perhaps better than any musician of his generation and that he can be a thoroughly effective one-man band, particularly when he shies away from obvious use of synthesizers and drum machines.

The up-tempo rock number "Fury" is an even stronger, musically tighter demonstration of Prince's one-man band talents. In a tale that swirls around a public figure—a pop star—apparently caught up in a broken relationship, Prince creates a musical aura that suggests Jimi Hendrix's version of the Bob Dylan composition "All along the Watchtower." Prince's song is based on a short chord riff, just as the famous Dylan song of the 1960s had been. He allows his voice to trail off in pitch at the end of some of the phrases in a way that sounds eerily like Hendrix. While Prince's lyrics pretty clearly revolve around a broken relationship, the imagery is impressionistic enough to suggest at least a touch of the nonlinear apocalyptic imagery of Dylan's "All along the Watchtower" lyrics. Prince goes so far as to adopt the electric guitar solo panning of the famous Hendrix recording. The piece is not, however, a mere remake of a classic 1960s song. For one thing, Prince's arrangement and performance on "Fury" (he sings all the vocal lines and plays all the instruments) generally is closer to pop rock than the acid rock of the Hendrix version of "All along the Watchtower." Prince, too, incorporates a descending figure at the end of the chorus sections that comes straight out of the post-punk new wave style of the Strangler's "Down in the Sewer." If the listener does not recognize the ties to the music of the past, this composition, performance, and production perfectly captures the feel of "a woman scorned" of the lyrics. Even if the listener hears the connections to the work of Hendrix and bands such as the Stranglers, the song—and Prince's vocal and guitar work—is so strong that it never sounds derivative. Somehow, it sounds more like a classic Prince song from the height of his popularity in the 1980s, just recorded 20 years or so later.

The album's next track, "The Word," focuses in directly on Prince's religious beliefs. Here, he tells the listener that the only chance for salvation comes from belief in "the Word" of God. It is a gentle, moderate-tempo piece that, while it is pleasant to listen to and fits in with the album's overarching theme, is not among Prince's best works. Some of the lines are set to such rapid-fire rhythm that it is easy to miss their significance, and the Latin-influenced background rhythmic and chordal accompaniment groove of the music seems to allow the listener's focus to wander. It is another track on which Prince plays all the instruments. It is not, however, as successful as the previous two songs. Particularly questionable is his decision to use a synthesized saxophone-like sound in the main instrumental countermelody figure, given the high-powered horn section that plays on some of the other tracks on the album.

Over the course of Prince's career, rarely have individual collaborators had their names appear as co-writers of Prince songs. Sure, there were some songs credited to Prince and the Revolution or the New Power Generation, but most Prince songs are . . . Prince songs. Prince and vocalist Támar share the writing credits for *3121*'s next track, "Beautiful, Loved, and Blessed." This song continues the religious theme of "The Word," at least on one level. The lyrics of redemption can be understood, however, to refer both to the sense of wholeness that one might find in a deep human love relationship or in a spiritual relationship with God. The music is pleasant, adult contemporary R&B. It is not, however, particularly distinctive in the manner of Prince's best-remembered songs. The next track, "The Dance," a love ballad, unfortunately sounds even more anonymous.

The album's closer, "Get on the Boat," is perhaps Prince's most consciously James Brown–influenced compositions in construction. In this old-school funk number, Prince pulls out all the Brown stops, including the guttural grunts and shouts, the horn riffs, the leader (Prince, in this case) calling out "bridge" to direct the band into the bridge section of the song, and so on.[3] The song has a more religious and spiritual aim than many up-tempo James Brown funk works, though. "The boat," which Prince exhorts the audience to board, is the boat of universal love, the boat of salvation. Listeners that think of Prince as "just" an ace guitarist and singer-songwriter had better listen to this track to be reminded that, when he lets down his guard, he can play keyboards. Prince also once again proves—as on several other songs on *3121*—that his religious messages are more effective when they are expressed in the form of more conventional metaphors than they are in the form of the esoteric settings and storyline of *The Rainbow Children*.

While *3121* contains a couple of less-than-completely-successful ballads, most of the songs sound more vital than those of the more-obviously retro-influenced *Musicology*. Prince provides his longtime fans with stylistic tastes of 1960s funk, 1970s new wave rock, the 1980s feel of the classic *Sign o' the Times* album, mixed in with just a little New Power Generation hip-hop–influenced funk. Despite the musical diversity, Prince's lyrics are remarkably consistent, focusing on the twin themes of the ups and downs of human-to-human love relationships and the utter solidity of human relationships with God.

PLANET EARTH

Released in July 2007, *Planet Earth* is Prince's most recent album to date. If nothing else, the album proves that Prince remains a creative force as he approaches age fifty. It is an album that finds Prince continuing to focus on creating tighter packages than what he was trying to put together in the late 1980s through the mid-1990s. The first track to be released, the single "Guitar," was offered free in June 2007 to subscribers to Verizon Wireless for trying a demonstration of the company's new music service. The full album also enjoyed a most unusual release. Prince arranged for the British newspaper *The Mail* to distribute the disc free with the July 15, 2007, issue. Prince's British distributor, Sony BMG U.K., refused to distribute the album for sale, fearing that Prince's deal with *The Mail* would undermine U.K. sales. While the means by which Prince released his latest material was cutting-edge and controversial, the music of *Planet Earth* by and large is not. However, the music is well crafted, engaging, and proves that Prince is still a vital artist.

The album begins with the title track. Of all of Prince's music of the new millennium, "Planet Earth" perhaps is the best example of a song that greatly benefits from multiple hearings, with different focal points for each listening. That is because the lyrics are challenging, the musical arrangement and use of contrasting styles and tone colors is so vivid, and the integration of music and lyrics creates such a powerful whole. Let us take a look at each of these features.

Prince begins the song by asking the listener to imagine that he or she holds the Earth "in the palm of [his or her] hand," and that the person also imagine that he or she has no political or geographical ties to any nation or land area. He then asks the listener to imagine what will be said in 50 years about people who inhabit the planet today—specifically, how they (we) treated the Earth and its resources. Prince then tells the listener that there are only two kinds of people: givers and takers, and in the chorus he tells us that now is the time for the planet to come into balance with "the one that caused it all to be." The focus, then, of the first third of the song is environmental stewardship as a way of honoring the Almighty. The second part of the song finds Prince challenging the listener to imagine that he or she could eradicate any people he or she chose and how the person would decide who would live and who would die. He then reminds us of Jesus' command not to judge "lest we be judged too." In the final third of the song, Prince asks the listener to image sending his or her first-born off to fight in a war that has no clear reason, and whether that would truly help to solve domestic problems such as poverty. The song concludes with a restatement of the chorus, which reminds the listener that Earth and its people must "come into balance with the one that caused it all to be" so that we "see his kingdom come."

Although it is not a novel technique, the fact that Prince puts the listener in the metaphorical shoes of the Almighty helps him make the points effectively—it keeps the message from getting preachy and alienating listeners who are adverse to being told what to do and what not to do. Although placing three submessages in one song runs the risk of diluting the message, such is not the case here. There seems to be little sense of a wandering purpose or message. Instead, the song can be heard as delivering the overarching, meta-message that everything in the universe—the spiritual world, the animal world, the plant world, the human world, and the worlds out in space—are all connected. While this concept is missing from some Western philosophies, it is common in Eastern philosophy, as well as in Native American philosophy.

One of the challenges the listener encounters in dealing with a piece such as "Planet Earth" is the sense of disconnection between the weightiness of the concepts and the structure of the lyrics as a poem. It is no secret that popular song lyrics—even those from wildly effective and well-loved songs—often pale as standalone poems. In the case of "Planet Earth," there are some awkward, moon-in-June-type moments, such as Prince's rhyming of "lose" and "choose," and "war" and "poor." It is just too obvious, too easy, and too lacking in rich imagery to be counted among Prince's best pieces of poetry. In particular, the linking of war and poverty does not hit with the same impact as, say, that of Marvin Gaye's "What's Going On." That does not mean, however, that the clipped poetic phrases and unsophisticated rhymes render "Planet Earth" a lost cause. As is so often the case with pop songs, the musical setting enhances the lyrics and takes at least some of the attention off the details of the rhyme scheme.

Although Prince does not spin the entire melody out in a single, organic melodic motive, he does use a motive and a slight variation of it to construct a good part of the melody of the verses of "Planet Earth." This lends some sense of an organic wholeness to the tune, which is supportive of the images and suggestions of interconnectedness that he explores in the text. What really makes this composition better than the sum of its parts, however, is the arrangement and production. Prince the arranger and producer juxtaposes distorted electric guitar with a clean-sounding acoustic piano. Stylistically, too, he balances jazz, pop, and hard rock references. The mixture of disparate timbres and styles suggests the interconnectedness of all humanity with the spiritual and natural worlds.

Given Prince's turn toward more serious topics (especially since the 1998 album *The Truth*...), lyrical sentiments that reflect middle age, and an increasing sophistication in his music and arrangements in the new millennium, the song "Guitar" represents a delightful return to youthful musical exuberance as well as lyrical sentiments that suggest youth. Prince gets away with this lyrical putdown, in which he tells his would-be lover that he doesn't love her as much as he loves his guitar, set to 1980s-style rock, because he does not dwell on nostalgia. Instead, he plays more of the role of the thirty-something Chuck Berry creating songs such as "School Days": "Guitar" is a here-and-now song that probably better reflects the attitudes of someone younger than Prince than it does someone of Prince's age. Ultimately, it is one of Prince's funniest songs and will satisfy those who consider him one of the more important guitar heroes of the past 30 years. It represents Prince at play, just cutting lose. He maintains the feeling of casualness throughout his performance as a player and as a singer. Especially notable is Prince almost (but not quite) telling his lover that she can "go to hell" until she understands that he doesn't love her as much as he loves his guitar. The chuckle Prince delivers at the end of the line—where he leaves out the word *hell*—suggests that he caught himself using an expletive that, mild as it might be in comparison with the language of some of Prince's songs of the 1980s and 1990s, is inappropriate within the context of his faith. He also adds to the conversational/casual nature of the song when he ends the last iteration of the vocals in the fadeout section with the aside, "you know the rest," instead of providing the expected last line of that particular section. The subtle beauty of this line—and one that is apt to be missed unless one is really paying close attention—is the way in which it matches what Prince does in his earlier guitar solo. The in-the-know, joking nature of the piece is also confirmed by the line "I'll send a letter when I learn how to spell." Any fan that has read Prince's lyrics as they are presented in the liner notes of his albums will likely connect this line with Prince's proclivity for using text messaging–type abbreviations—something he has done consistently since the 1980s, well before text messaging existed. It all fits the spirit of the playfulness and fun of the song.

The next track, "Somewhere Here on Earth," begins with the sound of vinyl record–era surface noise. This is followed by one of the gentlest old-school ballads Prince has ever written and recorded. Like some of Prince's classic melodies of the 1980s—the height of his popularity—this tune clearly emphasizes a descent from a high point, in this case, the fourth scale-step, to tonic. It seems a little disconcerting to hear Prince mention that this is the "digital age" and to suggest that his yet-to-be-found future lover could page him, because the musical setting (which includes a jazzy muted trumpet) and the use of vinyl-era noise make the song sound so deliberately old.

Prince returns to a rock style for "The One U Wanna C." Here, he conjures up the musical image of John Cougar Mellencamp in his "Hurts So Good" (1982) through "Small Town" (1985) period. The short, hook-laden phrases, narrow melodic range, and hint of neo-rockabilly all suggest the elements that defined the Mellencamp sound in the early 1980s. Prince's lyrics find his character trying to pick up a woman, while assuring her that he does not just want a one-night stand. This suggests a variant on the "I Could Never Take the Place of Your Man" lyrical theme. In this song, however, Prince's character clearly stands a chance of success in love.

The next piece, "Future Baby Mama," does not wear well. The R&B ballad style is pleasant enough, but the lyrics are problematic. Prince's character tells the woman whom he has decided is the love of his life that his former lovers just did not have what it takes. She, however, does have what it takes to be a "future baby mama." A male listener can only imagine or make an educated guess at how women would perceive this image. However, the suggestion that the defining factor for Prince's character to find his ideal lover revolves entirely around the image of a baby-making machine is disconcerting.

The song "Mr. Goodnight," which continues the R&B ballad feel, is another pickup song. This links it with "The One U Wanna C." In this case, though, Prince makes it clear that the lyrics represent his personal fantasy. In the rap, he says that "all over the world" he is "known as Prince," but that she can call him "Mr. Goodnight." The suave superlover Prince portrays tells his would-be lover that he will satisfy her and, in fact, tells her that he will match his suit to the dress she wears. He betrays, however, a touch of paternalism and objectification.

"All the Midnights in the World" places Prince into an entirely different rhetorical setting. Here, he asks his lover to make a commitment to accept his proposal for marriage "tonight," or else admit that the two will have to live out the rest of their lives as friends. The contrast of this near-chivalrous character with those of previous songs on the album—in particular, "Future Baby Mama" and "Mr. Goodnight"—suggests that a subtheme of the album is Prince's depiction of a wide range of male responses to love for and sexual desire for women.

The funk composition "Chelsea Rodgers" concerns the title character, who was a party-going model that apparently gave up the party life to devote her life to God. Prince's lyrics are somewhat confusing, and the Internet has continued to be abuzz from July 2007 into early 2008 about the real identity of Rodgers. The apparently real-life title character is either a protégé of Prince, his new girlfriend, or simply a model who is playing a role in generating interest in *Planet Earth*, depending on which line of Internet speculation one believes. No matter what the ultimate truth about the real-life story of the song's title character, Prince and the New Power Generation's arrangement on the song, which includes punchy brass figures and a decidedly disco-style electric bass, perfectly captures the go-go lifestyle of a party-girl fashion model. The story of Rodgers's salvation represents a break from the previous several songs, which had explored a range of male responses to female sexuality. However, it also represents a return to the theme of the first track on the album, which focused on humankind's relationship with God.

The song "Lion of Judah" is introduced by Prince's flanger-laden electric guitar. The melodic motion in the verses of the song is minimal, and that of the chorus is somewhat abstract, but that is because the story Prince tells seems to be more important to him than making a popish connection. The lyrics are written from the autobiographical standpoint of a male pop music star that wants to take a woman out on the town to all the places that she wants to go. He informs her that the press likely will follow their every move, but that "like the Lion of Judah," he will strike down his foes. Although the song speaks to the intensely personal nature of Prince's private life and his often-frosty relationship with the press, it is one of the less memorable tracks on the album.

Planet Earth ends with "Revelation," a song that evokes the spiritual, peace-love-and-universal-brotherhood-of-humankind work of George Harrison. Even Prince's use of some tasty chromatic chords suggests the work of the late Harrison. Prince's great revelation is that conflict never results in anyone being happy—whether on the interpersonal or on the global level. While the song can be interpreted as a commentary on the war in Iraq or even the broader Bush administration's war on terror (mostly because of the song's timing), it is general enough that the message could be understood within a wide range of references. And, it does tend to put the various relationship songs of the album into context. Prince builds the melody from a short, engaging motive. The composition is tuneful and invites multiple hearings. It forms an effective bookend to *Planet Earth* in that it brings back the social and environmental concerns that Prince raised in the first track.

All in all, *Planet Earth* contains engaging music and lyrics; however, it finds Prince jumping between three themes—humankind's relationships with God, the variety of men's responses to women, and autobiography—that only seem to tie together after the song "Revelation" puts them into context. The album's packaging, with its cover photo of Prince hovering over the Earth, suggests a grand concept album. Because of the loose ties between the songs and the multiple thematic focal points, however, *Planet Earth* tends to sound more like a collection of individual songs than a concept album.

Conclusions: The Importance of Being Prince

It is easy to find people who are familiar with at least one Prince song. Radio hits such as "Purple Rain," "Little Red Corvette," "1999," and "When Doves Cry," however, only tell a very small part of the story about Prince's importance in the music world of the late twentieth century and early twenty-first century. He is one of the most prolific songwriters and recording artists of the rock era, a skilled arranger and producer, and he has transcended stylistic boundaries like no other artist of the era. Because of his lyrics and music, his work as an actor, and his public stances for vegetarianism and against racism and corporate control over artists' product, and because of his unique sense of identity and fashion, Prince is one of the most iconic figures in popular culture. In order to sum up Prince's importance as a singer-songwriter and pop culture icon, it is important to review his contributions in all these areas.

It is important for the reader to keep in mind that the words and music of Prince—or any songwriter, for that matter—exist entirely within a context. In other words, Prince's lyrics and music are always tied together. What's more, because Prince aims his material so specifically at particular performers—himself, in most cases—the arrangement and production of the definitive recordings of his works also play a crucial role in creating the feel of each and every song. While it may be artificial, then, to consider the words and music of Prince separately, it is necessary in order to summarize his contributions.

As a lyricist, Prince's main contributions to American popular music over the past 30 years revolve principally around his subject matter. His frank and sometimes explicit references to human sexuality and sexual desire broke new ground in the 1980s. In fact, his explicit references to masturbation in the song "Darling Niki" are cited as the primary motivation behind Tipper

Gore's formation of the Parents Music Resource Center. Although it might appear to be ironic, Prince has also explored spiritual and religious themes throughout his career. While the most obvious example of this aspect of his work as a lyricist can be found in the songs of *The Rainbow Children*, his Jehovah's Witness album, it is found to much better effect in individual songs that are not impeded by the science fiction-esque nature of *The Rainbow Children*.

The most intriguing thing about what might at first appear to be a conceptual conflict between the twin focus on spirituality and sexuality is that Prince completely integrates the two subjects. Without him having to say it in so many words, Prince's lyrics tell the listener that sexuality and sexual desire are gifts from the Almighty that are meant to be celebrated and enjoyed. In Prince songs, sexual experiences of a wide variety of types between consenting adults are not a sin; rather, they are an affirmation of God's gift to humankind.

In his lyrics and costumes Prince also explores the sexual ambiguity of early 1970s glam rock pioneers Marc Bolan and David Bowie. Visually, this can be seen in the colorful purple motorcycle and frilly shirts of *Purple Rain*, as well as hints of eye makeup on other album covers. Lyrically, Prince mixes hyper-masculinity in some of his New Power Generation songs of the 1990s with references to adopting feminine personae in songs such as "If I Was Your Girlfriend" and "I Wanna Be Your Lover." In his 1999 retrospective look back at Prince's album *Dirty Mind*, *Rolling Stone* contributor Fred Schruers wrote that Prince "feminized" rock in the 1980s the same way as Mick Jagger in the 1960s and David Bowie in the 1970s. In particular, Schruers highlighted the album's cover art (which showed Prince in a black jock strap), his seeming obsession with sex, and concert and video performances that featured "falsetto, coy struts and eyelash-batting."[1]

Prince's active exploration of sexual ambiguity as an artist fits within an even wider theme in his music: identity. Some of Prince's songs, most obviously, "My Name Is Prince" and "Sexy M.F.," overtly deal with definition of self. The broad range of male character types—from vulnerable, to hypermasculine and misogynistic; from sensible and logical, to wildly illogical; and so forth—Prince portrays in his songs suggest that he intends to show his audience as universal a picture of the late twentieth/early twenty-first-century Western human male as possible. For the most part, Prince does not tell the listener whether the actions and attitudes of these male characters are right or wrong; it simply is. He provides snapshots of his view of the reality of the spectrum of male existence and male-female relationships of our time, and by juxtaposing a broad range of personality types forces the listener to deal on her or his own terms with the very real presence of these types in the real world.

Prince's musical compositions have exhibited a wide stylistic range. The most remarkable thing about his incorporation of heavy metal, Quiet Storm

R&B, hip-hop, new wave rock, hard rock, funk, soul, pseudo-1960s psyche-delia, and jazz is that he so frequently turns to all of these colors of the pop music stylistic palette. And, he does not just dabble in these disparate styles; he has written and recorded significant hit songs in every category. This makes *the* Prince sound difficult, if not impossible, to characterize. It also makes Prince stand apart from every popular musician of his generation.

One of the great controversies of American music has been the merger of black and white influences in popular music. This did not originate with Prince; it did not originate with Jimi Hendrix, or even with the development of rock and roll. Writer Ken Emerson traces questions of racial authentic-ity in American popular music well back into the nineteenth century in his book *Doo-Dah: Steven Foster and the Rise of American Popular Culture.*[2] Cer-tainly, Prince has generated controversy among his wide-ranging fan base, certain segments of which tend to gravitate to his funk and hip-hop music, and certain segments of which tend to gravitate to his pop and psychedelic rock sound. But, this stylistic diversity is one of Prince's greatest contribu-tions. Just as his integration of sexuality and spirituality breaks down tradi-tional social barriers, his integration of so-called black and white styles (to the extent there really are such entirely racially defined categories) breaks down barriers between people.

In order fully to appreciate the overall contribution Prince has made to popular music over the past three decades, it is also helpful to consider the importance of some of his specific compositions. Certainly, songs such as "Kiss" and "Sugar Walls" redefined the careers of Tom Jones and Sheena Easton, respectively, and the Bangles' recording of "Manic Monday" remains a radio staple. Most of the classic songs Prince has written, however, were given their definitive recorded treatment by Prince himself—Chaka Khan's Grammy Award-winning cover of "I Feel for You," notwithstanding. Let us briefly recap in a bit more detail just a very few of his compositions, some recorded by Prince, and some most closely associated with other performers as a brief overview of the significance of his work.

The aforementioned Bangles recording of "Manic Monday" will probably continue to be a staple of oldies radio for a good long time because its mes-sage of the drudgery of the work week is, if not a universal, at least some-thing that has been part of American society for decades and probably will be for many more. But, it also includes the sexual subtext: the reason that the woman is late to work is because she had a late night making "some noise" in the bedroom with her lover. And, the singer acknowledges that she enjoyed the physical lovemaking ("Time goes by so fast when you're having fun.") This captures the spirit of the fuller acknowledgment of women's sexual plea-sure that entered popular culture in the wake of the 1970s women's move-ment. Musically, although the song clearly is derived from "1999," there are enough subtle touches that make it succeed far beyond what might be expected from a rewrite of an older hit. Most notably, every time the word

Monday (the start of the dreary work week) occurs in the chorus, Prince sets it to a two-note descending figure; however, every time the word *Sunday* (the singer's "fun day") occurs, Prince sets it to a two-note ascending figure. To top it off, the narrow melodic range of the verses and chorus make it easily singable, and the entire *gestalt* of the musical style works within the context of pop music of the 1960s into the twenty-first century.

Prince's song "1999" captured the end-of-the-millennium angst that was already building at the time of its release: 1983. For one thing, the year 1984 loomed large on public consciousness as a result of the impact of George Orwell's famous novel *1984*. While Orwell's novel may have been a response to what he saw around him during the World War II era, the specter of Big Brother grew in public consciousness as the actual year 1984 approached. Not only was the Prince song, with its vision of the end of the world, part of this, but it is also evidenced by the enormous impact of Apple Computer's famous "*1984*" television ad that premiered in January 1984. The sense of tension was not merely tied to a novel from the late 1940s, however. International tension, particularly between the United States and the Soviet Union, rose through the time of the Carter administration (1977–1981) and the first term of the Reagan administration (1981–1985). In fact, the level of tension between the two nuclear superpowers perhaps was higher than at any time except during the Cuban Missile Crisis of the early 1960s. Prince's vision of the end of the world hit uncomfortably close: the song was very much a product of its time. However, the more general theme of living one's life to its fullest because one never knows when life will end is a universal. As the year 1999 and the year 2000 approached, "1999" enjoyed a second wave of popularity. While some people undoubtedly still feared just what the end of the millennium would bring, the spirit of partying that underlies the song seemed more to be what was felt in its second wave of popularity.

Although "I Could Never Take the Place of Your Man" might not be Prince's best-known song, it is in some respects one of the stronger songs of the 1980s new wave. In fact, a songwriter could have made a name in pop culture history by having authored the new wave style songs: "I Could Never Take the Place of Your Man," "When You Were Mine," "Uptown," and "Manic Monday." So, why might "I Could Never Take the Place of Your Man" be one of Prince's supreme achievements? First of all, the music completely captures the prevailing pop/rock style of the time and the performance is strong, a little overuse of studio reverb notwithstanding. Prince's guitar solo moves deftly from improvisation to prearranged melodic figures, and then back into (what appears to be) spontaneous improvisation. The whole thing is handled so smoothly that it is easy to miss its importance. What it really tells us is that Prince is always thinking and performing like a composer (as opposed to a songwriter). His work on the song—and especially on the extended *Sign o' the Times* album version—tells the listener in no uncertain terms that he conceives of the *whole* of the piece.

Various lists of the most significant singles of the rock era include Sinéad O'Connor's recording of "Nothing Compares 2 U." While O'Connor deserves a great deal of credit for making this recording a classic, part of the song's strength comes from Prince's merger of lyrics and music. The text painting, in particular the contrast in rhythmic and melodic activity between the phrases in which the singer bares the depth of her inner hurt and those in which she sings of all the fun things she will be able to do now that her relationship has ended, is stark. It is also highly effective.

Prince's other principal contribution is as a performing musician, particularly as a singer and guitarist. In his writing, singing, and instrumental work, he manages to maintain clear links to the musical traditions with which he grew up (psychedelic rock, R&B, and funk) while moving with the times. He has not always emphasized his guitar playing, particularly in the 1990s, but he remains a vital instrumental force and is widely acknowledged as one of the most important electric guitarists of the 1980s.

When I speak to groups, students, or colleagues about my research, one question that sometimes arises is, "If I had to select an artist's most essential work, what should I buy?" In the case of an artist as prolific as Prince, this is a particularly daunting challenge. The reader should keep in mind that any such list is by necessity going to be highly subjective. Personally—for what it is worth—if my collection of Prince records and CDs suddenly disappeared, I would immediately replace (in no particular order) *Sign o' the Times, Purple Rain* (and the film, too—it is an essential part of the Prince canon), "The Love Symbol Album," and *The Truth*…disc from the *Crystal Ball* multidisc set. While *Emancipation* is a challenging collection, because of its size, it shows off Prince's ability to assimilate the styles of earlier performers, writers, and producers better than perhaps any of his other albums, and it includes several songs that are especially strong examples of Prince's ability to establish mood by means of highly artistic juxtapositions of words and music. Of Prince's most recent recordings, I would make sure that I had the single "Guitar" available and the album *3121*. Add to that list the Bangles' single "Manic Monday" and Sinéad O'Connor's recording of "Nothing Compares 2 U."

That list misses some strong lyrical and musical work from each decade of Prince's career; however, even with that small sampling of Prince's total artistic contribution to the popular culture as a core, it would be clear why Prince is a formidable iconic figure and one of the most important musicians of his time.

Selected Discography

The Albums of Prince

For You. Prince, keyboards, guitars, bass, drums, various other instruments, and vocals. "For You" (Prince), "In Love" (Prince), "Soft and Wet" (Prince, Chris Moon), "Crazy You" (Prince), "Just As Long As We're Together" (Prince), "Baby" (Prince), "My Love Is Forever" (Prince), "So Blue" (Prince), "I'm Yours" (Prince). Produced by Prince; Executive Producer, Tommy Vicari. 33–1/3 rpm LP. Warner Bros. BSK 3150, 1978. Reissued on compact disc, Warner Bros., 3150–2, 1987.

Prince. Prince, keyboards, guitars, bass, drums, various other instruments, and vocals. "I Wanna Be Your Lover" (Prince), "Why You Wanna Treat Me So Bad?" (Prince), "Sexy Dancer" (Prince), "When We're Dancing Close and Slow" (Prince), "With You" (Prince), "Bambi" (Prince), "Still Waiting" (Prince), "I Feel for You" (Prince), "It's Gonna Be Lonely" (Prince). Produced by Prince. 33–1/3 rpm LP. Warner Bros. BSK 3366, 1979. Reissued on compact disc, Warner Bros. 3366–2, 1987. Also issued on compact disc as George V 3081502, 2003.

Dirty Mind. Prince, keyboards, guitars, bass, drums, percussion, vocals; various assisting musicians. "Dirty Mind" (Prince, Doctor Fink), "When You Were Mine" (Prince), "Do It All Night" (Prince), "Gotta Broken Heart Again" (Prince), "Uptown" (Prince), "Head" (Prince), "Sister" (Prince), "Partyup" (Prince). Produced by Prince. 33–1/3 rpm LP. Warner Bros. BSK 3478, 1980. Reissued on compact disc, Warner Bros. 3478–2, 1986.

Controversy. Prince, keyboards, guitars, bass, drums, percussion, vocals; various assisting musicians. "Controversy" (Prince), "Sexuality" (Prince), "Do Me, Baby" (Prince), "Private Joy" (Prince), "Ronnie, Talk to Russia" (Prince), "Let's Work" (Prince), "Annie Christian" (Prince), "Jack U Off" (Prince). Produced by Prince. 33–1/3 rpm LP. Warner Bros. BSK 3601, 1981. Reissued on compact disc, Warner Bros. 3601-2, 1986.

1999. Prince, keyboards, guitars, drums, percussion, vocals; various assisting musicians. "1999" (Prince), "Little Red Corvette" (Prince), "Delirious" (Prince), "Let's Pretend We're Married" (Prince), "D.M.S.R." (Prince), "Automatic" (Prince), "Something in the Water (Does Not Compute)" (Prince), "Free" (Prince), "Lady Cab Driver" (Prince), "All the Critics Love U in New York" (Prince), "International Lover" (Prince). Produced by Prince. Two 33–1/3 rpm LPs. Warner Bros. 1–23720, 1983. Reissued on compact disc as Warner Bros. 9–23720-2, 1984. Note: Some copies of the compact disc reissue do not include the song "D.M.S.R."

Purple Rain. Prince and the Revolution. "Let's Go Crazy" (Prince and the Revolution), "Take Me with U" (Prince and the Revolution), "The Beautiful Ones" (Prince), "Computer Blue" (Prince and the Revolution), "Darling Nikki" (Prince), "When Doves Cry" (Prince), "I Would Die 4 U" (Prince and the Revolution), "Baby, I'm a Star" (Prince and the Revolution), "Purple Rain" (Prince and the Revolution). Produced by Prince and the Revolution. Simultaneously issued on 33–1/3 rpm LP, Warner Bros. 1–25110; and compact disc, 9–25110-2, 1984.

Around the World in a Day. Prince and the Revolution; various accompanying musicians. "Around the World in a Day" (David Coleman, John L. Nelson, Prince), "Paisley Park" (Prince and the Revolution), "Condition of the Heart" (Prince and the Revolution), "Raspberry Beret" (Prince and the Revolution), "Tamborine" (Prince and the Revolution), "America" (Prince and the Revolution), "Pop Life" (Prince and the Revolution), "The Ladder" (John L. Nelson, Prince), "Temptation" (Prince and the Revolution). Produced by Prince and the Revolution. Simultaneously issued on 33–1/3 rpm LP, Paisley Park 25286–1; and compact disc, Paisley Park 9–25286-2, 1985.

Parade: Music from the Motion Picture "Under the Cherry Moon." Prince and the Revolution; various other accompanying musicians. "Christopher Tracy's Parade" (Prince, John L. Nelson), "New Position" (Prince and the Revolution), "I Wonder U" (Prince and the Revolution), "Under the Cherry Moon" (Prince, John L. Nelson), "Girls & Boys" (Prince and the Revolution), "Life Can Be So Nice" (Prince and the Revolution), "Venus De Milo" (Prince and the Revolution), "Mountains" (Prince and the Revolution), "Do U Lie?" (Prince and the Revolution), "Kiss" (Prince and the Revolution), "Anotherloverholenyohead" (Prince and the Revolution), "Sometimes It Snows in April" (Prince and the Revolution). Produced by Prince and the Revolution. Simultaneously issued on 33–1/3 rpm LP, Paisley Park 1–25395; and compact disc, Paisley Park 9–25395-2, 1986.

Sign o' the Times. Prince, vocals, guitars, keyboards, drums, percussion; various assisting musicians. "Sign o' the Times" (Prince), "Play in the Sunshine" (Prince), "Housequake" (Prince), "The Ballad of Dorothy Parker" (Prince), "It" (Prince), "Starfish and Coffee" (Prince, Susannah), "Slow Love" (Prince, Carol Davis), "Hot Thing" (Prince), "Forever in My Life" (Prince), "U Got the Look" (Prince), "If I Was Your Girlfriend" (Prince), "Strange Relationship" (Prince), "I Could Never Take the Place of Your Man" (Prince), "The Cross" (Prince), "It's Gonna Be a Beautiful Night" (Prince, Dr. Fink, Eric Leeds), "Adore"

(Prince). Produced by Prince. Two compact discs. Paisley Park 9–25577–2, 1987.

The Black Album. Prince, vocals, guitars, keyboards, drums, percussion; various assisting musicians. "Le Grind" (Prince), "Cindy C." (Prince), "Dead on It" (Prince), "When 2 R in Love" (Prince), "Bob George" (Prince), "Superfunky-califragisexi" (Prince), "2 Nigs United 4 West Compton" (Prince), "Rock Hard in a Funky Place" (Prince). Produced by Prince. 33–1/3 rpm LP. Erotic City NOIR-69, 1987. Released on compact disc, Warner Bros. 2–45793, 1994.

Lovesexy. Prince, keyboards, guitars, drums, percussion, vocals; various assisting musicians. "I [Eye] No" (Prince), "Alphabet St." (Prince), "Glam Slam" (Prince), "Anna Stesia" (Prince), "Dance On" (Prince), "Lovesexy" (Prince), "When 2 R in Love" (Prince), "I Wish U Heaven" (Prince), "Positively" (Prince). Produced by Prince. Simultaneously issued on 33–1/3 rpm LP, Paisley Park 9 25720–1; and compact disc, Paisley Park 9 25720–2, 1988.

Batman. Prince, keyboards, guitars, keyboards, drums, percussion, vocals; various assisting musicians. "The Future" (Prince), "Electric Chair" (Prince), "The Arms of Orion" (Prince, Sheena Easton), "Partyman" (Prince), "Vicki Waiting" (Prince), "Trust" (Prince), "Lemon Crush" (Prince), "Scandalous" (Prince, John L. Nelson), "Batdance" (Prince). Produced by Prince. Simultaneously issued on 33–1/3 rpm LP, Warner Bros. 25936–1; and compact disc, Warner Bros. 9 25936–2, 1989.

Graffiti Bridge. Prince, keyboards, guitars, drums, percussion, vocals; various assisting musicians. "Can't Stop This Feeling I Got" (Prince), "New Power Generation" (Prince), "Release It" (Prince, Levi Speacer, Jr.), "The Question of U" (Prince), "Elephants & Flowers" (Prince), "Round and Round" (Prince), "We Can Funk" (Prince, George Clinton), "Joy in Repetition" (Prince), "Love Machine" (Prince, Levi Speacer, Jr., Morris Day), "Tick, Tick, Bang" (Prince), "Shake!" (Prince), "Thieves in the Temple" (Prince), "The Latest Fashion" (Prince), "Melody Cool" (Prince), "Still Would Stand All Time" (Prince), "Graffiti Bridge" (Prince), "New Power Generation, Pt. II" (Prince). Produced by Prince. Simultaneously issued on two 33–1/3 rpm LPs, Paisley Park 1–27493; and compact disc, Paisley Park 9 27493–2, 1991.

Diamonds and Pearls. Prince and the New Power Generation. "Thunder" (Prince and the New Power Generation), "Daddy Pop" (Prince and the New Power Generation), "Diamonds and Pearls" (Prince and the New Power Generation), "Cream" (Prince and the New Power Generation), "Strollin'" (Prince and the New Power Generation), "Willing and Able" (Prince and the New Power Generation), "Gett Off" (Prince and the New Power Generation), "Walk Don't Walk" (Prince and the New Power Generation), "Jughead" (Prince and the New Power Generation), "Money Don't Matter 2 Night" (Prince and the New Power Generation), "Push" (Prince and the New Power Generation), "Insatiable" (Prince and the New Power Generation), "Live 4 Love" (Prince and the New Power Generation). Produced by Prince and the New Power Generation. Simultaneously issued on two 33–1/3 rpm LPs, Paisley Park WX432; and compact disc, Paisley Park 25379–2, 1991.

⚤ ("The Love Symbol Album"). Prince and the New Power Generation. "My Name Is Prince" (Prince), "Sexy M.F." (Prince, Tony M., Levi Speacer, Jr.,), "Love 2 the 9's" (Prince), "The Morning Papers" (Prince), "The Max" (Prince), "Blue

Light" (Prince), "I [Eye] Wanna Melt with U" (Prince), "Sweet Baby" (Prince), "The Continental" (Prince), "Damn U" (Prince), "Arrogance" (Prince), "The Flow" (Prince), "7" (Prince, with samples of material by Lowell Fulsom and Jimmy McCrackin), "And God Created Woman" (Prince), "3 Chains of Gold" (Prince), "The Sacrifice of Victor" (Prince). Produced by Prince and the New Power Generation and various assisting producers. Simultaneously issued on two 33–1/3 rpm LPs, Paisley Park 9362–45037–1; and compact disc, Paisley Park 9 45037–2, 1992.

Come. Prince, keyboards, guitars, keyboards, drums, percussion, vocals; the New Power Generation; various assisting musicians. "Come" (Prince), "Space" (Prince), "Pheromone" (Prince), "Loose!" (Prince), "Papa" (Prince), "Race" (Prince), "Dark" (Prince), "Solo" (Prince, David Henry Hwang), "Letitgo" (Prince), "Orgasm" (Prince). Produced by Prince. Compact disc. Warner Bros. 9 45700–2, 1994.

The Gold Experience. ⚥ (Prince), keyboards, guitars, keyboards, drums, percussion, vocals; the New Power Generation; various assisting musicians. "P Control" (Prince),[1] "NPG Operator" (Prince), "Endorphinmachine" (Prince), "Shhh" (Prince), "We March" (Prince, Nona Gaye), "NPG Operator" (Prince), "The Most Beautiful Girl in the World" (Prince), "Dolphin" (Prince), "NPG Operator" (Prince), "Now" (Prince), "NPG Operator" (Prince), "319" (Prince), "NPG Operator" (Prince), "Shy" (Prince), "Billy Jack Bitch" (Prince), "I [Eye] Hate U"[2] (Prince), "NPG Operator" (Prince), "Gold" (Prince). Produced by Prince, with various assisting producers. Compact disc. Warner Bros./NPG 9 45999–2, 1995.

Chaos and Disorder. Prince, keyboards, guitars, drums, percussion, vocals; the New Power Generation; various assisting musicians. "Chaos and Disorder" (Prince), "I Like It There" (Prince), "Dinner with Delores" (Prince), "The Same December" (Prince), "Right the Wrong" (Prince), "Zannalee" (Prince), "I Rock, Therefore I Am" (Prince), "Into the Light" (Prince), "I Will" (Prince), "Dig U Better Dead" (Prince), "Had U" (Prince). Produced by Prince. Compact disc. Warner Bros. 46317–2, 1996.

Emancipation. Prince, keyboards, guitars, drums, percussion, vocals; various assisting musicians. "Jam of the Year" (Prince), "Right Back Here in My Arms" (Prince), "Somebody's Somebody" (Prince, Brenda Lee Eager, Hilliard Wilson), "Get Yo Groove On" (Prince), "Courtin' Time" (Prince), "Bettcha By Golly Wow!" (Thomas Randolph Bell, Linda Creed), "We Gets Up" (Prince), "White Mansion" (Prince), "Damned If I [Eye] Do" (Prince), "I [Eye] Can't Make U Love Me" (James Allen Shamblin II, Michael Barry Reid), "Mr. Happy" (Prince), "In This Bed I [Eye] Scream" (Prince), "Sex in the Summer" (Prince), "One Kiss at a Time" (Prince), "Soul Sanctuary" (Prince, Sandra St. Victor), "Emale" (Prince), "Curious Child" (Prince), "Dreamin' about U" (Prince), "Joint 2 Joint" (Prince), "The Holy River" (Prince), "Let's Have a Baby" (Prince), "Saviour" (Prince), "The Plan" (Prince), "Friend, Lover, Sister, Mother/Wife" (Prince), "Slave" (Prince), "New World" (Prince), "The Human Body" (Prince), "Face Down" (Prince), "La, La, La Means I [Eye] Love You" (Thomas Randolph Bell, William Hart), "Style" (Prince), "Sleep Around" (Prince), "Da, Da, Da" (Prince), "My Computer" (Prince), "One of Us" (Eric M. Bazilian), "The Love We Make" (Prince), "Emancipation" (Prince). Produced by Prince with various associate producers. Three compact discs. NPG Records E2–54982, 1996.

Crystal Ball. Prince, keyboards, guitars, drums, percussion, vocals; various assisting musicians. "Crystal Ball" (Prince), "Dream Factory" (Prince), "Acknowledge Me" (Prince), "Ripopgodazippa" (Prince), "Love Sign" (Prince), "Hide the Bone" (Brenda Lee Eager, Hilliard Wilson), "2morrow" (Prince), "So Dark" (Prince), "Movie Star" (Prince), "Tell Me How U Wanna B Done" (Prince), "Interactive" (Prince), "Da Bang" (Prince), "Calhoun Square" (Prince), "What's My Name" (Prince), "Crucial" (Prince), "An Honest Man" (Prince), "Sexual Suicide" (Prince), "Cloreen Bacon Skin" (Prince), "Good Love" (Prince), "Strays of the World" (Prince), "Days of the Wild" (Prince), "Last Heart" (Prince), "Poom Poom" (Prince), "She Gave Her Angels" (Prince), "18 and Over" (J., Prince), "The Ride" (Prince), "Get Loose" (Prince), "P Control" (Prince), "Make Your Momma Happy" (Prince), "Goodbye" (Prince), "The Truth" (Prince), "Don't Play Me" (Prince), "Circle of Amour" (Prince), "3rd Eye" (Prince), "Dionne" (Prince), "Man in a Uniform" (Prince), "Animal Kingdom" (Prince), "The Other Side of the Pillow" (Prince), "Fascination" (Prince), "One of Your Tears" (Prince), "Comeback" (Prince), "Welcome 2 the Dawn" (Prince). Produced by Prince. Four compact discs. NPG Records, 1997.

New Power Soul. New Power Generation. "New Power Soul" (Prince and the New Power Generation), "Mad Sex" (Prince and the New Power Generation), "Until U're in My Arms Again" (Prince and the New Power Generation), "When You Love Somebody" (Prince and the New Power Generation), "Shoo-Bed-Ooh" (Prince and the New Power Generation), "Push It Up" (Prince and the New Power Generation), "Freaks on This Side" (Prince and the New Power Generation), "Come On" (Prince and the New Power Generation), "The One" (Prince and the New Power Generation), "(I [Eye] Like) Funky Music" (Prince and the New Power Generation), "Wasted Kisses" (Prince and the New Power Generation). "Circumcised" [produced] by Prince and Hans-Martin Buff. Compact disc. NPG Records 7 85337 98722, 1998.

The Vault: Old Friends 4 Sale. Prince, keyboards, guitars, drums, percussion, vocals; various assisting musicians. "The Rest of My Life" (Prince), "It's about That Walk" (Prince), "She Spoke 2 Me" (Prince), "5 Women +" (Prince), "When the Lights Go Down" (Prince), "My Little Pill" (Prince), "There Is Lonely" (Prince), "Old Friends 4 Sale" (Prince), "Sarah" (Prince), "Extraordinary" (Prince). Produced by Prince, with various assisting producers. Compact disc. Warner Bros. 2–47522, 1999.

Rave Un2 the Joy Fantastic. Prince, keyboards, guitars, drums, percussion, vocals; various assisting musicians. "Rave Un2 the Joy Fantastic" (Prince), "Undisputed" (Prince), "The Greatest Romance Ever Sold" (Prince), "Segue" (Prince), "Hot Wit U" (Prince), "Tangerine" (Prince), "So Far, So Pleased" (Prince), "The Sun, the Moon and Stars" (Prince), "Everyday Is a Winding Road" (Sheryl Crow, Jeff Trott, Brian McLeod), "Segue" (Prince), "Man o' War" (Prince), "Baby Knows" (Prince), "I [Eye] Love U, but I [Eye] Don't Trust U Anymore" (Prince), "Silly Game" (Prince), "Strange but True" (Prince), "Wherever U Go, Whatever U Do" (Prince). Produced by Prince. Compact disc. NPG Records 14624–2, 1999.

The Rainbow Children. Prince, keyboards, guitars, drums, percussion, vocals; various assisting musicians. "Rainbow Children" (Prince), "Muse 2 the Pharaoh" (Prince), "Digital Garden" (Prince), "The Work, Pt. 1" (Prince), "Everywhere" (Prince), "The Sensual Everafter" (Prince), "Mellow" (Prince), "1+1+1 Is 3"

(Prince), "Deconstruction" (Prince), "Wedding Feast" (Prince), "She Loves Me 4 Me" (Prince), "Family Name" (Prince), "The Everlasting Now" (Prince), "Last December" (Prince). Produced by Prince. Compact disc. NPG Records 70004–2, 2001.

N.E.W.S. Prince, keyboards, guitars; various assisting musicians. "North" (Prince), "East" (Prince), "West" (Prince), "South" (Prince). Produced by Prince. Compact disc. NPG Records, 2003.

Musicology. Prince, keyboards, guitars, drums, percussion, vocals; various assisting musicians. "Musicology" (Prince), "Illusion, Coma, Pimp & Circumstance" (Prince), "A Million Days" (Prince), "Life 'o' the Party" (Prince), "Call My Name" (Prince), "Cinnamon Girl" (Prince), "What Do U Want Me 2 Do?" (Prince), "The Marrying Kind" (Prince), "If I [Eye] Was the Man in Ur Life" (Prince), "On the Couch" (Prince), "Dear Mr. Man" (Prince), "Reflection" (Prince). Produced by Prince. Compact disc. NPG Records CK 92560, 2004.

3121. Prince, keyboards, guitars, drums, percussion, vocals; various assisting musicians. "3121" (Prince), "Lolita" (Prince), "Te Amo Corazón" (Prince), "Black Sweat" (Prince), "Incense and Candles" (Prince), "Love" (Prince), "Satisfied" (Prince), "Fury" (Prince), "The Word" (Prince), "Beautiful, Loved and Blessed" (Prince, Támar), "The Dance" (Prince), "Get on the Boat" (Prince). Produced by Prince. Compact disc. Universal Music 64039531, 2006.

Planet Earth. Prince, keyboards, guitars, drums, percussion, vocals; various assisting musicians. "Planet Earth" (Prince), "Guitar" (Prince), "Somewhere Here on Earth" (Prince), "The One U Wanna C" (Prince), "Future Baby Mama" (Prince), "Mr. Goodnight" (Prince), "All the Midnights in the World" (Prince), "Chelsea Rodgers" (Prince), "Lion of Judah" (Prince), "Revelation" (Prince). Produced by Prince. Compact disc. NPG Records 88697 12970 2, 2007.

Notes

INTRODUCTION

1. Stephen Thomas Erlewine, "Prince," *All Music Guide,* http://www.allmusic.com/cg/amg.dll?p=amg&sql=11:p9z8b5n4tsqs~T1 (accessed May 2, 2007).

2. Brock Helander, "Prince (Rogers Nelson)," *Baker's Biographical Dictionary of Musicians* (New York: Schirmer Books, 2001), p. 2871.

3. Not only does Prince pay tribute to Nikki's bumping and grinding, he also includes references to masturbation.

CHAPTER 1

1 Liner notes to *Prince,* compact disc, Warner Bros. 3366–2, 1987.

2. The composition does include minimal vocalization; however, the focus is entirely on the instrumental groove.

3. Stephen Thomas Erlewine, "Prince," *All Music Guide,* http://allmusic.com/cg/amg.dll?p=amg&sql=10:fne097q7krst (accessed February 12, 2007).

4. Frank Zappa, with Peter Occhiogrosso, *The Real Frank Zappa Book* (New York: Poseidon Press, 1989), p. 188 (capitalizations and italics in the original). Quoted in Albin J. Zak III, "'Edition-ing' Rock," *American Music* 23, Spring 2005, p. 96.

5. Stephen Thomas Erlewine, "*Dirty Mind,*" in *All Music Guide to Soul* (San Francisco: Backbeat Books, 2003), p. 549.

CHAPTER 2

1. See, for example, "100 Top Music Videos, The," *Rolling Stone* no. 667, October 14, 1993, pp. 76ff, and "Pop 100," *Rolling Stone* no. 855, December 7, 2000, p. 91.

2. Although the song is credited to "Christopher," it was widely known that Prince was the true source of the song.

3. Stephen Thomas Erlewine, "1999," in *All Music Guide to Soul* (San Francisco: Backbeat Books, 2003), p. 550.

4. Listen to the baritone saxophone figure in the chorus on David Bowie's 2003 recording of the Richman song on the Bowie album *Reality*.

5. See, for example, "Pop 100," *Rolling Stone* no. 855, December 7, 2000, p. 79.

6. The real names of Prince's bandmates Wendy Melvoin and Lisa Coleman. Significantly, of the characters who are members of the supposedly fictitious band, only Prince's character, The Kid, does not use his real first name.

7. The Mixolydian mode, known in European music since the Middle Ages, sounds like a major scale with a lowered seventh scale-step. The notes C, D, E, F, G, A, B-flat, C, would be an example of the scale.

CHAPTER 3

1. "Christopher" was the pseudonym Prince used for his composition "Manic Monday," a hit for the Bangles.

2. "Pop 100," *Rolling Stone* no. 855, December 7, 2000. O'Connor's recording of "Nothing Compares 2 U" is ranked at No. 16 overall.

3. This song suggests that the influence of funk pioneer Sly Stone (composer of "Thank You [Falettinme Be Mice Elf Agin]") went beyond music, extending into Stone's predilection for unusual, phonetic spellings of song titles and lyrics.

4. In its conventionally most simple form, twelve-bar blues consists of three, four-measure phrases, with the following chord progression: Phrase One—I, I, I, I; Phrase Two—IV, IV, I, I; Phrase Three—V, IV, I, I (where the Roman numerals refer to the scale degree on which the chords are built). The third phrase of "U Got the Look" uses the following progression: V, V, I, I.

5. The Mixolydian mode (or scale) closely resembles the major scale, except that the seventh note is a half-step lower. For example, while the C major scale consists of the notes C, D, E, F, G, A, B, C, the C Mixolydian mode consists of C, D, E, F, G, A, B-flat, C.

6. Although the same basic pulse is felt throughout virtually the entire song, the first section gives the listener the impression of two, slow beats per measure, while the hard rock section feels like four faster beats per measure.

7. Stephen Thomas Erlewine, Review of *The Black Album*, *All Music Guide*, http://allmusic.com/cg/amg.dll?p=amg&sql=10:kvftxqw5ldfe~T0 (accessed May 7, 2007).

8. *Rough Guide to Cult Pop* (London: Rough Guides, 2003), p. 152.

9. Stan Hawkins, "Prince: Harmonic Analysis of 'Anna Stesia,'" *Popular Music* 11, no. 3, October 1992, pp. 325–335. Reprinted in Richard Middleton, *Reading Pop: Approaches to Textual Analysis in Popular Music* (Oxford and New York: Oxford University Press, 2000), pp. 58–70.

10. The liner notes and album cover present the title as a hand-drawn picture of a human eye, followed by the word *No*. While I have retained the vast majority of Prince's text-message–style spellings (e.g., *4* for *for*), I have used *I [Eye]* whenever he uses the graphic of an eye in his titles.

11. Hawkins, "Prince," pp. 325–335.

12. "Pop 100," *Rolling Stone* no. 855, December 7, 2000.

CHAPTER 4

1. Stephen Thomas Erlewine, Review of *Diamonds and Pearls, All Music Guide,* http://allmusic.com/cg/amg.dll?p=amg&token=&sql=10:d9fqxqr5ldfe (accessed May 29, 2007).

2. The chord also concludes each stanza in the James Brown classic.

3. Stan Hawkins, "Stylistic Diversification in Prince of the Nineties: An Analysis of *Diamonds and Pearls*" (PhD diss., University of Oslo, 1992), p. 10.

4. "Gett Off" reached No. 21 on the *Billboard* pop charts; however, it reached No. 8 in sales, but only No. 56 in radio airplay. Joel Whitburn, *The Billboard Book of Top 40 Hits,* 6th ed. (New York: Billboard Books, 1996), p. 488.

5. The album booklet uses a picture of an eye for the word *I* in the title of this song, as well as each time the word occurs in the lyrics.

6. Tom Moon, "Oh, Whoever," *Rolling Stone* no. 690, September 8, 1994, p. 75.

7. Stephen Thomas Erlewine, "*Come,*" in *All Music Guide to Soul* (San Francisco: Backbeat Books, 2003), p. 551.

8. Ibid.

9. Jim Walsh, Liner notes to *The Gold Experience,* compact disc, Warner Bros./ NPG 9 45999–2, 1995.

10. Stephen Thomas Erlewine, "*The Gold Experience,*" in *All Music Guide to Soul* (San Francisco: Backbeat Books, 2003), p. 551.

11. In musical terms, a *motive* is a small, easily identifiable set of notes. There may be a distinctive melodic shape and/or rhythm associated with the motive.

12. Originally an album track on *The Youngbloods,* the song was reissued and became a hit single in 1969.

CHAPTER 5

1. Melinda Newman, "The Beat," *Billboard* 106, October 29, 1994, p. 14.

2. A term usually used in jazz/pop music context as an abbreviation for "accompanying" on piano or guitar.

3. Prince Rogers Nelson, Liner notes to *Emancipation,* three compact discs, NPG Records E2 54982, 1996.

4. Ibid.

5. Ibid.

6. Prince uses the British spelling.

7. Nelson, Liner notes to *Emancipation.*

8. Ibid.

9. Greil Marcus, *Rock and Roll Will Stand* (Boston: Beacon Press, 1969).

10. Nelson, Liner notes to *Emancipation.*

11. *New Oxford Annotated Bible with the Apocrypha* (New York: Oxford University Press, 1973), p. 1206.

12. Nelson, Liner notes to *Emancipation.*

Chapter 6

1. Barney Childs, "Time and Music: A Composer's View," *Perspectives of New Music* 15, no. 2, Spring-Summer 1977, p. 195.

2. See, for example, Steven Thomas Erlewine, Review of *Musicology, All Music Guide,* http://wm10.allmusic.com/cg/amg.dll?p=amg&token=&sql=10:knfoxqual dhe (accessed September 27, 2007).

3. Prince directs his band on other, earlier tracks, such as the well-known "Sexy M.F.," but rarely does he key in major sectional changes to the extent he does on "Get on the Boat." On a song such as "Sexy M.F.," too, Prince plays an ultraunderstated cool role: a style that is the antithesis of James Brown's.

Conclusions

1. Fred Schruers, "Recordings: *Dirty Mind,*" *Rolling Stone* no. 821, September 16, 1999, p. 119.

2. Ken Emerson, *Doo-Dah: Steven Foster and the Rise of American Popular Culture* (New York: Da Capo Press, 1998).

Selected Discography

1. The liner notes of *The Gold Experience* give Prince's name as the infamous "love symbol."

2. The album booklet and the compact disc itself use a picture of a human eye every time the word *I* appears in song titles and song lyrics on *The Gold Experience*.

Annotated Bibliography

"A to Z of the Eighties, The—A Definitive Guide to the Decade." *Melody Maker* 65, December 1989, p. 45. Prince is included.

Aaron, C. "The 50 Greatest Rock Frontmen of All Time." *Spin* 20, August 2004, pp. 70–74. Prince is included in this list of esteemed rock musicians.

"Albums: *1999*." *Melody Maker* 58, May 26, 1983, p. 27. A review of the album.

"Albums: *Around the World in a Day*." *Melody Maker* 60, May 4, 1985, p. 33. A review of the album.

"Albums: *Diamonds and Pearls*." *Melody Maker* 67, October 5, 1991, p. 34. A review of the album.

"Albums: *Exodus*." *Melody Maker* 72, July 1, 1995, p. 38. A review of the album.

"Albums: *Graffiti Bridge*." *Melody Maker* 66, August 25, 1990, p. 34. A review of the album.

"Albums: Ho-Hum, More Sex." *Melody Maker* 73, July 6, 1996, p. 45. A mixed review of *Chaos and Disorder*.

"Albums: *The Legendary Black Album*." *Melody Maker* 71, December 10, 1994, p. 30. A review of the album.

"Albums: *Lovesexy*." *Melody Maker* 64, May 14, 1988, p. 38. A review of the album.

"Albums: *Music from the Motion Picture 'Purple Rain.'*" *Melody Maker* 59, July 28, 1984, p. 28. A favorable review of the album.

"Albums: *Prince*." *Melody Maker* 54, December 22, 1979, p. 21. A review of the album.

"Albums: Symbollocks." *Melody Maker* 68, October 17, 1992, p. 32. A review of "The Love Symbol Album."

Aletti, V. "Riffs: The Genius of Love." *The Village Voice* 26, December 2, 1981, p. 87. A review of *Controversy*.

Altrogge, Michael. "*Alphabet Street*: Prince oder die Kunst der Re-de-Konstruktion." In *VIVA MTV! Popmusik im Fernsehen*. Frankfurt am Main, Germany:

Suhrkamp, 1999, pp. 230–255. A scholarly analysis of Prince's *Alphabet Street* music video.

Amendola, Billy. "John Blackwell: Heavy Heart, Strong Soul." *Modern Drummer* 29, January 2005, pp. 44–46. A profile of John Blackwell, the drummer on Prince's *Musicology* album.

———. "Prince: School of Funk." *Modern Drummer* 29, January 2005, pp. 40–43. A profile of Prince and his album *Musicology*.

"Beat, The: Prince's *Black Album* a Real Beauty." *Billboard* 100, April 2, 1988, p. 33. A favorable review of the album.

Begun, Bret, and Dana Thomas. "Newsmakers: This Week, a Royal Flush." *Newsweek* May 29, 2000, p. 76. This article concerns in part the expiration of Prince's contract with Warner Bros. Records.

Bessman, Jim. "A Prince of a Teenager." *Billboard* 97, October 5, 1985, p. 4. A report on the release of Prince's early recordings with the band 94 East.

Blackwell, J. "Prince Talks Drums." *Modern Drummer* 25, October 2001, p. 74.

Boehlert, Eric. "Prince's Big Payoff." *Rolling Stone* no. 832, January 20, 2000, p. 19. A report on the royalties (in excess of six figures) Prince received for the song "1999" at the end of the millennium.

Bos, Alfred, and Tom Engelshoven. *Prince Roger [sic] Nelson: de biografie*. Utrecht, Netherlands: Uitgeverij Luitingh, 1988. A Dutch-language biography of Prince.

"*BP* Recommends: *Rave Un2 the Joy Fantastic*." *Bass Player* 11, March 2000, p. 70. A favorable review of the album.

Bream, Jon. *Prince: Inside the Purple Reign*. New York: Collier Books, 1984. A brief biography of Prince.

"Call Me . . ." *Time* 141, June 21, 1993, p. 18. A brief report on Prince's name change to an unpronounceable symbol.

"Capsule Reviews: *For You*." *Crawdaddy* no. 88, September 1978, p. 79. A review of the album.

Carcieri, Matthew. *Prince: A Life in Music*. New York: IUniverse, 2004. A brief biography of Prince.

Childs, Barney. "Time and Music: A Composer's View." *Perspectives of New Music* 15, no. 2, Spring-Summer 1977, pp. 194–219.

Christgau, Robert. "Consumer Guide." *The Village Voice* 40, November 14, 1995, p. 82. Includes a review of *The Gold Experience*.

———. "Consumer Guide." *The Village Voice* 41, September 17, 1996, p. 60. Includes a review of *Chaos and Disorder*.

———. "Consumer Guide." *The Village Voice* 42, January 28, 1997, p. 56. Includes a review of *Emancipation*.

———. "The Rise of the Corporate Single." *The Village Voice* 30, February 19, 1985, pp. 29–30.

———. "Rock & Roll: In the Court of the Sun King." *The Village Voice* 38, January 12, 1993, p. 76. An analysis and review of Prince's "The Love Symbol Album."

Christman, E., and G. Mayfield. "Prince CD Sparks Debate." *Billboard* 116, May 8, 2004, p. 1. A report on the marketing of *Musicology* alongside concert tickets for Prince's tour.

Cobb, Jerry, and David Alessandri. "Cover Me: '1999.'" *Gig Magazine* 3, September 1999, p. 54. A brief study of Prince synthesizer arrangements on "1999."

Conniff, Tamara. "6 Questions with Prince." *Billboard* 118, March 25, 2006, p. 62. A brief email interview with Prince about his *3121* album.

Cooper, C. "Riffs & Licks: King Prince 2U." *The Village Voice* 30, May 14, 1985, p. 69. A review of *Around the World in a Day.*

Cott, Jonathon. "The *Rolling Stone* Interview: Michael Tilson Thomas." *Rolling Stone* nos. 828–829, December 16, 1999, p. 76. Among the popular compositions praised by symphonic conductor Michael Tilson Thomas is Prince's "Nothing Compares 2 U."

Danielson, Anne. "His Name Was Prince: A Study of *Diamonds and Pearls.*" *Popular Music* 16, October 1997, pp. 275–291. A detailed study of the music and lyrics of Prince's *Diamonds and Pearls* album. The author compares her analysis with that of Stan Hawkins in his 1992 dissertation.

Darling, C. "Closeup." *Billboard* 93, November 21, 1981, p. 92. A profile of Prince on the occasion of the release of *Controversy.*

DeCurtis, Anthony. "80s." *Rolling Stone* no. 591, May 15, 1990, pp. 59–60. Prince figures prominently in DeCurtis's overview of pop music in the 1980s. In particular, *Purple Rain* is praised, and Prince is given credit for his groundbreaking frankness in dealing with sexuality on *Dirty Mind* and other albums.

———. "Burning Down the House." *Rolling Stone* no. 949, May 27, 2004, pp. 56–58. An interview with Prince to coincide with his *Musicology* album and tour. In particular, the profile of Prince highlights his new emphasis on sexual decorum and responsibility. DeCurtis praises the listener-friendly nature of the album.

———. "Free at Last." *Rolling Stone* no. 748, November 28, 1996, pp. 61–63. A report on Prince's *Emancipation* and his release from his contract with Warner Bros.

———. "He's Back—But Don't Call It a Comeback." *New York Times* September 12, 1999, p. 89. A report on *Rave Un2 the Joy Fantastic.*

———. "In the Studio." *Rolling Stone* no. 745, October 17, 1996, p. 36. A report on the upcoming release of *Emancipation.* The author deals with the difficulty Prince had with Warner Bros. because of the prolific nature of his writing and recording.

———. "*Sign o' the Times:* Prince Bounces Back with Bold Concert Movie." *Rolling Stone* no. 514, December 3, 1987, p. 16. A report on Prince's *Sign o' the Times* concert film.

Denisoff, R. Serge. "Video Review: The Not So Holy *Batman:* The Film." *Popular Music and Society* 14, no. 3, 1990, pp. 113–122. A review of *Batman* by one of the best-known scholars on popular music.

Doerschuk, Robert L. "Portrait of the Artist." *Musician* no. 221, April 1997, p. 29. An interview with Prince that follows the release of *Emancipation* and the death of his son.

———. "The View from *Graffiti Bridge:* Matt Fink and Rosey Gaines Expose Prince's Keyboard Secrets." *Keyboard* 17, January 1991, pp. 84–88. A study of Prince's keyboard arrangements for songs on the *Graffiti Bridge* album.

Duffy, Thom. "Home & Abroad." *Billboard* 107, May 18, 1995, p. 46. Includes information about Prince's March 3, 1995, performance in London. According to the reviewer, Prince's material from *The Gold Experience,* "Days of Wild," "Now," "Dolphin," and "Gold," "rank among the best stuff heard in some years from the prolific yet eccentric artist."

————. "Prince Shows Off *Diamonds & Pearls.*" *Billboard* 103, September 7, 1991, p. 71. A favorable review of the album.

"Eighties, The—A Vinyl Documentary: *1999.*" *Melody Maker* 65, February 11, 1989, p. 33.

"Eighties, The—A Vinyl Documentary: *Around the World in a Day.*" *Melody Maker* 65, February 25, 1989, p. 24.

"Eighties, The—A Vinyl Documentary: *Parade.*" *Melody Maker* 65, February 25, 1989, pp. 24–25.

"Eighties, The—A Vinyl Documentary: *Purple Rain.*" *Melody Maker* 65, February 18, 1989, p. 28.

"Eighties, The—A Vinyl Documentary: *Sign o' the Times.*" *Melody Maker* 65, March 4, 1989, p. 28.

Emerson, Ken. *Doo-Dah: Steven Foster and the Rise of American Popular Culture.* New York: Da Capo Press, 1998. Emerson deals extensively with the question of racial authenticity in nineteenth-century American music.

Erlewine, Stephen Thomas. "*Come.*" In *All Music Guide to Soul.* San Francisco: Backbeat Books, 2003, p. 551.

————. "Prince." *All Music Guide.* http://allmusic.com/cg/amg.dll?p=amg&sql=10:fne097q7krst. Accessed February 12, 2007.

————. "Prince," *All Music Guide.* http://www.allmusic.com/cg/amg.dll?p=amg&sql=11:p9z8b5n4tsqs~T1. Accessed May 2, 2007.

————. Review of *1999.* In *All Music Guide to Soul.* San Francisco: Backbeat Books, 2003, p. 550. A favorable review of the album.

————. Review of *The Black Album. All Music Guide.* http://allmusic.com/cg/amg.dll?p=amg&sql=10:kvftxqw5ldfe~T0. Accessed May 7, 2007.

————. Review of *Diamonds and Pearls. All Music Guide.* http://allmusic.com/cg/amg.dll?p=amg&token=&sql=10:d9fqxqr5ldfe. Accessed May 29, 2007.

————. Review of *Dirty Mind.* In *All Music Guide to Soul.* San Francisco: Backbeat Books, 2003, p. 549. A favorable review of the album.

————. "*The Gold Experience.*" In *All Music Guide to Soul.* San Francisco: Backbeat Books, 2003, p. 551.

————. Review of *Musicology. All Music Guide.* http://wm10.allmusic.com/cg/amg.dll?p=amg&token=&sql=10:knfoxqualdhe. Accessed September 27, 2007. A generally favorable review of what is labeled a "comeback" album for Prince.

Evans, Paul. "Recordings: *Graffiti Bridge.*" *Rolling Stone* no. 585, August 23, 1990, pp. 125–126. A favorable review of the album.

Ewing, Jon. *Prince.* Miami Springs, Fla.: MSI Corp., 1994. A brief biography of Prince.

Feldman, Jim. *Prince.* New York: Ballentine, 1985. A biography.

"Film Reviews." *Variety* 329, November 18, 1987, p. 14. Includes a review of Prince's *Sign o' the Times* concert film.

Flanagan, Bill. "1987: The Year Rock 'n' Roll Came Back . . . and Wouldn't Leave." *Musician* no. 111, January 1988, p. 76. Prince's *Sign o' the Times* is included.

————. "Pop Life." *Musician* no. 170, December 1992, pp. 58–66. A report on the working relationships between Prince and the members of the New Power Generation.

Flick, Larry. "The Artist Steps out on Arista." *Billboard* 111, November 6, 1999, p. 1. A feature article on Prince's new contract with Arista and the album *Rave Un2 the Joy Fantastic.*

Fraser, Julia. "NPG Hornz's Alter Ego: The Hornheads." *Windplayer* no. 64, 2002, pp. 20–25. A profile of trombonist Michael B. Nelson and Prince's other wind players.

George, Nelson. "Music: Whose Time Was It?" *The Village Voice* 35, September 11, 1990, pp. 70–71. A report on the controversy surrounding the appearance of the Time in Prince's film *Under the Cherry Moon.*

———. "*Purple Rain* Storms Silver Screen." *Billboard* 96, July 28, 1994, p. 60.

———. "Record Reviews: *Parade.*" *Musician* no. 90, April 1986, pp. 83–84. A review of the soundtrack album.

———. "Rhythm & Blues: Prince Is Brilliant in His Debut Garden Performance." *Billboard* 98, August 23, 1986, p. 74. A favorable review of Prince's performance at New York's Madison Square Garden. I include this review as an indication that even at the time when his film *Under the Cherry Moon* was being widely panned and labeled a failure in the press, his live performances generated favorable public and critical reaction.

———. "The Rhythm and the Blues: New Prince Album Harks Back to *1999.*" *Billboard* 99, March 7, 1987, p. 28. A favorable review of *Sign o' the Times.*

———. "The Rhythm and the Blues: Prince Is Back on Wings of 'Batdance.'" *Billboard* 101, June 17, 1989, p. 21.

Gibbs, V. "Time for the Prince Who Would Be King." *Creem* 14, May 1983, pp. 40–42.

Goaty, Frédéric. "Prince côté jazz." *Jazz Magazine* no. 526, May 2002, pp. 16–23. An interview with and profile of members of Prince's band.

Gold, Richard. "*Purple Rain* Sells Rock at Boxoffice." *Variety* 316, August 1, 1984, p. 5. Deals with the popular appeal of the film *Purple Rain.*

Goldberg, Michael Alan. "Paisley Is Out." *Rolling Stone* no. 678, March 24, 1994, p. 18. A report on the termination of Prince's record label, Paisley Park Records, by parent company Warner Bros. Records.

———. "Prince Scores *Batman* Film." *Rolling Stone* no. 555, June 29, 1989, p. 21. A brief report on Prince's original songs for the film *Batman.*

Goodman, Fred L. "Prince Ignores Industry Marketing Wisdom." *Billboard* 98, May 22, 1986, p. 50. A report on *Parade* being Prince's third album in less than two years. Prince's prolific writing and recording would soon cause much conflict between him and Warner Bros. Records.

Guzman, P. "Riffs: Rock's New Prince." *The Village Voice* 25, December 17, 1980, p. 95. A report on the importance of *Dirty Mind.*

Hahn, Alex. *Possessed: The Rise and Fall of Prince.* New York: Billboard Books, 2003. A biography aimed at teen readers.

Hardy, Camille. "*Billboards.*" *Dance Magazine* 68, March 1994, pp. 106ff. A mixed review of the Joffrey Ballet's production of *Billboards,* a modern dance production based on the music of Prince.

Harris, J. "The Greatest Songwriters of All Time (as Judged by Peers)." *Q* no. 219, October 2004, pp. 73–75. Prince is included in this list of popular songwriters of the past and present.

Hawkins, Stan. "Prince: Harmonic Analysis of 'Anna Stesis.'" *Popular Music* 11, no. 3, October 1992, pp. 325–335. Reprinted in Middleton, Richard. *Reading Pop: Approaches to Textual Analysis in Popular Music.* Oxford and New York: Oxford University Press, 2000, pp. 58–70.

———. *Setting the Pop Score: Pop Texts and Identity Politics.* Aldershot, England: Ashgate, 2002. A study of sexual politics and stereotypes in the work and public images of Prince, Annie Lennox, Madonna, Morrissey, and Pet Shop Boys.

———. "Stylistic Diversification in Prince of the Nineties: An Analysis of *Diamonds and Pearls.*" PhD diss., University of Oslo, 1992. A detailed deconstruction of the Prince album.

Helander, Brock. "Prince (Rogers Nelson)." *Baker's Biographical Dictionary of Musicians.* New York: Schirmer Books, 2001, p. 2871.

Hill, Dave. *Prince: A Pop Life.* New York: Harmony Books, 1989. A biography and discography.

Hiltbrand, David. "*Come.*" *People Weekly* 42, August 29, 1994, p. 23. A brief review of the Prince album that focuses on Prince's lyrical focus on sex. According to Hiltbrand, the highlights are "Pheromone" and Prince's vocal work on "Solo."

Hoberman, J. "Film: Valley of the Dolls." *The Village Voice* 32, November 24, 1987, pp. 67–68. A report on Prince's concert film *Sign o' the Times.*

Holdship, Bill. "The Wit & Wisdom of Prince Rogers Nelson." *Creem* 17, July 1985, pp. 28–33. A feature on Prince and the way in which he breaks sexual and musical boundaries in his recordings.

Horwitz, Carolyn. "The Artist Sues Nine Web Sites, Search Engine." *Billboard* 111, May 13, 1999, p. 24. A report on Prince's lawsuit against fan Web sites for unauthorized use of his image and music.

Howe, Rupert. "Hail to the Chief." *Q* no. 217, August 2004, pp. 68–72. A report on Prince's comeback.

Hughes, Ken. "Prince's 2004 ever Tour." *Keyboard* 30, August 2004, pp. 28–30. A report on the keyboard/synthesizer set-ups used on Prince's tour.

Isler, S. "Record Reviews: *Around the World in a Day.*" *Musician* no. 81, July 1985, pp. 104–105. A review of the album.

Ivory, Steven. *Prince.* Paris: Carrer, M. Lafon, 1984. A French-language biography of Prince.

Jisi, Chris. "Artistic Aristocrat." *Bass Player* 15, June 2004, pp. 46–48. A profile of Rhonda Smith, the bass guitarist on Prince's *Musicology.*

Jones, Liz. *Purple Reign: The Artist Formerly Known as Prince.* London: Little, Brown, 1997. Secaucus, N.J.: Carol Publishing Group, 1998. A biography.

Kael, P. "The Current Cinema." *The New Yorker* 60, August 20, 1984, p. 84. A report on the film *Purple Rain.*

Karlen, Neal. "Prince Talks." *Rolling Stone* no. 456, September 12, 1985, pp. 24–26. A feature-length interview with Prince at the time of the psychedelic album *Around the World in a Day.*

———. "Prince Talks." *Rolling Stone* no. 589, October 18, 1990, pp. 56–60. A feature-length interview. Prince discusses *Graffiti Bridge,* the intensity of his work schedule, the various intrigues that surrounded the former members of the Time who did not participate in *Purple Rain,* and a host of other topics.

King, W. "Prince's Spaghetti Musical." *Record* 3, October 1984, p. 38. A review of *Purple Rain.*

Kintner, Thomas. "Baby, I'm Still a Star." *Goldmine* 27, December 14, 2001, pp. 14–17. An assessment of Prince's work in the 1990s, which includes a discography of his work in the decade.

Knopper, Steve. "Fresh Prince: The Purple One Reclaims His Crown with New CD, Hot Tour." *Rolling Stone* no. 948, May 13, 2004, p. 14. A favorable review of the *Musicology* album and tour.

Kordosh, J. "Prince's *Purple Rain:* 'scuse Me While I Get Some Popcorn." *Creem* 16, September 1984, pp. 30–31.

Kushner, D. "*RS* NetBook: The Best Artist Sites." *Rolling Stone* no. 842, June 8, 2000, p. 4. Prince's Web site (npgon@ineltd.com) is included in this list of the best artist Web sites.

LaFranco, Robert. "Music's Top Fifty Moneymakers." *Rolling Stone* no. 968, February 24, 2005, pp. 52–54. Prince is included in this report on the highest-earning musicians of 2004, largely as a result of his highly successful tour that packaged the CD *Musicology* with concert tickets.

Leo, Christie. "Singapore Bans New GN'R, Prince Sets." *Billboard* 103, October 19, 1991, p. 71. A report on censorship because of Prince's sexually explicit lyrics.

Lester, P. "Singles: 'Thieves in the Temple.'" *Melody Maker* 66, July 28, 1990, p. 31.

Lichtman, Irv. "Prince Enters into New Label, Pub. Ventures with Warner." *Billboard* 104, September 12, 1992, p. 100. A report on Prince's $100,000,000 multialbum deal with Warner Bros.

Linder, Greg. "Prince of Minneapolis?" *Creem* 16, September 1984, p. 33.

Loder, Kurt. "David Bowie." *Rolling Stone* no. 498, April 23, 1987. Reprinted in *Rolling Stone* no. 641, October 15, 1992, pp. 141ff. Among the topics David Bowie discusses in this feature-length interview is Prince's ties to the aesthetics of early 1970s glam rock.

———. "Prince Reigns." *Rolling Stone* no. 429, April 30, 1984, pp. 16ff. A detailed review of the film *Purple Rain*. Loder discusses the complexities and contradictions of Prince's work and public persona.

———. "Prince Stunning in *Purple Rain*." *Rolling Stone* no. 428, August 16, 1984, p. 31. A highly favorable review of the film *Purple Rain*.

Mack, B. "I'm Too Sexy for Your TV: The Prince Video You'll Probably Never See." *Spin* 8, September 1992, p. 48. A report on Prince's *Sexy M.F.* music video.

Marcus, Greil. "Real Life Rock Top Ten." *The Village Voice* 33, August 9, 1988, p. 67. A report on Prince's Lovesexy Tour 1988 opening concert.

———. *Rock and Roll Will Stand*. Boston: Beacon Press, 1969. A seminal work that deals in part with how to define meaning in popular music.

McAdams, J. "The Rhythm and the Blues: Prince Crosses *Graffiti Bridge* and Leaves behind Much of *Purple*'s Passion, Spirit." *Billboard* 102, November 17, 1990, p. 20. As this article's title suggests, this review finds that *Graffiti Bridge* pales in comparison to Prince's film debut: *Purple Rain*.

McGee, D. "The *Rolling Stone* 200: *Dirty Mind*." *Rolling Stone* no. 760, May 15, 1997, p. 92. Prince's *Dirty Mind* is included among *Rolling Stone* magazine's most significant albums.

———. "The *Rolling Stone* 200: *Purple Rain*." *Rolling Stone* no. 760, May 15, 1997, p. 92. Prince's *Purple Rain* is included among *Rolling Stone* magazine's most significant albums.

————. "The *Rolling Stone* 200: *Sign o' the Times.*" *Rolling Stone* no. 760, May 15, 1997, p. 92. Prince's *Sign o' the Times* is included among *Rolling Stone* magazine's most significant albums.

McInnis, C. Liegh, Jr. *The Lyrics of Prince Rogers Nelson.* Jackson, Miss.: Psychedelic Literature, 1995. A study of Prince's literary techniques in his lyrics.

McLane, D. "Music: Glyph Notes." *The Village Voice* 41, December 10, 1996, p. 65. A review of *Emancipation.*

Miller, Debby. "Prince: The Secret Life of America's Sexiest One-Man Band." *Rolling Stone* no. 394, April 28, 1983, pp. 18–21. A feature-length profile of Prince fairly early in his career.

Mitchell, Gail. "The *Billboard* Reviews." *Billboard* 119, July 28, 2007, p. 47. Includes a brief favorable review of *Planet Earth.*

Moon, Tom. "Oh, Whoever." *Rolling Stone* no. 690, September 8, 1994, p. 75. A lukewarm review of *Come* and *1–800 New Funk.*

Morris, Chris. "The Beat: Prince Courts Success at Album Preview." *Billboard* 103, August 31, 1991, p. 26. A report on the *Diamonds and Pearls* album.

————. "Time for a Prince Film." *Billboard* 99, November 21, 1987, p. 3. A report on the Prince concert film *Sign o' the Times.*

————, and Geoff Mayfield. "*Lovesexy* Too Sexy for Some." *Billboard* 100, May 21, 1988, p. 1. A report on public reaction to the cover art of Prince's *Lovesexy* album.

"Music: Prince Makes Capitol Deal." *Variety* 21, October 1996, p. 78. A report on Prince's new recording contract with Capitol/EMI.

"Music Publishing: The Top Pop Songwriters of the Year." *Billboard* 104, May 16, 1992, p. 4. Prince is included in the list.

"Music Publishing: The Top R&B Songwriters of the Year." *Billboard* 104, May 16, 1992, p. 6. Prince is included in the list.

"Music Video Review: *Sexy M.F.*" *Billboard* 104, July 18, 1992, p. 53.

Nelson, Prince Rogers. Liner notes to *Emancipation.* Three compact discs. NPG Records E2-54982, 1996.

New Oxford Annotated Bible with the Apocrypha, The. New York: Oxford University Press, 1973.

"New Releases: *Crystal Ball.*" *Goldmine* 24, April 24, 1998, p. 56. A review of the album.

"New Releases: *Newpower Soul.*" *Goldmine* 24, September 25, 1998, p. 58. A mixed review of the album credited to the New Power Generation.

Newman, Melinda. "The Beat." *Billboard* 106, October 29, 1994, p. 14. Included is a report on Prince's troubled negotiations with Warner Bros. In reaction to Prince's assertion that his $100,000,000 deal was "a way to lock him into 'institutionalized slavery'" with the label, Newman writes, "Well, all we can say is that for $100,000,000, we'd walk barefoot across hot coals singing 'Raspberry Beret' in Swahili. Or maybe we'd realize we were getting paid way more than we ever deserved and graciously shut up and cash the check."

————. "Holy Soundtracks: *Batman!* There's Two!" *Billboard* 101, June 24, 1989, p. 4.

"News." *Melody Maker* 71, September 17, 1994, p. 6. Included is a brief report that *Purple Rain* has broken the U.S. record for film soundtrack sales.

"News." *Melody Maker* 72, March 11, 1995, p. 3. Includes a report that Prince has purchased the London Astoria club.

"News." *Melody Maker* 72, April 1, 1995, p. 6. A report that Warner Bros. has threatened to sue Prince.

"News: Paisley Park Shuts Down for Prince." *Melody Maker* 71, February 12, 1994, p. 4. A report on the dropping of Prince's Paisley Park label by Warner Bros. Records.

"News: Prince Gets Vertigo." *Melody Maker* 69, February 13, 1993, p. 2. A brief report on Prince's purchase of the Vertigo nightclub in Los Angeles.

"News: Sexy Motherf***er Joins the Board." *Melody Maker* 68, September 19, 1992, p. 5. A report on Prince's $100,000,000 multialbum deal, which gave him a seat on the Warner Bros. Board of Directors.

Nilsen, Per. *Dancemusicsexromance: Prince: The First Decade*. Wembley, England: Firefly, 1999; London: Firefly, 2004. A biography of Prince.

"Nothing Compares 2 Him." *Rock & Rap Confidential* no. 110, October 1993, pp. 2–3. A favorable review of the compilation albums, *The Hits* and *The B-Sides*.

"100 Top Music Videos, The." *Rolling Stone* no. 667, October 14, 1993, pp. 76ff. Three Prince music videos, "Kiss" (No. 18), "Gett Off" (No. 21), and "Little Red Corvette" (No. 85) are included in the magazine's top 100 videos. In addition, Sinéad O'Connor's video performance of Prince's composition "Nothing Compares 2 U" was ranked at No. 5.

Pareles, Jon. "Still Moaning, Still Shimmying." *New York Times* September 17, 1995, Section 2, p. 30. A review of Prince's *The Gold Experience*.

Peel, M. "Purple Prince." *Stereo Review* 49, October 1984, p. 81.

Perry, Steve. "The 10 Most Interesting Musicians of the Last 5 Years." *Spin* 6, April 1990, pp. 36–37. Prince is included.

———. "The Early Years: Creating the Minneapolis Myth." *Musician* no. 94, August 1986, pp. 11–12. A report on Prince's early years as a musician.

Poet, J. "Reviews: *1999*." *Trouser Press* 10, March 1983, p. 38. A review of the album.

Pollard, Alton B., III. "Religion, Rock, and Eroticism: Prince." *Black Sacred Music* 3, no. 2, 1989, pp. 133–141. A scholarly study of Prince's integration of what many people consider to be conflicting themes.

"Pop CD: *Rave Un2 the Joy Fantastic*." *Stereoplay* December 1999, p. 179. A review of the Prince album in this German publication.

"Pop 100." *Rolling Stone* no. 855, December 7, 2000, pp. 79, 91. Two Prince performances are included in *Rolling Stone*'s list of the greatest pop songs of the rock era: "When Doves Cry" (No. 27) and "Little Red Corvette" (No. 50). In addition, Sinéad O'Connor's recording of Prince's composition "Nothing Compares 2 U" is ranked No. 16.

"Popular Music: *Emancipation*." *Stereo Review* 62, March 1997, p. 80. A review of the album.

"Popular Music: *Graffiti Bridge*." *Stereo Review* 55, December 1990, p. 105. A review of *Graffiti Bridge*.

"Popular Music: The 'Love Symbol' Album." *Stereo Review* 58, January 1993, p. 84. A review of the album.

"Popular Music Reviews: *Come*." *Stereo Review* 59, December 1994, p. 132. A review of the album.

"Popular Music Reviews: *Diamonds and Pearls*." *Stereo Review* 57, February 1992, p. 132. A review of the album.

Poulson-Bryant, S. "Fresh Prince." *Spin* 7, September 1991, pp. 36–38. An interview with and profile of Prince's recent activity.

Powers, Ann. "The Ten That Matter Most '85–'95: Prince." *Spin* 11, April 1995, p. 54. Prince in included in this listing of the most important musical artists of the period 1985–1995.

Prince: Unauthorized. VHS Videocassette. 50 minutes. Plymouth, Minn.: Simitar Entertainment, 1992. A biography of Prince up through the success of *Purple Rain.*

"Prince & the Dells Inducted into the Rock & Roll Hall of Fame." *Jet* 105, April 5, 2004, pp. 30ff. This brief report includes excerpts from Prince's acceptance speech.

"Prince Blacked." *Melody Maker* 64, February 6, 1988, p. 4. A report on the shelving of the "*Black Album.*"

"Prince Film a Flop." *Rolling Stone* no. 481, August 28, 1986, p. 25. An unfavorable review of *Under the Cherry Moon.*

"Prince Sues His Own Fans." *Q* no. 152, May 1999, p. 24. A brief report on Prince suing fans for unauthorized use of his image and music on their Web sites.

"Prince's *1999* Still Sells Well a Year after Release of Album." *Variety* 313, November 9, 1983, p. 73.

?uestlove. "The Immortals 28: Prince." *Rolling Stone* no. 946, April 15, 2004, p. 112. Musician ?uestlove (Ahmir Khalib-Thompson) pays tribute to Prince in this brief article.

"Rebellion Rocks the Music Biz." *Musician* no. 195, January 1995, p. 32. This article includes information on Prince's battles with Warner Bros.

"Record & CD Reviews: *Graffiti Bridge.*" *Down Beat* 58, January 1991, pp. 46–47. A review of the *Graffiti Bridge* album.

"Record Reviews: *1999.*" *Down Beat* 50, May 1983, p. 28. A review of the album.

"Record Reviews: *1999.*" *Popular Music and Society* 9, no. 2, 1983, pp. 63–64. A review of the album.

"Record Reviews: *Around the World in a Day.*" *Down Beat* 52, August 1985, p. 30. A review of the album.

"Record Reviews: *Dirty Mind.*" *Musician, Player & Listener* no. 31, March 1981, p. 86. A review of the album.

"Record Reviews: *Sign o' the Times.*" *Down Beat* 54, July 1987, p. 33. A review of the album.

"Recordings: *Batman.*" *Rolling Stone* no. 559, August 24, 1989, pp. 121–123. A review of the soundtrack album.

"Recordings: *Chaos and Disorder.*" *Rolling Stone* no. 741, August 22, 1996, p. 98. A review of the album.

"Recordings: *Crystal Ball.*" *Rolling Stone* no. 785, April 30, 1998, p. 68. A review of the four-disc set.

"Recordings: *Diamonds and Pearls.*" *Rolling Stone* no. 615, October 17, 1991, p. 92. A review of the album.

"Recordings: *The Gold Experience.*" *Rolling Stone* no. 720, November 2, 1995, p. 66. A review of the album.

"Recordings: *Graffiti Bridge.*" *Musician* no. 144, October 1990, p. 120. A review of the album.

"Recordings: 'The Love Symbol Album.'" *Rolling Stone* no. 644, November 26, 1992, pp. 70–71. A review of the album.

"Recordings: Prince Wants to Take U Higher." *Musician* no. 156, October 1991, pp. 95–96. A review of *Diamonds and Pearls.*

"Recordings: *Rave Un2 the Joy Fantastic.*" *Rolling Stone* no. 832, January 20, 2000, p. 57. A review of the album.

"Records: *Around the World in a Day.*" *Creem* 17, August 1985, pp. 44–45. A review of the album.

"Records: *Around the World in a Day.*" *Rolling Stone* no. 449, December 19, 1985, pp. 149+. A review of the album.

"Records: *Batman.*" *Musician* no. 131, September 1989, p. 92. A review of the album.

"Records: *Chaos and Disorder.*" *Musician* no. 215, October 1996, pp. 82–83. A profile of the album.

"Records: *Controversy.*" *Creem* 13, February 1982, p. 52. A review of the album.

"Records: *Controversy.*" *Rolling Stone* no. 361, January 21, 1982, pp. 51–52. A review of the album.

"Records: *Dirty Mind.*" *Rolling Stone* no. 337, February 19, 1981, pp. 54–55. A review of the album.

"Records: *Lovesexy.*" *Musician* no. 117, July 1988, pp. 111–112. A review of the album.

"Records: *Lovesexy.*" *Rolling Stone* no. 528, June 16, 1988, p. 117. A review of the album.

"Records: *1999.*" *Rolling Stone* no. 384, December 9, 1982, p. 65. A review of the album.

"Records: *Parade.*" *Creem* 17, July 1986, p. 24. A review of the album.

"Records: *Parade: Music from 'Under the Cherry Moon.'*" *Rolling Stone* no. 472, April 24, 1986, p. 53. A review of Prince's soundtrack album.

"Records: *Purple Rain.*" *Creem* 16, October 1984, pp. 52–53. A review of the album.

"Records: *Purple Rain.*" *Rolling Stone* nos. 426–427, July–August 1984, p. 102. A review of the album.

"Records: *Sign o' the Times.*" *Creem* 18, August 1987, p. 18. A review of the album.

"Records: *Sign o' the Times.*" *Rolling Stone* no. 498, April 23, 1987, pp. 145–146. A review of the album.

"Reviews: *Come.*" *Musician* no. 192, October 1994, pp. 77–78. A review of Prince's *Come* album.

"Reviews: *Crystal Ball.*" *Request* May 1998, pp. 44–45. A review of the album.

"Reviews: *Graffiti Bridge.*" *Guitar Player* 24, November 1990, p. 151. A review of the album.

"Reviews: *Purple Rain.*" *High Fidelity/Musical America Edition* 34, October 1984, pp. 106–107. A review of the album.

"Reviews: *The Rainbow Children.*" *Spin* 18, February 2002, p. 112. A review of the album, *The Rainbow Children.*

Reynolds, Simon. "Sidelines: *Graffiti Bridge.*" *Melody Maker* 66, November 17, 1990, p. 12. A review of the Prince album and film.

"Rock 'n' Roll News: You Say You Want No Revolution." *Creem* 18, February 1987, p. 4. A report on Prince's decision to disband the Revolution.

Rodgers, Lissa. "Performance." *Rolling Stone* no. 832, January 20, 2000, p. 28. A brief report on the live performance of Prince's *1999* album at the Brooklyn Academy of Music, on December 11, 1999.

Rosen, Craig. "Prince Being Sued over *Diamonds* Cut." *Billboard* 103, December 21, 1991, p. 97.

————. "Prince 'Getts Off' Special Pre-*Diamonds & Pearls* Vid." *Billboard* 103, August 31, 1991, p. 82. A report on the video *Gett Off*, which previews the forthcoming *Diamonds and Pearls* album.

Rough Guide to Cult Pop, The. London: Rough Guides, 2003. Prince is one of the artists featured in this irreverent guidebook.

Schruers, Fred. "Recordings: *Dirty Mind*." *Rolling Stone* no. 821, September 16, 1999, p. 119. In this retrospective look back at Prince's *Dirty Mind*, the author recalls that the album's cover art (Prince in a black jock strap), the obsession with sex, and Prince's concert and video performances that featured "falsetto, coy struts and eyelash-batting" made listeners wonder "which way he swung." According to the author, Prince feminized rock in the 1980s the same way as Mick Jagger in the 1960s and David Bowie in the 1970s.

Simonart, S. "The One and Only." *Guitar World* 18, October 1998, pp. 38–40. A profile of and interview with Prince on the occasion of the release of *New Power Soul*.

"Singles: 'Alphabet St.'" *Spin* 4, July 1988, p. 94. A review of the song.

Smith, R. J. "Music: Imagine Life without Him." *The Village Voice* 33, May 24, 1988, p. 85. A report on Prince's *Lovesexy* album.

————. "Swing Shift: Prince's Black Booty." *The Village Voice* 33, March 22, 1988, p. 82. A review of the "*Black Album*."

"Someday Our Prince Will Run Dry." *Rock & Rap Confidential* no. 152, May 1998, p. 1. A report on Prince's mammoth four-CD album *Crystal Ball*.

Spencer, M. "Riffs: Dream Lover Takes It to the Floor." *The Village Voice* 27, November 16, 1982, p. 93. A review of *1999*.

"Spins: *Batman*." *Spin* 5, September 1989, p. 86. A review of the album.

"Spins: *Diamonds and Pearls*." *Spin* 105, November 1991, p. 105. A review of the album.

"Spins: *Emancipation*." *Spin* 12, February 1997, p. 85. A review of the album.

"Spins: 'The Love Symbol Album.'" *Spin* 8, November 1992, p. 109. A review of the album.

"Spotlight: Music Publishing." *Billboard* 103, April 27, 1991, pp. 6, 8. Prince is named as one of the top pop and top R&B songwriters of the year.

Stark, Phyllis. "Managers' Royalty Rights Debated." *Billboard* 103, November 23, 1991, p. 83.

Sutcliffe, P. "The Artist Formerly Known as Successful." *Q* no. 144, September 1998, pp. 62–65. A report on the relative lack of commercial success of Prince's *Crystal Ball* album, as well as other late 1990s releases.

Sutherland, Sam. "Prince 'Rains' Supreme as Star." *Billboard* 96, August 4, 1984, p. 45. A favorable review of *Purple Rain*.

Swenson, J. "Records: *Around the World in a Day*." *Saturday Review* 11, July–August 1985, p. 83. A review of the album.

Tabor, Lisa. "Rock On: Prince's *Batman* Soundtrack Is No Joker." *International Musician* 88, August 1989, p. 18. A report on Prince's film score in the official organ of the American Federation of Musicians.

"Takin' It to the *Bridge*." *Rock & Roll Confidential* no. 82, October 1990, p. 7. A review of *Graffiti Bridge*.

Tannenbaum, Rob. "Music: The Artistry." *The Village Voice* 43, April 21, 1998, pp. 85–86. A review of *Crystal Ball* and Prince's concert at Irving Plaza.

————. "The Sound of the City: Like It's *1999*." *The Village Voice* 44, December 21, 1999, p. 139. A report on the *Party at the End of Time,* a live performance of the songs from Prince's *1999.*

Tate, Greg. "Music: Painted Black." *The Village Voice* 32, April 14, 1987, p. 81. A report on the *Sign o' the Times* album.

————. "Stagolee vs. the Proper Negro." *The Village Voice* 29, September 11, 1984, p. 1. A report on the popular acceptance by white audiences of Prince, actor/comedian Eddie Murphy, and trumpet virtuoso Wynton Marsalis.

Terry, Ken. "Prince Tour Seems Unstoppable." *Variety* 317, December 12, 1984, p. 123. A report on the enormous commercial and critical success of Prince's "Purple Rain" concert tour.

"Testing the Barriers of Dance." *Maclean's* 107, May 30, 1994, p. 41. A report on the dance work *Billboards,* which features the music of Prince.

Thompson, Art. "Crown of Creation." *Guitar Player* 38, July 2004, pp. 50–54. A review of *Musicology.*

————. "The Once & Future Prince." *Guitar Player* 34, January 2000, pp. 86–92. A feature article on Prince and *Rave Un2 the Joy Fantastic.*

"Top 100, The." *Rolling Stone* no. 507, August 27, 1987, pp. 78, 102. Prince's *Dirty Mind* and *Purple Rain* are included.

"Top 100, The." *Rolling Stone* no. 534, September 8, 1988, pp. 90, 118. Prince's "Little Red Corvette" and "When Doves Cry" are included.

"Top 100, The." *Rolling Stone* no. 565, November 16, 1989, pp. 56, 76, 77, 127. Prince's *Purple Rain, 1999, Dirty Mind,* and *Sign o' the Times* are included in this countdown of significant albums of the 1980s.

Tucker, Mark. "Behind the Beat: Michael Jackson and Prince." *Institute for Studies in American Music Newsletter* 14, November 1984, pp. 12–14. An analysis of Jackson's "Billie Jean" and Prince's "When Doves Cry."

Udovitch, M. "Film: Take It to the Bridge." *The Village Voice* 35, November 13, 1990, p. 88. A review of Prince's film *Graffiti Bridge.*

————. "Music: Before Swine." *The Village Voice* 36, October 8, 1991, p. 82. A report on *Diamonds and Pearls.*

Vail, Mark. "25 Giants of Keyboard Music." *Keyboard* 26, January 2000, pp. 32–42. Prince is among the prominent keyboard artists profiled.

Waddell, Ray. "Ticket/Album Bundle Pushes Prince CD to Platinum." *Billboard* 116, June 5, 2004. A report on the packaging of *Musicology* with tickets to Prince's tour performances.

Walls, Jeannette. "Prince Doesn't Tire of the Name Game." *New York* 26, November 15, 1993, p. 16. A report on Prince's name change to a symbol and the ridicule he received because of the name change.

Walser, Robert Anton. "Prince as Queer Poststructuralist." *Popular Music and Society* 18, no. 2, 1994, pp. 79–89.

Walsh, Chris M. "Sony BMG U.K. Drops Prince Album." *Billboard* 119, July 14, 2007, p. 10. A brief report on Sony BMG U.K.'s refusal to distribute Prince's *Planet Earth* in the U.K. because of Prince's deal with the newspaper *The Mail* to distribute the disc as a giveaway in its July 15, 2007, edition.

————. "Verizon Nabs Prince Exclusive." *Billboard* 119, June 9, 2007, p. 8. A brief report that Verizon Wireless will distribute the single "Guitar" free to any subscriber who demos the company's new music service.

Walsh, Jim. "15 Years: *Spin* Flashes Back." *Spin* 16, April 2000, pp. 166–167. A report on the Minneapolis music scene in 1985–1986.

———. Liner notes for *The Gold Experience*. Compact disc. Warner Bros./NPG 9 45999–2, 1995.

———. "The Toaster Formerly Known as His—The Artist's Paisley Park Yard Sale." *Rolling Stone* no. 822, September 30, 1999, p. 22. A report on the sale of memorabilia from Prince's Paisley Park studio.

Weisbard, E. "Music: Jams of the Year." *The Village Voice* 42, January 21, 1997, p. 56.

Whitburn, Joel. *The Billboard Book of Top 40 Hits*, 6th ed. New York: Billboard Books, 1996.

Wimberley, Richard E. "Prophecy, Eroticism, and Apocalypiticsm in Popular Music: Prince." *Black Sacred Music* 3, no. 2, 1989, pp. 125–132.

Winters, Marty. "Five Star Records." *Goldmine* 29, December 12, 2003, p. 68. A favorable comparison of the Beatles' "White Album" (real title, *The Beatles*) and Prince's *Black Album*.

———. "This Issue's Five Star Record." *Goldmine* 25, May 7, 1999, p. 20. A highly complimentary retrospective of Prince's *1999*.

Wolff, Daniel. "Music." *The Nation* 245, December 12, 1987, pp. 728–729. Includes a report on Prince's *Around the World in a Day, Parade*, and *Purple Rain*. According to the author, Prince turned inward on *Around the World in a Day* and *Parade* in response to the enormous success of *Purple Rain*.

"Wonder Years, The." *Guitar Player* 35, April 2001, pp. 86–115. Prince is included in this study of the most important 32 guitar players "who defined the sound of '80s guitar."

Woodward, J. "Purple Maze." *Down Beat* 61, January 1994, p. 52.

"Year in Recordings, The: *The Gold Experience*." *Rolling Stone* nos. 724–725, December 1995, p. 124. A review of the album.

"Year in Records, The: *Batman*." *Rolling Stone* nos. 567–568, December 1989, p. 215. A review of the soundtrack album.

"Year in Records, The: *Graffiti Bridge*." *Rolling Stone* nos. 593–594, December 1990, p. 205. A favorable review of the "demon funk, heavy-metal hallelujah, sugary psychedelia, and incandescent soul" of *Graffiti Bridge*.

"Year in Records, The: *Lovesexy*." *Rolling Stone* nos. 541–542, December 1988, p. 191. The Prince album is included in this annual review.

"Year in Records, The: *Sign o' the Times*." *Rolling Stone* nos. 515–516, December 1987, p. 183. The Prince album is included in this annual review.

Zappa, Frank, with Peter Occhiogrosso. *The Real Frank Zappa Book*. New York: Poseidon Press, 1989. I have included this book in the bibliography because of the insight Zappa provides on the importance of arrangement and record production in establishing the true "meaning" of a pop song. Zappa's observations play a role in the thorough understanding of more than a few Prince songs.

Zimmerman, Kevin. "Bootlegged 'Black Album' Competes in Stores with Latest." *Variety* 331, June 8, 1988, p. 69. A report on the competition between Prince's official new release, *Lovesexy*, and the bootleg version of the unissued *Black Album*.

Index

"Acknowledge Me," 113–14
"Adore," 48–49
"All Along the Watchtower," 154
Allen, Woody, 84
"All the Critics Love U in New York," 23
Alomar, Carlos, 108
"Alphabet St.," 52–53
"America," 32, 33
"America, the Beautiful," 33
America Online, 110
Anderson, Laurie, 26–27
"And God Created Woman," 76
"Animal Kingdom," 119–20
"Anna Stesia," 52, 53–54
"Annie Christian," 15–16, 122, 148
"Anotherloverholenyohead," 40–41
Arista Records, 131
"Arms of Orion, The," 56
Around the World in a Day, 22,
    29–35, 45
"Around the World in a Day," 30, 32,
    35, 74
"Arrogance," 75
"Automatic," 22

"Baby," 4
"Baby, I'm a Star," 28

"Baby Knows," 134–35
Badfinger, 6, 42
"Ballad of Dorothy Parker, The,"
    44–45
"Bambi," 7
"Bang a Gong (Get It On)," 65
Bangles, The, 20, 47, 163, 165
Bartòk, Béla, 143
"Batdance," 55, 56–57
Batman, 55–57
Bazilian, Eric, 111
Beatles, The, 24, 28, 38, 41, 42, 46,
    55, 110, 111
"Beautiful, Loved, and Blessed," 155
"Beautiful Ones, The," 26
Bee Gees, The, 40
Bell, Thom, 99, 101, 108
Benson, George, 4
Bernstein, Leonard, 42, 74–75
Berry, Chuck, 42, 157
"Betcha By Golly Wow!," 99–100
"Better Than You Think," 2
Billboards, 78
Billy Jack, 89
"Billy Jack Bitch," 89
Black Album, The, 42, 49–51, 81
Black Sabbath, 7, 85

"Black Sweat," 153
Blackwell, John, 144
Bland, Michael, 85
Blondie, 40
"Blue Light," 73
"Bob George," 49, 50
"Bohemian Rhapsody," 3
Bolan, Marc, 65, 162
Bowie, David, 14, 65, 91, 108, 120, 162
Boyz II Men, 121
Brill Building, 53
Brown, James, 14, 22, 38, 40, 50, 64,
    71, 109, 126, 130, 137, 147, 155
Burton, Tim, 56
Bush, Kate, 110

"Call My Name," 149
Campbell, Tevin, 59
"Can't Stop This Feeling I Got," 58
Capital Records, 97
Cat (rap artist), 53
C.F.M. Band, The, 75
Chandler, Raymond, 130
Chaos and Disorder, 91–95
"Chaos and Disorder," 91–92
"Chelsea Rodgers," 159
"Christopher Tracy's Parade," 38
Chuck D., 131
"Cindy C.," 50
"Cinnamon Girl," 149
"Circle of Amour," 118
Clinton, George, 50, 59, 81, 126
"Cloreen Bacon Skin," 115
Cobain, Kurt, 95
Coleman, David, 30
Coleman, Lisa, 11–12, 13, 28, 33, 45
Coleman, Ornette, 143
Coltrane, John, 51, 143
Comden, Betty, 74–75
Come, 78–82, 91
"Come," 79
"Comeback," 121
"Come On," 125–26
"Computer Blue," 26
"Condition of the Heart," 32
"Continental, The," 74
Controversy, 13–16
"Controversy," 13–14

Costello, Elvis, 10, 39, 42, 77
"Could It Be I'm Falling in Love," 9
Country Joe and the Fish, 15
"Courtin' Time," 99
Crawford, Cindy, 50
"Crazy You," 4
"Cream," 65, 68
"Cross, The," 48, 74
Crow, Sheryl, 131, 134
Crystal Ball, 112–23, 127, 165
"Crystal Ball," 113, 115
"Curious Child," 104

"Da, Da, Da," 109–10
"Daddy Pop," 64, 68
"Damned If I [Eye] Do," 101
"Damn U," 74–75
"Dance, The," 155
"Dance On," 54
"Dance to the Music of the World," 1–2
Daniels, Charlie, 5, 6
"Dark," 81, 82
"Darling Nikki," 26–27
Davis, Clive, 131
Davis, Miles, 146
Day, Morris, 57, 58
"Dead on It," 50
"Dear Mr. Man," 150
Deep Purple, 84–85
"Delirious," 21, 24
Delphonics, The, 99, 109
"Devil's Radio," 13–14
Diamonds and Pearls, 63–69
"Diamonds and Pearls," 64–65
Difranco, Ani, 131
"Digital Garden," 141
"Dig U Better Dead," 94–95
"Dinner with Delores," 92
"Dionne," 118–19
Dirty Mind, 9–13
"Dirty Mind," 9–10
"D.M.S.R.," 22
"Do It All Night," 10
"Dolphin," 86–87
"Do Me, Baby," 15
"Don't It Make My Brown Eyes Blue," 8
"Don't Play Me," 117–18
"Do U Lie?," 40

"Down in the Sewer," 154
"Dream Factory," 113
"Dreamin' about U," 104
Dressed to Kill (record label), 1
Dylan, Bob, 154

Eager, Brenda Lee, 98
Eagles, The, 152
Easton, Sheena, 45–46, 56, 153
"Electric Chair," 56
"Elephants & Flowers," 59
Elfman, Danny, 55
Elgar, Edward, 148
Ellington, Duke, 141–42
"Emale," 103–4
Emancipation, 97–112, 124, 165
"Emancipation," 112
"Endorphinmachine," 84–85
"English Country Garden,"
Eric B & Rakim, 75
Escovedo, Sheila (Sheila E.), 33
Eve (rap artist), 133
"Everyday Is a Winding Road," 134
"Everyday People," 8, 14, 18
"Extraordinary," 130

"Face Down," 108, 109
"Fame," 108
"Fascination," 120–21
Fink, Matthew (Dr. Fink), 11, 13, 48
"Fire," 7
Fisher, Clare, 38, 135
"5 Women +," 128–29
"Flow, The," 75
Fogerty, John, 2
"Footloose," 58
Foreigner, 28, 111
"Forever in My Life," 45
For You, 2–5
"For You," 2–3
"4 Blank Seconds," 132–33
"Freaks on This Side," 125
"Free," 22
"Friend, Lover, Sister, Mother/Wife,"
    106–7
Fripp, Robert, 23
Fugs, The, 15
Fulsom, Lowell, 75

"(I [Eye] Like) Funky Music," 126
"Fury," 154
"Future, The," 55–56
"Future Baby Mama," 158

Gaines, Rosie, 64
Galdo, Joe, 107
"Games," 2
Garcia, Mayte, 72
Garrett, Betty, 75
Gaye, Marvin, 4, 85, 102, 149,
    150–51, 157
Gaye, Nona, 85
Gayle, Crystal, 8
Geils, J., Band, 25, 43
"Get on the Boat," 155
"Gett Off," 66
"Get Yo Groove On," 99
"Girls & Boys," 39, 41
"Glam Slam," 53
Glover, Savion, 105
Goethe, Wolfgang von, 110
Goffin, Gerry, 53
"Gold," 90
Golden Gate Park, San Francisco, 31
Gold Experience, The, 82–91, 123,
    134, 136
Gore, Tipper, 12, 26, 161–62
"Gotta Broken Heart Again," 10–11
Graffiti Bridge, 57–62
"Graffiti Bridge," 61
Grainger, Percy, 61
"Greatest Romance Ever Sold, The,"
    132–33
Green, Al, 81, 106, 149
"Guitar," 130, 135, 155–56,
    157–58, 165

"Had U," 95
Hall, Daryl and John Oates, 10
Handel, George Frederic, 42
Harrison, George, 13–14, 58, 87,
    122, 159
Hart, William, 108
Hayward, Justin, 72
"Head," 11–12
Hendrix, Jimi, 6, 7, 25, 29, 59, 81, 82,
    117, 154, 163

Holy Modal Rounders, the, 40
"Holy River, The," 105, 106
Hooty & the Blowfish, 101
"Hotel California," 152
"Hot Thing," 45
"Hot Wit U," 133
"Housequake," 44
"Human Body, The," 107–8
Human League, The, 40
"Hush," 85

"I Can't Make You Love Me," 101, 102
"I Could Never Take the Place of Your Man," 47–48, 49, 76, 87, 126, 149, 158, 164
"I Feel for You," 7, 8–9, 163
"I-Feel-Like-I'm-Fixin'-to-Die Rag," 15
"If I [Eye] Was the Man in Ur Life," 150
"If I Was Your Girlfriend," 46, 65, 107, 162
"If You Feel Like Dancin'," 2
"If You See Me," 2
"I [Eye] Hate U," 90–91
"I [Eye] Know," 52, 53
"I Like It There," 92
"Illusion, Coma, Pimp & Circumstance," 148
"I [Eye] Love U, But I [Eye] Don't Trust U Anymore," 135
"I'm Yours," 5
"Incense and Candles," 153
"In Love," 3, 4
"Insatiable," 68
"International Lover," 23–24
"In the Mood," 7
"In This Bed I [Eye] Scream," 102
"Into the Light," 94
"I Rock, Therefore I Am," 93–94
"I Second That Emotion," 9
"It's about That Walk," 128
"It's Gonna Be a Beautiful Night," 48
"It's Gonna Be Lonely," 9
"I Wanna Be Your Lover," 5–6, 7, 9, 107, 162
"I [Eye] Wanna Melt with U," 73–74

"I Will," 94
"I Wish U Heaven," 55
"I Wonder U," 38–39
"I Would Die 4 U," 28

Jackson, Mahalia, 102
Jackson Five, The, 52
"Jack U Off," 16
Jagger, Mick, 162
"Jam of the Year," 98
James, Rick, 10, 22, 45, 130
Jesus of Nazareth, 58, 77, 105, 156
Jobim, Antonio Carlos, 118
Johnson, Kirk A., 109
Johnson, Robert, 116
"Joint 2 Joint," 104–6
Joplin, Janis, 95
"Joy in Repetition," 59, 61
"Jughead," 64, 67
"Just As Long As We're Together," 4

Kane, Bob, 56
Keaton, Michael, 56
Khan, Chaka, 9, 163
"Kill for Peace," 15
King, Carole, 44, 53, 136
"Kiss," 40, 41, 163
Klaatu, 121
Kotero, Apollonia, 25–26

"Ladder, The," 34
"Lady Cab Driver," 22–23, 104
"La, La, La (Means I Love You)," 108
"Latest Fashion, The," 60
Laughlin, Tom, 89
Leeds, Eric, 48, 66, 100, 125, 144
"Le Grind," 50
Leiber, Jerry, 93
"Lemon Crush," 56
Lennon, John, 14, 16, 108, 110
"Letitgo," 82
"Let's Dance," 14
"Let's Go Crazy," 24–25, 28
"Let's Have a Baby," 106
"Let's Pretend We're Married," 21–22
"Let's Work," 15
"Life Can Be So Nice," 39–40
"Life 'o' the Party," 148–49

"Lion of Judah," 159
Liquid Sky, 15
"Little Red Corvette," 17, 21, 24, 161
"Little Wing," 29
"Live 4 Love (Last Words from the
    Cockpit)," 68
Loggins, Kenny, 58
Lolita, 152
"Lolita," 152–53
"Loose!," 80–81
"Love," 153
"Love Machine," 58
Lovesexy, 51–55
"Lovesexy," 54
♀ ("The Love Symbol Album"),
    69–78, 79, 83, 84, 93, 114, 165
"Love 2 the 9's," 71–72, 74
"Love We Make, The," 111
Luther, Martin, 117
Lynch, Brian, 100
Lynyrd Skynyrd, 6

M., Eddie, 34
M., Tony, 67, 69, 75
Mac, Michael, 105
"Machine Gun," 81
"Mad Sex," 123–24
Mahavishnu Orchestra, The, 146
Mahler, Gustav, 110
Mail, The, 155–56
"Manic Monday," 20, 31, 35, 47, 163
"Man in a Uniform," 119, 125
Mann, Barry, 53
"Man o' War," 134
Manzarek, Ray, 82
Marley, Bob, 73
"Marrying Kind, The," 150
Marsalis, Branford, 51
Martin, George, 38
"Max, The," 72–73
Mayte. *See* Garcia, Mayte
McCartney, Paul, 2
McCrackin, Jimmy, 75
McLaughlin, John, 146
McLeod, Brian, 134
Mellencamp, John Cougar, 158
"Melody Cool," 60
Melvoin, Wendy, 28, 33, 45

Mendelssohn, Felix, 46
Miller, Glenn, 7
"Million Days, A," 148
Mingus, Charles, 51, 143
Minneapolis, Minnesota, 1
Minogue, Kylie, 9
Mitchell, Joni, 44
"Money Don't Matter 2 Night," 67
Moody Blues, The, 72
Moon, Chris, 2, 3
"Morning Papers, The" 72–73
Morrison, Jim, 95
"Most Beautiful Girl in the World,
    The," 86
"Mother's Little Helper," 129
"Mountains," 40
"Mr. Goodnight," 158–59
"Mr. Happy," 101, 102
"Muse 2 the Pharaoh," 141
Musicology, 147–51, 155
"Musicology," 147–48
"My Computer," 110–11
"My Little Pill," 129
"My Love Is Forever," 4
"My Name Is Prince," 60, 69, 72, 101,
    108, 114, 116, 123

Nabokov, Vladimir, 152
Najee, 141
Nelson, John L., 1, 30, 38, 39
Nelson, Prince Rogers. *See* Prince
Neto, Renato, 144
"New Position," 38
"New Power Generation," 58
New Power Generation, The,
    57, 58, 63–64, 66–68,
    69, 78, 82, 91, 101,
    114, 123, 125, 126, 129, 131,
    152, 159
New Power Soul, 123–27
"New Power Soul," 123
N.E.W.S., 142–47
"New World," 107
New York Dolls, The, 65
1984, 19, 164
1999, 17–24
"1999," 12, 13, 17–20, 24, 28, 31,
    92, 139, 153, 161, 163, 164

94 East, 1–2
94 East, 1
Northern Exposure, 121
"Nothing Compares 2 U," 39, 61–62, 148, 165
"Now," 87–88
"NPG Operator," 84, 86, 87, 88, 90
N.W.A., 75

O'Connor, Sinéad, 39, 61–62, 148, 165
"Old Friends 4 Sale," 130
"One, The," 126
"One Kiss at a Time," 103
"One Man Jam," 1
"One of Us," 111
"One of Your Tears," 121
"One U Wanna C," 158
Ono, Yoko, 14, 82
"On the Couch," 150
"Orgasm," 82
Orwell, George, 19, 164
Osborne, Joan, 111
"Other Side of the Pillow, The," 120

"Pablo Piccaso," 26
Page, Jimmy, 7
"Paisley Park," 31–32, 33–34, 61
"Papa," 81, 82
"Papa's Got a Brand New Bag," 64
Parade, 37–41
Parents Music Resource Center, 12, 26, 161–62
Parker, Maceo, 131, 137
Parliament/Funkadelic, 50
Parsons, Gram, 95
"Partyman," 55, 56
"Partyup," 12
"P Control," 83–84, 114–15, 124
"Pheromone," 80, 84
Planet Earth, 155–60
"Planet Earth," 156
"Play in the Sunshine," 43–44
Poet 99, 98, 105
Police, The, 45, 136
"Pop Life," 33–34, 120
"Positivity," 55
Presley, Elvis, 24, 108

"Pretty Man," 137
Prince: as arranger, 6, 27, 31, 32, 34, 43, 45, 51, 52, 74, 79–80, 115, 129, 134, 156–57; ballad style of, 26, 54–55, 61–62, 86, 103, 124, 148; change of name to a symbol, 78–79, 83, 87–88; compositional technique of, 8, 10, 18, 20, 27, 28–29, 30–31, 34, 39, 41, 42–43, 47, 53, 60–61, 62, 66, 75–76, 86, 95, 102–5, 113, 116–18, 122, 135, 142–46, 157, 163–64; eclecticism in the music of, 3, 6, 11, 75, 76, 136, 162–63; funk style in the music of, 10, 18, 38, 40–41, 49–50, 58, 64, 80–81, 147–48; gender roles and gender neutrality in the lyrics of, 11, 46, 62, 64–65, 73–74, 103, 158–59, 162, 163; gospel style in the music of, 28–29, 34, 60, 81, 93, 150; as guitarist, 4, 6, 7, 11, 29, 59, 87, 111, 130; hard rock and heavy metal style in the music of, 7, 84–85; hip-hop style in the music of, 50, 69, 81, 115, 135–36; humor in the music of, 44, 50; identity as a theme in the lyrics of, 70–73, 74, 76–78, 82, 83, 87–88, 103–4, 113–15, 117, 120, 124–25, 128–29, 158–59, 162; jazz style in the music of, 4–5, 40, 51, 65–66, 79, 99, 130, 141–47; as keyboardist, 51, 101, 135; metaphor in the lyrics of, 16, 21, 27, 30, 39–40, 60, 67, 82, 103–4, 120–21, 151–52, 159–60; millennial angst and the songs of, 20, 91–92, 164; new wave style in the music of, 10, 39, 45, 47–48, 136, 164; as percussionist, 33, 147–48; as producer, 20, 26, 51, 57, 141, 157; psychedelic style in the music of, 22, 29–32, 35, 45, 81; racism as a theme in the lyrics of, 16, 85–86, 88, 93, 107; as rapper, 23, 64, 69–70; religious and spiritual imagery and references in the lyrics of, 18–19, 22, 25, 28, 31, 34, 48, 52–53, 55, 58–59,

60–61, 64, 70, 75–78, 79–80, 94, 103–6, 111–12, 116–18, 121–22, 131, 133–34, 140–42, 149, 155, 156, 162; sexual explicitness in the lyrics of, 3–4, 9–11, 12, 15, 21–23, 52–53, 67, 78, 79–80, 82, 93, 118, 161–62; as singer, 26, 29, 40, 43, 77, 81, 100, 102, 135, 153; social commentary in the lyrics of, 14, 16, 19, 23, 31, 33, 43–44, 53–54, 81, 85–86, 88–89, 93–94, 100, 103–5, 109–11, 118, 120, 130, 149, 150–51, 156; Southern rock style in the music of, 5–6; use of synthesizers by, 18, 22, 39–40
Prince, 5–9
Prince Rogers Trio, 1
"Private Joy," 15
"Promo to Website," 136
Purple Rain, 24–29, 57–58, 122, 165
"Purple Rain," 24, 25, 28–29, 122, 161
"Push," 67
"Push It Up," 125

Queen, 3, 75
"Question of U, The," 58

Rainbow Children, The, 140–42, 155
"Rainbow Children, The," 140–41
Raitt, Bonnie, 101
"Raspberry Beret," 32–34, 35, 124–25
Rave Un2 the Joy Fantastic, 131–37
"Rave Un2 the Joy Fantastic," 131
Reagan, Ronald, 15, 16, 19–20
"Reflection," 151
Reid, Michael Barry, 101
"Release It," 58
"Rest of My Life, The," 127–28
"Revelation," 159–60
Revolution, The, 13, 24–25, 28, 37, 38, 41, 48, 66, 131, 153
Richie, Lionel, 54
Richman, Jonathan, 26
"Right Back Here in My Arms," 98
"Right the Wrong," 93

Robinson, Smoky, 5–6, 9, 40, 59, 99, 102, 128
"Rockhard in a Funky Place," 51
Rodgers, Nile, 14
Rolling Stones, The, 42, 129
"Ronnie, Talk to Russia," 15
"Round and Round," 59

Sacre du printemps, Le, 32
"Sacrifice of Victor, The," 77–78
"Same December, The," 92
Santana, Carlos, 7, 29, 59, 120, 131, 132, 144
"Sarah," 130, 131
"Satisfied," 153–54
"Saviour," 106
"Scandalous," 56
Schubert, Franz, 110
Scrap D, 109
"Segue," 73, 75, 77
"Segue to Man o' War," 134
"7," 75–76
"Sex in the Summer," 102–3
Sex Pistols, The, 91
"Sexuality," 14
"Sexual Suicide," 114, 115
"Sexy Dancer," 6
"Sexy M. F.," 70–71, 74, 101, 108, 109, 114
"Shake!," 58
Shamblin, James Allen, 101
Shaw, Mattie, 1
"She Spoke 2 Me," 128
"Shhh," 85
"Shoo-Bed-Ooh," 125
Sign o' the Times, 41–49, 122, 165
"Sign o' the Times," 16, 42–43, 66, 73, 126
"Silly Game," 135
Simon, Paul, 66, 136
Sinatra, Frank, 75
"Sister," 12, 133–34
"Sister Popcorn," 64
"Slave," 107
"Sleep Around," 109
"Slow Love," 45
Sly and the Family Stone, 8–9, 14, 18, 38, 39, 54, 91, 107, 131

Smith, Rhonda (Rhonda S.), 100, 144
"So Blue," 4–5
"So Far, So Pleased," 132, 133
"Soft and Wet," 3–4
Sogbe, Cesar, 107
"Solo," 81–82
"Somebody's Somebody," 98–99
"Something in the Water (Does Not
    Compute)," 22
"Sometimes It Snows in April," 41
"Somewhere Here on Earth," 158
Sony BMG U.K., 155–56
"Soul Sanctuary," 103
"Space," 80
Speacer, Levi, 71
Spinners, The, 9
"Squibcakes," 109
Staples, Mavis, 60
"Starfish and Coffee," 45
Steeles, The, 60, 66
Stefani, Gwen, 133
"Still Waiting," 8, 75
"Still Would Stand All Time," 60, 61
Stoller, Mike, 93
Stone, Sly, 6, 8–9, 14, 15, 64, 81, 85,
    91, 126, 147. See also Sly and the
    Family Stone
"Strange but True," 132, 135–36
"Strange Relationship," 47
Stranglers, The, 154
Stravinsky, Igor, 32
Stray Cats, The, 43
"Strollin'," 65–66
St. Victor, Sandra, 103
"Style," 109
Stylistics, The, 98–100
"Sub Rosa Subway," 121
"Sugar Walls," 46, 163
"Sun, the Moon, the Stars, The," 132,
    133–34
"Super Freak," 10
"Superfunkycalifragisexy," 50
Supremes, The, 27
"Sweet Baby," 74, 76

"Take Me with U," 25–26, 29
Talking Heads, 11
Támar, 153, 154–55

"Tamborine," 32, 33
"Tangerine," 133
"Te Amo Corazón," 153
"Temptation," 34, 44–45, 48
Temptations, The, 128
"There Is Lonely," 129–30, 131
"Thieves in the Temple," 59–60, 61, 64
"3rd Eye," 118
3121, 151–55, 165
"3121," 151–52
Thorogood, George, 93
"3 Chains of Gold," 76–77
"319," 88–89
"Thunder," 64, 66
"Tick Tick Bang," 59
Time, The, 57–60
"Tower of Power," 109
T. Rex, 65
Trott, Jeff, 134
"Trust," 56
Truth, The. See Crystal Ball
"Truth, The," 116–17
"2 Nigs United 4 West Compton,"
    50–51, 52

"U Got the Look," 45–46, 152
Under the Cherry Moon, 37, 38, 41. See
    also Parade
"Under the Cherry Moon," 39, 41
"Undisputed," 132
"Until U're in My Arms Again," 124
"Uptown," 11, 164

Vault: Old Friends 4 Sale, The, 127–31
Veloso, Gaetano, 118
"Venus De Milo," 40
Verizon Wireless, 155
"Vicki Waiting," 55

"Walk Don't Walk," 66–67
War, 66
Warner Bros. Records, 2, 37, 41–42,
    49, 63, 78–79, 82, 83, 88, 91, 94,
    97, 107, 127, 130
"Wasted Kisses," 126
"Way You Do the Things You Do,
    The," 128
Weather Report, 146

"We Can Funk," 59
"We Gets Up," 100
Weil, Cynthia, 53
"Welcome 2 the Dawn," 121–22
"We March," 85–86
"We're All Water," 14
West Compton, Los Angeles Country,
    California, 51
"What Do U Want Me 2 Do?," 150
"What's My Name," 114
"When Doves Cry," 24, 25, 27,
    153, 161
"When the Lights Go Down," 129
"When 2 Are in Love," 50, 54–55
"When U Love Somebody," 124–25
"When We're Dancing Close and
    Slow," 7
"When You Were Mine," 10, 164
"Wherever U Go, Whatever U Do," 136
White, Barry, 101
"White Mansion," 100–101
Who, The, 74, 84

"Why You Wanna Treat Me So Bad?,"
    6, 7, 9
Williams, Hank, 42
"Willing and Able," 66
Wilson, Brian, 3, 40
Wilson, Hilliard, 98
Winter, Edgar, 146
"With You,"
"Woman from Tokyo," 84
Wonder, Stevie, 2, 27, 32, 41, 54, 58,
    73, 85, 98, 99, 101, 120, 140–41,
    147
"Word, The," 154
Wray, Link, 31

"You Keep Me Hangin' On," 27
Youngbloods, The, 92
"You're Awful," 74–75

"Zannalee," 93
Zappa, Frank, 2, 51, 146
Z., Bobby, 13

About the Author

JAMES E. PERONE is currently Professor of Music at Mount Union College, where he teaches American music and music theory, and chairs the Department of Music. He is the series editor for the Praeger Singer-Songwriter Collection, for which he has also written three volumes: *The Sound of Stevie Wonder* (2006), *The Words and Music of Carole King* (2006), and *The Words and Music of David Bowie* (2007). He is also the author of several Greenwood Press books, including *Music of the Counterculture Era* (2004) and *Woodstock: An Encyclopedia of the Music and Art Fair* (2005).